Praise for *Managing Software Debt*

"If you work in technology, you're probably familiar with terms like 'technical debt.' The metaphor seems easy, but using it to influence change can be remarkably hard. To do that, you're going to want to present options to decision makers, backed up by evidence. I've been impressed watching Chris Sterling research and refine his work in just this area for several years, and I'm pleased to see him release it as a book. If you want to go beyond clichés to talk about how to deal with the problem of software debt, this is the seminal work in the field—and it's also the book for you."

—*Matthew Heusser, Software Process Naturalist*

"Inertia: It's what restricts change and leads to a cost of making a change or starting a change after a period of no investment or maintenance. This book explains in great detail what the different types of debt are that lead to inertia and, ultimately, to a cost to the business in managing software maintenance and development. The richness of explanation in this book of how to manage the virtual debt that every business incurs is unmatched. Every business-focused CIO, enterprise architect, software architect, or project manager should have a copy."

—*Colin Renouf, Enterprise Architect*

"Software debt is an important concept and Sterling does a sterling job of explaining what it is, why it is bad, and how to avoid it. A healthy dose of theory sprinkled with lots of pragmatic examples."

—*Roger Sessions, CTO, ObjectWatch (objectwatch.com)*

"Chris Sterling's experience in Agile architecture and his focus on software debt make this book a must-read for architects and engineers on Agile teams."

—*Jan Bosch, VP Engineering Process, Intuit*

"This book offers highlights and shortcomings of managing inherited software code and the debts that come with quality software. The author offers a unique perspective on dealing with software development issues. A must-read for all software developers."

—*Leyna Cotran, Institute for Software Research, University of California, Irvine*

"The vital importance of rapid feedback to the software process is a fundamental premise of modern software methods. When such feedback is quantified in the form of software debt, the software process becomes most effective. Chris Sterling's book holds the details you need to know in order to quantify the debt and pay it back. Moreover, it will teach you how to avoid debt in the first place."

—*Israel Gat, The Agile Executive (theagileexecutive.com and on Twitter at @agile_exec)*

"This book represents a wonderful opportunity for a larger community to take advantage of Chris's many years of experience and his innovative approaches to Agile architecture and continuous quality. . . . His book distills many of his principles and techniques into practical guidelines, and he manages to convey very powerful ideas in accessible prose, despite the inherent complexity of architecture and technical debt. . . . Chris's book will help architects, leaders, and teams see their way to better systems and better organizational performance."

—*Evan Campbell, Founder of Chinook Software Consulting*

Managing Software Debt

The Agile Software Development Series

Alistair Cockburn and Jim Highsmith, Series Editors

Addison-Wesley

Visit **informit.com/agileseries** for a complete list of available publications.

Agile software development centers on four values, which are identified in the Agile Alliance's Manifesto:

1. Individuals and interactions over processes and tools
2. Working software over comprehensive documentation
3. Customer collaboration over contract negotiation
4. Responding to change over following a plan

The development of Agile software requires innovation and responsiveness, based on generating and sharing knowledge within a development team and with the customer. Agile software developers draw on the strengths of customers, users, and developers to find just enough process to balance quality and agility.

The books in The Agile Software Development Series focus on sharing the experiences of such Agile developers. Individual books address individual techniques (such as Use Cases), group techniques (such as collaborative decision making), and proven solutions to different problems from a variety of organizational cultures. The result is a core of Agile best practices that will enrich your experiences and improve your work.

MANAGING SOFTWARE DEBT

BUILDING FOR INEVITABLE CHANGE

Chris Sterling

With contributions from Brent Barton

✦Addison-Wesley

Upper Saddle River, NJ • Boston • Indianapolis • San Francisco
New York • Toronto • Montreal • London • Munich • Paris • Madrid
Capetown • Sydney • Tokyo • Singapore • Mexico City

Cover photograph reused with the permission of Earl A. Everett.

The quotation on page 227 is excerpted from Beck, EXTREME PROGRAMMING EXPLAINED: EMBRACING CHANGE, © 2000 by Kent Beck. Reproduced by permission of Pearson Education, Inc.

The publisher offers excellent discounts on this book when ordered in quantity for bulk purchases or special sales, which may include electronic versions and/or custom covers and content particular to your business, training goals, marketing focus, and branding interests. For more information, please contact:

U.S. Corporate and Government Sales
(800) 382-3419
corpsales@pearsontechgroup.com

For sales outside the United States please contact:

International Sales
international@pearson.com

Visit us on the Web: informit.com/aw

Library of Congress Cataloging-in-Publication Data
Sterling, Chris, 1973–
  Managing software debt : building for inevitable change / Chris
Sterling ; with contributions from Brent Barton.
       p.   cm.
  Includes bibliographical references and index.
  ISBN-13: 978-0-321-55413-0 (hardcover : alk. paper)
  ISBN-10: 0-321-55413-2 (hardcover : alk. paper)
  1. Computer software—Quality control. 2. Agile software development.
  3. Software reengineering. I. Barton, Brent. II. Title.
  QA76.76.Q35S75 2011
  005.1'4—dc22
                                                      2010037879

ISBN-13: 978-0-321-55413-0
ISBN-10:   0-321-55413-2
Text printed in the United States on recycled paper at Courier in Westford, Massachusetts.
First printing, December 2010

Thank you to my children, Ashon, Diya, and Aman, who put up with their daddy writing so much, and especially thank you to my beautiful wife, Shivani, who enabled me to write this book.

CONTENTS

FOREWORD

OF FAIRY RINGS, CATHEDRALS, SOFTWARE ARCHITECTURE, AND THE TALLEST LIVING LIFE FORM ON EARTH

The imposing, luxuriant, and verdant groves of the coast redwood (*Sequoia sempervirens*) are found today mostly in the foggy valleys along the Pacific Coast of North America from southern Oregon to just south of Monterey, California, in a strip approximately 450 miles long and 20 or so miles wide (725 by 32 km). They are the tallest living species on Earth, reaching heights of 300 to 350 feet (91 to 107 m). The tallest redwood known measures 367 feet (112 m), slightly taller than the *Saturn V* rocket. Redwood forests possess the largest biomass per unit area on Earth, in some stands exceeding 1,561 tons/acre (3,500 metric tons/hectare).

They can also be ancient, predating even the earliest FORTRAN programmers, with many in the wild exceeding 600 years. The oldest verified tree is at least 2,200 years of age, and some are thought to be approximately 3,000 years old. Redwoods first appeared on our planet during the Cretaceous era sometime between 140 and 110 million years ago, grew in all parts of the world, and survived the KT (Cretaceous–Tertiary) event, which killed off more than half the Earth's species 65 million years ago.

Clearly, the coast redwood has been successful. But how? After all, these trees require large amounts of water (up to 500 gallons or 1,893 liters per day), with the significant requirement of transporting much of that up to the height of the tree. Their height turns them into lightning rods, and many fires are struck at their bases during the dry season, fires that often spread underground along their root systems to their neighbors, as well. Rabbits and wild hogs would sneer disdainfully at their reproductive rate, because the trees produce seeds but once per year, and although a mature tree may produce as many as 250,000 seeds per year, only a minuscule number (0.23% to 1.01%) will germinate.

As you would guess, the redwoods have developed a number of architectural features and adaptations to survive and thrive.

The Pacific Coast region they inhabit provides a water-rich environment, with seasonal rains of 50 to 100 inches (125 to 250 cm) annually, and a coastal fog that helps keep the forests consistently damp. Adapting to this fog, redwoods obtain somewhere between 25% and 50% of their water by taking it in through their needles, and they have further adapted by sprouting canopy roots on their branches, getting water from lofty spongelike "soil mats" formed by dust, needles, seeds, and other materials trapped in their branches. Redwoods also have a very sophisticated pumping capability to transport water from their roots to their tops. In the tallest trees, the water's journey can take several weeks, and the tree's "pump" overcomes a negative pressure of 2,000,000 pascals, more than any human pump system is capable of to date.

This abundant fog and rainfall have a downside, however, creating (along with several other factors) a soil with insufficient nutrients. The redwoods have adapted by developing a significant interdependence with the whole biotic forest community to obtain sufficient nutrients, an interdependence that is only beginning to be understood.

The redwood has built bark that is tough and thick—up to 1 foot (30.5 cm) in some places—thickness that, among other things, shields against woodpeckers. Imbued with a rich cocktail of tannins, it is unappetizing to termites and ants. The bark also functions as an ablative heat shield, similar to the heat shields of the Mercury/Gemini/Apollo capsules, and protects the tree from fire.

Young redwoods use sunlight very efficiently (300% to 400% more so than pines, for example) and are capable of rapid growth. With optimal conditions, a sapling can grow more than 6 feet (2 m) in height and 1 inch (2.5 cm) or more in diameter in a growing season. Mature trees under optimal conditions can grow at a rate of 2 to 3 feet (.6 to 1 m), per year, but if the tops are exposed to full sun and drying winds, they will grow only a few inches/centimeters per year. They simply out-compete other trees for the sun's energy.

A major component in the coast redwoods' responsiveness to environmental conditions is their high genetic variability. Like most plants, they can reproduce sexually with pollen and seed cones, with seed production generally beginning at 10 to 15 years of age.

Yet the seeds don't get very far. While the seeds are winged and designed for wind dispersal, they are small, and light (around 5,600 to 8,500 seeds per ounce [200 to 300 seeds/g]), and are dispersed a distance of only 200 to 400 feet (60 to 120 m) around the parent. When they land, the thick amount of duff (decaying plant debris on the ground) prevents most seeds from ever making it to the dirt.

This accounts for a part of the 1% or less seed germination rate, but a much more significant factor is at work. A large number of the seeds are actually empty! Scientists speculate this could be an adaptation to discourage seed predators, which learn that too much time is wasted sorting the "wheat" (edible seeds) from the "chaff" (empty seeds). It is estimated that only 20% of redwood reproduction occurs sexually through seeds.

The other 80% comes from their capability to reproduce asexually through sprouting, even after severe damage, a feature that has likely played a large part in making the coast redwood such a vibrant and resilient species.

If a redwood is damaged by a fire, lightning strike, or ax, or is dying, a number of sprouts erupt and develop around the circumference of the tree. This nearly perfect circle is known colloquially as a "fairy ring." The sprouts can use the root system and nutrients of the parent and therefore can grow faster than seedlings, gaining 8 feet (2.3 m) in a single season. The sprouts are really "clone trees," and their genetic information may be thousands of years old, dating back to the first parent. Surprisingly, genetic analysis has found diverse gene stocks in the rings, where non-clones (seedlings) have "completed" the circle.

These fairy rings are found around the parent tree's stump, or a depression in the middle of the circle if the stump has decayed completely. They can also be found circling their still-alive and recovered parent tree. The stump of a parent tree inside a fairy ring is known colloquially as a "cathedral," and the fairy rings themselves are also known as "cathedral spires."

Walking through a redwood grove inspires awe. As one stands within the tall columnar trees, the canopy vault overhead dappling and chromatically filtering the light, enveloped in the pervasive and meditative quiet, it is not hard to appreciate the sense of being within a cathedral of nature.

The cathedral analogy is understandable but somewhat ironic, given that most of these trees existed long before the first cathedrals built by humans. Cathedrals are one of humans' archetypal and iconic architectures, with a unifying and coherent structure designed and built especially to be habitable by both the people and spirit of their region.

The concept of architecture has been adapted to include computer and software systems. At its mid-twentieth-century beginning, software system architecture meant algorithms and data structures. As our skills evolved and allowed increasing software system size and complexity, gotos came to be considered harmful, and domain-specific systems became mainstream. Just like the coastal redwoods, our systems are becoming rich and interconnected ecosystems, and our understanding of the richness and complexities of these systems and their development continues to evolve.

The *Encyclopedia Britannica* says this about architecture:

> *The characteristics that distinguish a work of architecture from other man-made structures are (1) the suitability of the work to use by human beings in general and the adaptability of it to particular human activities, (2) the stability and permanence of the work's construction, and (3) the communication of experience and ideas through its form.*[1]

The first two definitions adapt perfectly to software architecture. When judged successful, our system architectures are usable and adaptable by humans and offer stability in usage, although the concept of "permanence" is perhaps considered too lightly at times, as Y2K taught us.

Applied to software, the third definition may be the richest. Obviously, our system architectures communicate our experience and ideas, but they also reflect and embed the organizational structures that build them. Conway's Law states:

> *. . . organizations which design systems . . . are constrained to produce designs which are copies of the communication structures of these organizations.*[2]

Ultimately system architecture is a human activity, perhaps the most human activity. Perhaps Agile's biggest contribution is the recognition of the humanness of systems development. Agile organizations connect software and the business, and Agile processes provide communication patterns connecting the system-building teams, and the teams with the business, as well as role definitions. Like the forest architecture of the redwoods, Agile organizations evolve ecosystems in which experience and ideas live and grow and

---

1. www.britannica.com/EBchecked/topic/32876/architecture
2. Melvin E. Conway, "How Do Committees Invent?" *Datamation* 14, no. 5 (April, 1968): 28–31, www.melconway.com/research/committees.html.

enable shared understanding of the problems we're trying to solve, and thereby provide the foundation to architect, design, and build solutions to the problems we're addressing.

Good architecture and Agile organizations help us build systems that provide fitting, innovative, and exceptional solutions to functional and nonfunctional requirements and a sense of accomplishment and joy to the system's builders, maintainers, and users, and they represent, in the very best sense, the culture that designed, built, and lives in and around the system. They help our evolution beyond the observation that Sam Redwine made in 1988:

> *Software and cathedrals are much the same—first we build them, then we pray.*[3]

—Earl Everett

---

3. Sam Redwine, *Proceedings of the 4th International Software Process Workshop*, Moreton-hampstead, Devon, UK, May 11–13, 1988 (IEEE Computer Society).

INTRODUCTION

The best architectures, requirements, and designs emerge from self-organizing teams.

—From "Principles behind the Agile Manifesto"[1]

WHY THIS BOOK?

Just as Agile software development methods have become mainstream to solve modern, complex problems, practices of software architecture must change to meet the challenges of the ever-changing technology ecosystem. Good Agile teams have undergone a mind-set shift that enables them to deal with changing requirements and incremental delivery. A similar mind-set shift to manage larger software architecture concerns is needed to keep systems robust. Software architecture is as important as ever. Modern product requirements, such as scaling to Internet usage, extending the enterprise beyond the firewall, the need for massive data management, polyglot applications, and the availability of personal computing devices, continue to challenge organizations. To keep up with this ever-changing landscape, modern practices, processes, and solutions must evolve.

To set the foundation for architectural agility, we explore how architecture is accomplished. In any significant enterprise, and certainly on the Internet, architecture functions as a federated system of infrastructure, applications, and components. Thus, many people contribute to the architectures involved in providing a solution to users. Agile software development teams are an excellent example of where sharing architectural responsibilities is essential. To address multiple people collaborating and producing high-quality, integrated software effectively, we must understand how cross-functional, self-organizing teams are involved with and support effective software architectures.

Teams should have "just enough" initial design to get started. A team should also understand what aspects of the software architecture are not well understood yet and what risk that poses to a solution. In Agile, the sequence of delivery is

---

1. "Principles behind the Agile Manifesto," www.agilemanifesto.org/principles.html, 2001.

ordered by business priority, one of the main reasons Agile is now mainstream. Elements of the software architecture are built and proven early to support the business priorities, and other parts are delayed until they rise in priority. In this way, software architecture is reviewed, updated, and improved in an evolutionary way. Learning how to cope with this process and produce high-quality, highly valued, and integrated software is the focus of this book. To illustrate, the "Manifesto of Agile Software Development" values describe its biases by contrasting two attributes of software development. Either extreme is bad. For example, "responding to change" is valued over "following a plan." Both are important, but the bias is toward the ability to respond to changes as they come. Another example is valuing "working software over comprehensive documentation." It is OK to document an initial architecture and subsequent changes to a level of detail needed for delivering valuable software. This balance could be affected by operational constraints such as compliance and regulatory concerns.

While "everything" is important to consider in software architecture, the ability of architecture to accommodate change is most important. Architecture must define an appropriately open system considering its continued evolution beyond the first release. If it is closed, every change becomes progressively more expensive. At some point the cost per feature added becomes too expensive, and people start to talk about rewriting or replacing the software. This should rarely happen if the architecture establishes an open system that supports an adequate level of changeability. Agile approaches to software development promote this kind of open architecture, provided the team members are equipped with the knowledge and authority to build quality in throughout development and maintenance of the software.

Evolutionary Design

Rather than supporting the design of significant portions of the software architecture before the software is built, Agile methods identify and support practices, processes, and tools to enable evolutionary design. This is not synonymous with undisciplined or "cowboy" coding of software. Agile methods are highly disciplined. One principle behind the "Manifesto for Agile Software Development" in particular identifies the importance of design:

> *Continuous attention to technical excellence and good design enhances agility.*[2]

---

2. Ibid.

Because design is continuously discussed while implementing features, there is less focus on documentation and handoffs to capture design. People who have traditionally provided designs to project teams are expected to work more closely with the teams. The best way to do this is to be part of the team. When documentation is necessary or supports the continued maintenance of the software, it is created alongside the implementation of the features that made the need visible. Designers may also take on other responsibilities within the team when necessary to deliver working software.

Agile teams are asked to think more broadly than in terms of a single component or application when planning, implementing, and testing features. It is important that they include any integration with external applications in their incremental designs. The team is also asked to continually incorporate enhancements to quality attributes of the software, such as

- **Suitability:** Functionality is suitable to all end users.
- **Interoperability:** Functionality interoperates with other software easily.
- **Compliance:** Functionality is compliant with applicable regulatory guidelines.
- **Security:** The application is secure: confidentiality, integrity, availability, accountability, and assurance.
- **Maturity:** Software components are proven to be stable by others.
- **Fault tolerance:** The software continues operating properly in the event of failure by one or more of its components.
- **Recoverability:** The software recovers from failures in the surrounding environment.
- **Understandability:** People are able to use the software with little training.
- **Learnability:** Functionality is learned with little external interfacing.
- **Operability:** The software is kept in a functioning and operating condition.
- **Performance:** Perceived response is immediate.
- **Scalability:** The software is able to handle increased usage with the appropriate amount of resources.
- **Analyzability:** It is easy to figure out how the software functions.
- **Changeability:** Software components can be changed to meet new business needs.
- **Testability:** Repeatable and specific tests of the software can be created, and there is potential for some to be automated.
- **Adaptability:** Software component functionality can be changed quickly.

- **Installability:** Installation and reinstallation are easy.
- **Conformance:** The software conforms to industry and operational standards.
- **Replaceability:** The software is replaceable in the future.

Taking into consideration external integrations, software quality attributes, and the internal design of components and their interactions is a lot of work. Agile teams look for clarity about what aspects of these areas they should focus more of their effort on. For external integrations, find out who in the organization can support your application integrations and coordinate efforts between teams.

In the case of software quality attributes, work with your business owner to decide which quality attributes are most important for your application. As for the software's internal design, decide how large design changes will be undertaken. Also, figure out how these design decisions will be communicated inside and, if needed, outside the team to external dependents. In all cases, an Agile team looks for ways to consolidate its efforts into practical focus areas that are manageable from iteration to iteration as the application and its design evolve.

In a phase-gate approach, all of the design effort that occurs before construction begins is sometimes referred to as "big design up front" (BDUF). The reason for specifying business requirements and technical design before construction is to reduce risk. I often hear the phrase "We have to get it right" from teams using this phased approach. The BDUF approach to software development, however, creates problems:

- Customers don't know all of the requirements up front, and therefore requirements emerge during implementation. When customers touch and feel the software after implementation, they have feedback for the development team. This feedback is essential to developing software that meets the actual needs of the customer and can be in conflict with the original requirements.
- The people who create business requirements and design specifications are not easily accessible once construction of the software begins. They are often busy specifying and designing other software at that time.
- Development teams, who read requirements and design specifications well after they were created, often interpret business requirements incorrectly. It is common for testers and programmers to have conflicting understandings of requirement details as they interact with existing components and application logic.

- Business needs change frequently, and therefore the requirement details specified weeks or months ago are not necessarily valuable today. Any changes to the requirements must be reflected in the technical design specifications so that the "correct" solution is developed. An adversarial relationship develops between business and technology groups because of these changes. Scope must be managed, or fixed so that the business is not able to make any more changes. Any modifications that the business wants must go through a costly change control process to detail the changes and estimate the impact on the current design, construction, and testing efforts.

Generally, these problems with BDUF are symptoms of feedback cycles that are too long in duration. The time needed to analyze, specify, and design software before constructing it allows requirements and designs to grow stale before they are implemented. One important aspect of an Agile approach is shortening the feedback cycle between customers, the development team, and working software that can be validated. Agile teams manage their development efforts to get working software into the hands of their customers so they can touch it, feel it, and provide feedback. Short iterations and feedback from customers increase the possibility that the software will align with customer desires and expectations as development progresses. This shorter feedback cycle is established using *self-organizing, cross-functional*, and *highly collaborative project teams* delivering working software to their customers incrementally using *evolutionary design*.

Self-organizing, Cross-functional Teams

In the seminal paper that profoundly influenced the development of Scrum, "The New New Product Development Game,"[3] Takeuchi and Nonaka provided three characteristics exhibited by self-organizing project teams, which I summarize here:

- **Autonomy:** External involvement is limited to guidance, money, and moral support, and top management rarely intervenes in the team's work. The team is able to set its own direction on day-to-day activities.
- **Self-transcendence:** Teams seem to be continually striving for perfection. Teams set their own goals that align with top management objectives and devise ways to change the status quo.

---

3. Hirotaka Takeuchi and Ikujiro Nonaka, "The New New Product Development Game," *Harvard Business Review*, January–February 1986.

- **Cross-fertilization:** The team members' different functional specializations, thought processes, and behavior patterns enhance product development once team members start interacting effectively.

In Scrum, the entire team is a self-contained unit, including the Product Owner and the ScrumMaster. The Scrum team members are expected to make incremental improvements to transcend their existing software delivery process capabilities, resulting in better quality and faster throughput of feature delivery over time. Multiple functional roles are represented on a Scrum team. Their cross-fertilizing tendencies and knowledge sharing about different aspects of the delivery process each iteration enable them to figure out how to optimize their interactions over time.

Teams (as opposed to teamwork) self-organize in response to significant challenges—audacious goals—because it energizes them. Leaders help by building a strong performance ethic. Individual responsibility and individual differences become sources of collective strength rather than barriers to team self-organization.

Software development involves the work of multiple functional disciplines: design, testing, programming, analysis, user experience, database, and more, depending upon the project. Agile team members are able to carry out all the work to deliver what is necessary for the project. Instead of optimizing functional disciplines, the team looks for ways to optimize the delivery of a feature from user experience to testing to code to database.

Continuous interaction among team members taking on different functional roles makes good things happen. Team members find ways to interact better, so they are neither overloaded nor starving for work items to take on. When someone on the team is overwhelmed with work items, another team member can look for ways to help that person finish the work. This person could have additional work cycles, depending on the type of work the team took on, and will learn how to execute the easier aspects of a functional discipline with which they help.

Agile teams look for ways to implement features that are verified and validated every iteration. This entails a high degree of collaboration among people across functional roles during the iteration. When the appropriate functional roles for the project are not represented on the team, or are limited, software delivery slows down. Team members have to either cover the work conducted in this functional area or let the work pile up to be done later. When work is left for later, it becomes more complicated, overwhelming, and error-prone.

Organizations taking an Agile approach must find ways for teams to increase collaboration across functional disciplines. Let's take the situation where a project has testers and programmers, but now they are on the same team. When both functional roles are represented on the team and are working together, a defect can be found much closer to the time that it was injected into the software. This reduces the amount of code created around the defect, puts the defect more into the context of current development efforts, and reduces the risk of unpredictability inherent in finding most defects at the end of a release. Highly collaborative teams enhance delivery, shorten feedback cycles, and improve quality.

Architectures should evolve toward simplicity. This is also true in a scaled environment that has many cross-functional teams. Simplicity emerges when teams spend time finding ways to deliver a complete feature, including the user interface and supporting infrastructure. If the architecture is too complicated, Agile teams make many small changes that lead to removal of unnecessary architectural components over time. This sort of simplification cannot be done in a vacuum by a single team because oversimplification can reduce business options too early and reduce the organization's ability to leverage existing assets for lower-cost solutions. Therefore, teams must work cross-organizationally to make architecture decisions that encompass diverse needs for similar assets. Also, there is a need in larger organizations to facilitate these cross-organizational interactions and communications to a larger audience.

WHY IS THIS TOPIC IMPORTANT?

Most books on Agile software development focus on either practices of the software development process, such as testing and programming techniques, or methods for project management. This book discusses how Agile software organizations can use these practices and methods with a holistic view of software development from team configurations to deployment and maintenance. Some might discuss parts of this book in terms of software or enterprise architecture, but this book is about how teams can take more responsibility for these aspects, taking software from vision to delivery and beyond. In this way, businesses can better understand the path to delivering valuable tools to users, and teams can build more integrity into what they deliver.

THIS BOOK'S TARGET AUDIENCE

This book is for everyone who is involved in delivering and maintaining software for users. Senior software leadership can find better ways to support and manage delivery of value to stakeholders. Software management can find ways to organize and support the work of development teams. Teams can find out more about how they can build integrity into the full software development life cycle. And team members can take away specific techniques, heuristics, and ideas that can help them improve their own capabilities.

HOW THIS BOOK IS ORGANIZED

This book is made up of 11 chapters and an appendix.

Chapter 1, "Managing Software Debt," is a primer on the types of software debt that can impede software changes with age. The topic of software debt is prevalent throughout the book as the main focus for attaining more architectural agility. Five areas of software debt are described in the chapter: technical, quality, configuration management, design, and platform experience. These five areas of software debt are detailed further in the rest of the book.

Chapter 2, "Technical Debt," Chapter 3, "Sustaining Internal Quality," and Chapter 4, "Executable Design," focus on how the internals of software, mostly the code, can be delivered in a way that reduces the friction of future changes.

Chapter 5, "Quality Debt," discusses the problem inherent in the break/fix mentality common in software development organizations. This chapter discusses the use of automation and putting tests toward the front of software delivery to progress toward zero bug tolerance.

Chapter 6, "Configuration Management Debt," presents the need for teams to take care of their software's configuration management needs. The point of this chapter is that teams should have two scripts that do the heavy lifting: deploy and roll back. To do this, many aspects of configuration management must be attended to along the way.

Chapter 7, "Design Debt," Chapter 8, "Designing Software," Chapter 9, "Communicating Architectures," and Chapter 10, "Technology Evaluation Styles," focus on how software is designed for changeability, including its structure, alignment to current business needs, integrity, and design communication.

Chapter 11, "Platform Experience Debt," looks at how people fit into software development and provides team configuration patterns and knowledge-sharing approaches to enable teams to be more effective.

This book is heavily focused on Agile software development, and therefore the expectation is that the reader has experience using an Agile approach such as Scrum or Extreme Programming (XP). For those who want a primer, Appendix A discusses the history of Agile software development along with Scrum and XP in more detail.

I hope that you enjoy this book and that it gives you tools, techniques, and heuristics to improve your daily work life in software development.

ACKNOWLEDGMENTS

I would first like to acknowledge content contributions from Brent Barton, Earl Everett, and Timothy Fitz. Brent helped review the book thoroughly and then edited the Introduction so that it pulled together themes in the book much better. Earl Everett took a photograph in the Redwoods that led to the one that adorns the front cover. Earl also wrote a wonderful foreword that aligns this image with the contents of the book. Timothy Fitz allowed for re-creating parts of his "Continuous Deployment" blog in Chapter 6 of the book.

Next, I would like to thank those people who provided significant reviews for parts of the book. Brad Appleton not only was a technical reviewer but also discussed particular aspects of his review via email with me, and I truly appreciate his input. Colin Renouf and a few other anonymous reviewers gave great input and enabled me to restructure the entire book after the technical review to better focus the book and its purpose. Bas Vodde provided direct feedback on early chapter drafts that guided me as I wrote what became the actual book; thank you for your directness, Bas. Jeff Sutherland, creator of the Scrum framework, reviewed Appendix A to ensure it does not misrepresent historical information or the framework itself.

For any book there are plenty of research sources that influence and inform the author before and during the book-writing process. Although I could never remember all of these sources, I would especially like to thank Steve McConnell, Ron Jeffries, Chet Hendrickson, Robert C. Martin, Martin Fowler, and Luke Hohmann for their great writing and passion for software development.

There are many folks who provided advice while I was writing this book. Naomi Karten discussed the book-writing process's difficulties and rewards with me at the AYE Conference so I could make an informed decision about whether to accept the offer from Addison-Wesley to write this book. Esther Derby, Diana Larsen, Johanna Rothman, and Will Iverson all gave me sage advice on the process of writing a book that got me through some of the toughest parts. I would like to thank Joshua Kerievsky for cheering me on over Twitter and then giving me advice on changing the name of the book once again at the last minute.

Of course, I could not have written this book without the unwavering support from my wife, Shivani. She is truly amazing and gave me the time and room to complete the book even when it was not so easy. I would also like to acknowledge my mom's support along the way, including reviewing the entire book and telling everyone she knows about it even though sometimes they didn't understand what I do.

About the Author

Chris Sterling is a Partner at Sterling Barton, LLC, where he works with clients as a Technology, Management, and Agile Consultant. Chris has an extensive technology, process, and consulting background which allows him to work with a diverse set of clients and teams. Chris brings his real-world experience and deep passion for software development to his engagements, enabling others to grasp important points and take away something that they can put into practice immediately.

In addition to consulting, Chris is a Certified Scrum Trainer and Innovation Games Facilitator. Chris has created and continues contributing to multiple open-source projects. He has been a speaker at many conferences and group meetings, including Agile Conferences, Better Software, SD West, Scrum Gatherings, PNSQC, and others. He has been a coordinator for multiple Puget Sound–area groups, including the International Association of Software Architects (IASA), Seattle Scrum, and most recently Beyond Agile. Chris also teaches the Advanced Topics in Agile Software Development course at the University of Washington for the Agile Developer Certificate extension program.

Chapter 1

MANAGING SOFTWARE DEBT

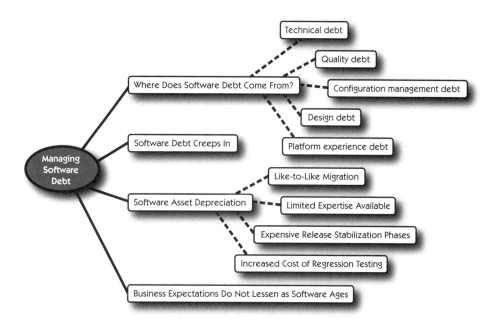

What he needs is some way to pay back. Not some way to borrow more.

—*Will Rogers*

WHERE DOES SOFTWARE DEBT COME FROM?

Many software developers have to deal with bad code at some point during their careers. Simple changes become frustrating endeavors. This results in more code that is difficult to read and unnecessarily complex. Test scripts and requirements are lacking and discordant with the existing system. The build is cryptic, minimally sufficient, and difficult to successfully configure and execute. It is almost impossible to find the proper place to make a requested change without breaking unexpected portions of the application. The people who originally worked on the application are long gone. Management expects delivery of predictable and frequent updates to the software but is continually disappointed with the progress.

How did the software get like this? It is almost certain that the people who developed the application did not intend to create such a mess. Did they?

Software debt accumulates when the focus is on immediate completion and changeability is neglected. The accumulation of debt does not impact software delivery immediately. At first, focusing on immediate completion creates a sense of rapid feature delivery with management, business stakeholders, and the team. Business stakeholders respond well to the pace of delivered functionality, and so the team attempts to continue this pace. What they don't understand is that this is only an illusion of speed in delivery.

Software debt creeps into systems slowly, allowing both the business and software delivery teams to maintain the illusion of rapid delivery far longer than they should. At some point small forms of decay in software become large enough to affect delivery to a point where working harder and longer doesn't result in successful outcomes. These results are not the fault of any one person. Usually many people are involved, there is poor communication, and ineffective software delivery practices allow decay to proliferate unmanaged throughout the software. Each time a team ignores the small but growing issues and thinks that this neglect will not affect the outcome, the team members are being dishonest with stakeholders and ultimately with themselves.

Although teams complain about quality issues that hinder progress on feature delivery, the complaints are not taken seriously enough until the issues present visible business challenges. Communication of software delivery issues that lead to future business challenges is not easy when the focus is usually on developing new features for users. The communication problem is exacerbated with the further separation of business and software delivery groups in companies. Business people are challenged with the lack of transparency provided by software projects. They learn about critical problems too late in the software development release cycle to make appropriate changes to their plans.

Software debt is made glaringly visible when the team works on stabilizing the software functionality late in the release cycle. Integration, testing, and bug fixing are unpredictable and the problems do not get resolved adequately before the release. People involved in the project stay late working to get the release out the door. At this point it is too late to pay back the debt accrued during feature development. It is found not only in the code. It is found in all aspects of software development. The following sources constitute what I call software debt:

- **Technical debt:**[1] These are the activities that a team or team members choose not to do well now and will impede future development if left undone.
- **Quality debt:** There is a diminishing ability to verify the functional and technical quality of software.
- **Configuration management debt:** Integration and release management become more risky, complex, and error-prone.
- **Design debt:** The cost of adding features is increasing toward the point where it is more than the cost of writing from scratch.
- **Platform experience debt:** The availability of people to work on software changes is becoming limited or cost-prohibitive.

Later chapters in this book will go into more detail about each specific type of software debt and ways to address them specifically. The rest of this chapter will describe what leads to software debt and how it affects software assets.

SOFTWARE DEBT CREEPS IN

Let's look at a fictional application, the relative location of software debt in it, and how new feature implementation is affected over time.

In Figure 1.1, we see an application that has some software debt but not enough to prolong implementation of upcoming features significantly. Two functional areas have no debt across the internal components needed to support their implementation. Only one functional area has accrued software debt across all internal application components so far.

As the team pushes toward the release date, they accrue software debt. They think there will be an opportunity to pay down the software debt, but application stakeholders are pushing for approximately the same amount of functionality in the next release. This is received as schedule pressure within the team. In response to this pressure, the team attempts to implement new features and bug fixes within the same amount of time. This attempt to stuff more work into the same amount of time leads to accelerated accrual of software debt.

As an application ages, software debt is ignored so the team can supposedly sustain its velocity of feature delivery. Everyone involved in the project knows that software debt is being ignored, but it is kept lower in priority and severity compared to functionality. Figure 1.2 shows an application that has incurred software debt across all functional areas and components. In five functional areas, the debt is significant enough that it will affect implementation

---

1. Ward Cunningham, "Technical Debt," http://c2.com/cgi/wiki?TechnicalDebt.

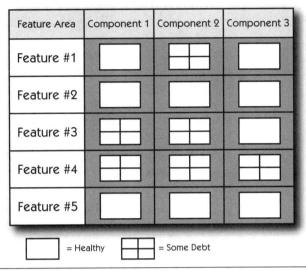

Feature Area	Component 1	Component 2	Component 3
Feature #1	Healthy	Some Debt	Healthy
Feature #2	Healthy	Healthy	Healthy
Feature #3	Some Debt	Some Debt	Healthy
Feature #4	Some Debt	Some Debt	Some Debt
Feature #5	Healthy	Healthy	Healthy

☐ = Healthy   ▦ = Some Debt

Figure 1.1   A relatively new system with little software debt accrued

of new features. No functional areas have avoided accrual of software debt at this time.

Business owners are starting to see small slowdowns in delivery. The development team notices this slowdown, too. The team asks for more "resources" so it can deliver functionality at the same velocity as in the past. This will increase the costs without any increase in value delivered. This means the return on investment (ROI) is affected negatively.

Even if the business sponsors were willing to cover the cost for additional people on the team, adding them would only reduce the rate of debt accrual and not the overall software debt. Continued feature development has surrounded the existing software debt with more and more code. This adds to the cost to remove the existing software debt. This means software debt increases in cost to pay back with age. The more software debt that persists in the software, the more difficult it is to address from a cost and duration perspective.

Software debt continues to accrue, as shown in Figure 1.3. Implementation of new features is affected significantly at this point. Business sponsors start minimizing feature development and put the software into "maintenance" mode. Applications with this designation usually stay in use until users complain that their ability to work within the application has slowed noticeably. At this point, perception of the software has degraded significantly and stakeholders are looking for ways to salvage or replace it.

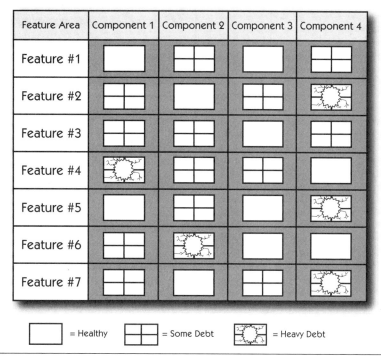

Feature Area	Component 1	Component 2	Component 3	Component 4
Feature #1	Healthy	Some Debt	Healthy	Some Debt
Feature #2	Some Debt	Healthy	Some Debt	Heavy Debt
Feature #3	Some Debt	Some Debt	Healthy	Some Debt
Feature #4	Heavy Debt	Some Debt	Some Debt	Healthy
Feature #5	Healthy	Some Debt	Healthy	Heavy Debt
Feature #6	Some Debt	Heavy Debt	Healthy	Healthy
Feature #7	Some Debt	Healthy	Some Debt	Heavy Debt

☐ = Healthy   ⊞ = Some Debt   ✳ = Heavy Debt

Figure 1.2   An aging software application that slowly incurs increased software debt across its functional areas and internal components

SOFTWARE ASSET DEPRECIATION

As software debt grows in an application, the increased cost of delivery will eventually overtake the value realized by implementing new features. Applications with this profile become liabilities to the organization that owns them. Organizations deal with these liabilities by decommissioning, upgrading, wrapping, or replacing the software. The following items are indicators of not realizing the effects of software debt early enough or outright ignoring the increased costs associated with continued maintenance of a software asset:

- Like-to-like migration
- Limited expertise available
- Expensive release stabilization phases
- Increased cost of regression testing

Each of these items will be discussed in more detail in the following sections.

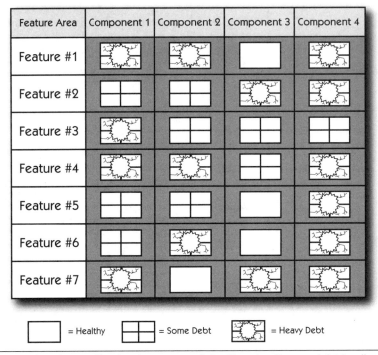

Figure 1.3   The application has accrued significant software debt in all functional areas and components.

Like-to-Like Migration

When software accrues too much debt, ways to continue adding value to the application diminish. The software becomes difficult to support and costs too much to work on. Some of these applications are still important to the business, but the cost to make even essential changes starts to outrun the value they provide. When an application starts showing these characteristics, teams and management start to discuss replacing it with a "better" and "newer" solution. This is sometimes called like-to-like migration, rewrite, system replacement, "next gen," or just a mess we've got to deal with some-day. Whatever it's called, the cost of such an endeavor is steep, and there are many misconceptions about how complicated it will be to deliver.

While consulting with teams and organizations taking on like-to-like migra-tions, I have heard the following justifications for such projects:

- *"It will be easy since we can just copy functionality from the current ver-sion."* This argument is usually not true since the team is crippled from the start by multiple factors. Once business sponsors are told about a like-to-like migration, they think that all the features can just be copied from the current version. Some stakeholders will have changes, additions, and updates. Also, it is common for requirements, mostly in those areas that are most complicated, to be out of date with the actual application. Along with the changes and out-of-date requirements, teams will also be developing the application on a new platform, which comes with its own complications. Although the team members understand the domain, they will be fighting with new technology, tools, and processes that always create unexpected costs.

- *"We need to update our technology."* Technology evolves quickly and there is considerable pressure to keep current. The problem with updating just to upgrade the technology is that significant portions of the development effort will not enhance the value of the software. In addition to the cost in effort, there tend to be fewer knowledgeable and experienced people to support the design, implementation, and maintenance of the updated technology.

- *"We don't have any other options."* Over the past decade, tools and platforms have become easy to find, learn, and use. This has moved our industry forward quickly. Although some of these tools and platforms have existed for some time, they have been packaged for mass consumption, reducing the learning curve. Refactoring and test automation tools are particularly interesting examples that give teams alternative options to like-to-like migrations. Refactoring,[2] changing the internal structure of the code without modifying its external behavior, can be used to make step-by-step improvements to the software over time. Test automation enables improvement in application verification by providing a safety net to check modifications more frequently for unexpected effects.

Like-to-like migrations always take longer than expected and therefore are surprisingly costly. Customers become frustrated with the amount of time taken to develop the migrated version of the application. It seems as if the development should be much easier if it is like-to-like. If multiple like-to-like migration projects are in progress at the same time, this is an indicator of systemic problems in software quality.

---

2. Martin Fowler, *Refactoring: Improving the Design of Existing Code* (Addison-Wesley, 1999).

Limited Expertise Available

An indicator of a software asset liability is when there is limited expertise available to work on an application. If the skills to work on the software are scarce in the industry, it is likely that the cost for someone with those skills is much higher than for people with more common skills. Organizations with extreme legacy software—I would suggest any software more than 20 years old—could also have liabilities on their hands. Some organizations have individuals who have been the only programmer on an application or component for 10, 15, 20 years or more. An application or component that is a liability because of limited available expertise is like a balloon that is ready to pop. At any time the person who is counted on to work on the software could be unavailable, and then a giant void is exposed.

It is common for organizations to hire a group of specialists to implement, configure, and alter a solution, for instance, with commercial off-the-shelf (COTS) products, based on the particular needs. The organization sponsors may not realize that continued maintenance will be needed for the specialized platform. A specialist comes with a higher price tag than people with other skill sets. This leads to hiring fewer people than are needed to maintain the solution satisfactorily. Now the customer has a single point of failure in the application, but migrating from this solution costs too much right now. At some point in the future, the cost to maintain this solution will not be easy to ignore anymore and the application will have to be replaced.

Limited expertise found in isolated software maintainers and platform specialists adds costs to application maintenance. Excessive software isolation and platform specialization in an organization is an indicator of optimizing locally without understanding the effects on maintaining the whole infrastructure. The total cost of ownership for applications with limited expertise available to maintain them continues to rise with time. Isolating development for particular parts of an application for an extended period of time increases the risk to future maintainability. Operating costs rise with excessive use of platform specialists because demand for their skills is high.

Expensive Release Stabilization Phases

Integration of components and functionality into a releasable package is a critical activity in any software development life cycle. The longer the wait to integrate, the more difficulties arise when generating a stabilized build of an application. Problems that were introduced earlier in development emerge during integration, such as duplicate code, merge conflicts, incompatible interfaces, and misaligned feature interpretations. These problems result in excessive defect logging and an unpredictable number of development revisions.

As software grows, integration strategies can become increasingly complex. This is evidenced in risk-based and time-boxed testing techniques. Risk-based testing is used because running a full regression suite takes too long to run frequently. Instead of running regression tests frequently, teams wait until there is "enough" software built to make a long-running regression test "worth" doing. During execution of the regression suite, a large number of defects are logged and categorized. Another strategy employed for testing is to simply restrict stabilizing the release to a fixed duration. This results in testers not having enough time to verify the software adequately. In both testing strategies, which are usually created in response to lack of value seen in testing, some defects will not be addressed. Over time this leads to a growing amount of known software debt that slows down delivery.

Configuration management also gets increasingly complex as software grows, attracts more dependencies, and deploys alongside more applications. Teams start using complicated branching strategies to deal with complexities across an application's components and long feedback cycles. These branches must be untangled and integrated to release some time after changes have been made. Additionally, compilation, packaging, and deployment may involve many manual steps to produce a valid build. Once a build is deployed to an environment and is deemed ready for verification to commence, it takes an extended period of time to execute an environment verification cycle. There is risk that the build pushed to this environment is unable to pass verification. A potentially even worse case is that the build does pass high-level verification but during regression test execution it fails early, thus exposing a hole in the verification process.

Driving toward a "code complete" date on software projects has been the predominant cause of these late-breaking integration issues. In early milestones and releases, the code complete date is sometimes fairly close to appropriate because the amount of software asset depreciation is still low. As the software grows in size and the liabilities increase, the code complete date becomes volatile and less attainable. Teams start pushing the code complete date out or just ignoring it to get a build into test. Testing these early builds results in a bunch of critical issues and problems executing a full regression suite. Figure 1.4 shows that when release stabilization phases increase in duration, the amount of effort geared toward feature delivery decreases.

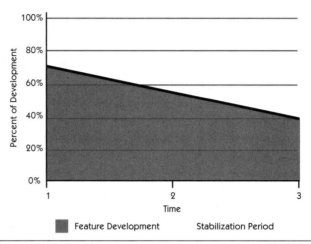

Figure 1.4   As more effort is devoted to the stabilization period for a
release, less effort is put into feature development.

An effect of increasing stabilization periods is unpredictable feature delivery.
The software accrues debt at an accelerated rate because decreased feature
delivery and compressed timelines culminate in removal of "noncritical"
processes such as full test verification, automation, documentation, and fixing of perceived lower-quality bugs.

You may have been part of a bug triage meeting in the past and had a conversation similar to this:

> Tester: "Now let's talk about the error that occurs in certain configura-
> tions of the software."
>
> Customer: "Do you think that priority 1 bug is really priority 1?"
>
> Project Manager: "No, we have a work-around for that particular bug.
> We can lower the severity to level 3 for now. We will fix this after the
> release."

This conversation occurs on projects that are behind schedule and getting
near their respective release dates. Quality decisions are being made based on
the plan rather than the severity of the issue being described. It is not
uncommon for organizations to have quality gates that dictate when software
is ready for production. If bugs at high priority or severity levels are not
addressed, the release will be delayed. In their haste to satisfy customers with
a release as planned, project teams cut quality, leaving the customers with
higher costs to maintain their software in the future.

Increased Cost of Regression Testing

With sufficient build and test automation, a project team is able to execute a full regression test suite in substantially less time compared to fully manual regression testing. Larger software applications take longer to run their full regression suite than smaller applications. As software ages, it grows in size and has a broader feature set to regression test. Automation is essential to keeping the cost of regression test execution manageable over time. Agile teams tend to put even more focus on build verification and testing, reducing integration issues, rework, and defects remaining in the software they develop.

As depicted in Figure 1.5, there is an ROI for test automation and continuous integration after some up-front cost. Depending upon the complexity, age, size, and platform an application is built on, the costs to realize a return on investment for build and test automation in the development of the application are different. Over time, the execution of manual regression test suites will take longer and slow down delivery. This slowdown may result in a reduction of testing to meet deadlines. This leads to a vicious cycle that accelerates the accumulation of software debt in the software that teams must deal with in the future.

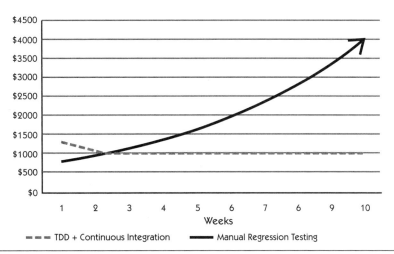

Figure 1.5   Average cost per similar-size feature per week as software systems age and increase in size

BUSINESS EXPECTATIONS DO NOT LESSEN AS SOFTWARE AGES

I was invited into an organization to deliver training on Agile software quality techniques and processes. The training was going well, but it seemed that the teams had already implemented many of the ideas being discussed. Halfway into the second day of the two-day course I asked, "What issues are you having that made you think your software quality practices needed to be improved?" This was not the first time I had asked the people who invited me this question, but I was surprised to hear a different answer from the one that was previously communicated to me. In response to the question, one of the software developers gave a quick high-level summary of the problems that led to our being there. The company's main product was an application that was over 15 years old. About a year prior to this course the company had made a release plan that included ten features to be delivered in six months. After six months, only six out of the ten features were deliverable, and they included quality issues. The company then created its next release plan with the goal of implementing six features in the next six months. To the company's dismay, only one out of the six planned features was delivered. Within one year the velocity of delivery had gone down 90%. The developers were stumped by these results and figured they must be doing something wrong. Figure 1.6 shows the decline in delivery over one year at this company.

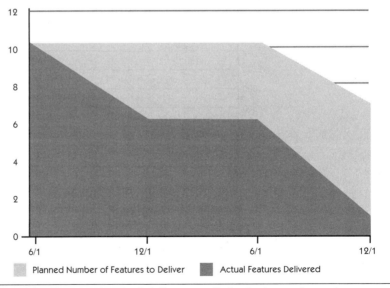

Figure 1.6   Company's actual delivery results for features planned over one year

This had been such a big problem that people from the business were also participating in this course. One of the business representatives added, "There is no way this product can survive if we can only implement one feature every six months. Our existing and potential customers will not trust that we can keep up with their evolving business needs. That is why you are here. We want to implement significantly more features during the next six months."

I must admit that I was initially overwhelmed by the situation this company was in. The expectations of the business representatives and teams in the room were obviously unrealistic.

The product in question was the company's flagship product. It represented 95% of its annual revenue. It had been actively developed over the past 15 years. About 70% of the product was written in C by the group's estimation. Over the past few years there had been a push toward object-oriented C++ code. Team members complained about the difficulties they were having working with the legacy code. Global variables were used as random data buffers, causing inexplicable problems in the application when they were modified. Naming conventions made reading the code nearly impossible without using a debugger to follow execution patterns. They were taking action to improve the situation, but there was not enough time to do it. Sometimes they just had to work around the issues rather than fix them.

Management had heard about these issues and more over the years. The business stakeholders did not see any ramifications to the problems in the previous product releases; therefore the problems were not perceived to be severe enough for action to be taken. What many people did not realize was that the teams were going above and beyond so that the releases would not fail. This additional effort, at the expense of not fixing the software debt, had left them in a state where software debt had become overwhelming.

If development teams and organizations are going to manage software debt, they must strike a balance between feature delivery for business gain and changeable software for the long haul. Doing whatever the business wants and dealing with the consequences of this decision by working additional hours so that the software delivery does not fail will lead to failure later on. As professionals we must find ways to manage software debt effectively while delivering additional business value. Business expectations will never lessen, but they can be prioritized.

SUMMARY

The rest of this book is dedicated to the topic of managing software debt at all levels: technical, quality, configuration management, design, and platform experience. It is my opinion that we cannot stop the creation of software debt while we are implementing each piece of code in the software. Instead, we must find ways to see indicators of software debt throughout the software development life cycle. Find out where the indicators of software debt are emerging in your organization. Do you have like-to-like migrations, limited expertise available, expensive release stabilization phases, or increased cost for regression testing your software assets? If so, find techniques in this book to try out to help manage the current software debt and slowly remove it over time.

Although there is no one-size-fits-all formula for managing software debt, a focus on creating potentially shippable software seems to lead toward reduced software debt. Performing the activities leading to releasable software frequently provides more transparency and focus to the software development process. Agile teams work in small batches and look for ways to reduce the feedback cycle for potentially shippable software. Teams start with short iterations, maybe one to four weeks in length. Over time, their technical feedback cycles could be shortened to days and minutes.

Managing software debt is the main way to attain architectural agility and enable software to be built for changing conditions. Consider the techniques in this book for your teams and organization with a focus on how they can reduce the feedback cycles for each component, application, and enterprise integration change that is committed. This is the way toward changeable software that continues to meet the needs of the business processes it supports.

Chapter 2

TECHNICAL DEBT

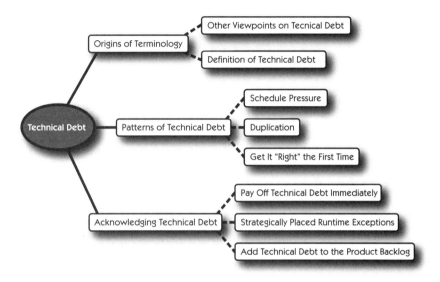

Technical Debt includes those internal things that you choose not to do now, but which will impede future development if left undone. This includes deferred refactoring.

Technical Debt doesn't include deferred functionality, except possibly in edge cases where delivered functionality is "good enough" for the customer, but doesn't satisfy some standard (e.g., a UI element that isn't fully compliant with some UI standard).

—Ward Cunningham[1]

---

1. Ward Cunningham, "Technical Debt," http://c2.com/cgi/wiki?TechnicalDebt. Reprinted with the permission of Ward Cunningham.

ORIGINS OF TERMINOLOGY

Technical debt emerged on the C2.com (also known as Cunningham & Cunningham, Inc.) wiki within a discussion on the "First Law of Programming." The ideas expressed on that wiki page regarding quality and software development throughput are enlightening. The first sentence professes in a simple and straightforward manner:

> *Lowering quality lengthens development time.*

The revisions of and responses to this sentence provided further clarity. There was also plenty of discussion about whether "quality" or "integrity" is the focal point and if the word *law* is appropriate. This kind of discussion is just up my alley, but I am going to focus on one particular point in the online conversation that links to a page on "Technical Debt":

> *Lowering quality lengthens development time in the long run, but can shorten development time in the short run if you're starting from a good place. It's a trick that you get to pull once, or maybe twice, before [technical debt] builds to the point of slowing down development. I've been part of pulling this trick a couple of times, when "making the numbers this quarter" at a startup had particularly high stakes.*[2]

This statement tells us that short-term technical debt comes with consequences. Teams that take on technical debt often or in large doses are challenged with potentially dire consequences to the sustainability of their software.

From this online discussion came an important corollary. The term *debt* has become a common metaphor to describe how deferring quality in software leads to slower delivery of changes to that software in the future. Technical debt focuses on the software debt pertaining to the internal quality of the software.

Other Viewpoints on Technical Debt

Martin Fowler makes an important point about technical debt in software.[3] Since we are unable to measure productivity, it is impossible to measure the

---

2. Ibid.
3. Martin Fowler, "TechnicalDebt," http://martinfowler.com/bliki/TechnicalDebt.html, original posting on August 3, 2004, with an update on February 26, 2009.

loss in productivity from taking on technical debt. Because technical debt cannot be measured, business stakeholders and management easily ignore it. If a project team anecdotally understands that cutting corners too many times will lead to costly software maintenance, they will have difficulty putting it into quantifiable terms that stakeholders and management can understand.

Fortunately, I have had fairly consistent success describing technical debt to business stakeholders and management for some time now. Whether or not their actions changed to more effectively manage their technical debt, the metaphor of "debt" at least made them aware and created a common language to discuss with development teams.

Steve McConnell provided his take on technical debt in an online article. Following is his technical debt taxonomy:

> *Here's a summary of the kinds of technical debt:*
>
>   I. *"Unintentional Debt." Debt incurred unintentionally due to low quality work*
>   II. *"Intentional Debt." Debt incurred intentionally*
>   II.A. *"Short-Term Debt." Short-term debt, usually incurred reactively, for tactical reasons*
>   II.A.1. *"Focused Short-Term Debt." Individually identifiable shortcuts (like a car loan)*
>   II.A.2. *"Unfocused Short-Term Debt." Numerous tiny shortcuts (like credit card debt)*
>   II.B. *"Long-Term Debt." Long-term debt, usually incurred proactively, for strategic reasons*[4]

Notice that he points out that lack of completeness does not constitute debt. This is similar to how Ward Cunningham originally defined technical debt. Adding more features to software that has structural integrity is always faster than working with code that is difficult to read and whose complexity hinders average changes.

Steve also makes a distinction between intentional and unintentional creation of debt. If a team lacks the ability and experience to identify when they are putting technical debt into software, it will be difficult to avoid adding technical debt. One way that technical debt can be managed is to put some

---

4. Steve McConnell, "Technical Debt," http://forums.construx.com/blogs/stevemcc/archive/2007/11/01/technical-debt-2.aspx, November 1, 2007.

people on the project with relevant experience and competency. Most teams are not made up entirely of domain experts. Finding the proper mix of experience and domain knowledge to establish satisfactory delivery of software that is also maintainable can make an enormous difference.

Talking about technical debt with your project team, business stakeholders, and management will heighten awareness of your software's health. As more technical debt is identified, it is important to make a continual effort to pay it back. If technical debt is not managed effectively, the costs for maintaining software will increase at a rate that will eventually outrun the value it delivers to customers.

Definition of Technical Debt

Ward Cunningham's clarification of technical debt is the definition used most often. Here it is again if you missed it at the start of this chapter:

> *Technical Debt includes those internal things that you choose not to do now, but which will impede future development if left undone. This includes deferred refactoring.*
>
> *Technical Debt doesn't include deferred functionality, except possibly in edge cases where delivered functionality is "good enough" for the customer, but doesn't satisfy some standard (e.g., a UI element that isn't fully compliant with some UI standard).*[5]

Although this definition could be left as is, I think it is important to put technical debt into context for this book. Technical debt is focused on components and how they interact within an application. The following definition is how this book will approach technical debt:

> *Technical debt is the decay of component and inter-component behavior when the application functionality meets a minimum standard of satisfaction for its users.*

Therefore, in this chapter we will focus on managing *debt* for the internal code of an application's components and the interactions between components, including external dependencies.

---

5. Ward Cunningham, "Technical Debt," http://c2.com/cgi/wiki?TechnicalDebt. Reprinted with the permission of Ward Cunningham.

PATTERNS OF TECHNICAL DEBT

There are some well-known patterns in software development that lead directly to increased technical debt. If teams are able to reduce or eliminate these patterns of work, they will deliver software with less technical debt. I can look back at projects I was affiliated with or consulted on in which the reduction or removal of the following patterns of work always resulted in better software delivery:

- Schedule pressure
- Duplication
- Get it "right" the first time

Each of these is the outcome of poor planning and ignoring the reality of past software development efforts. The next few sections will go into more detail about how these patterns add to the technical debt in software.

Schedule Pressure

When teams are held to a commitment that is unreasonable, they are bound to cut corners in order to meet the expectations of management. Many situations can cause a commitment to become unreasonable:

- **Scope creep:** Additional features are added to the project release plan without removing scope, which affects the schedule, cost, and quality of the project.
- **Third-party estimates:** A technical lead or architect makes an initial estimate of how long it will take and how much it will cost to deliver the scope of the release, and then the actual team is held to those estimates.
- **Change in team makeup:** Members of the team are added, removed, or replaced after a release plan has been put together.
- **Artifact of the estimation process:** Estimation is a guess, an educated guess at best, and therefore making exact commitments with no reasonable variability built in is problematic.
- **Late integration:** When integration happens late in the release cycle, surprising issues are usually found that must be addressed and stabilized within the time allotted by the release plan.

Schedules are put together based on numerous assumptions. It is impossible to know what will happen in the future. It is also impossible to fully comprehend a complex system like software before it is built. Therefore, plans are tools to help guide us toward our goals. This has been mentioned throughout history in many variations, including this one:

> *No battle plan survives contact with the enemy.*
> —*Nineteenth-century German military strategist Field Marshall Helmuth von Moltke*

Plans are bound to change once they are put into practice. We learn how our plans are flawed as we go. Organizations should adopt more flexible and adaptive planning strategies to help manage software debt better.

Cutting corners is a natural reaction of teams when schedule pressure becomes a driver of delivery. Their inclination is to "hurry up" and "just get it done." You may have heard these phrases used when a team is under schedule pressure. This mentality pushes teams to focus on the fastest way to modify the code and make the functionality "work." This is faster initially, but it leads to increased technical debt. It will not take long for further changes to be slowed by extensive debugging and inconspicuous defects. Schedule pressure leads to cutting corners, growing technical debt, and slower delivery of valuable features.

Duplication

There are many reasons that duplication of code occurs in software development:

- Lack of experience on the part of team members
- Copy-and-paste programming
- Conforming to existing software's poor design
- Pressure to deliver

Duplication is difficult to avoid completely, but there are tools that can help identify it. Tools that implement algorithms for finding duplicate code in most popular modern languages have become mature in the past few years. In Chapter 3, there is a section on static code analysis that will go into more detail about how these tools can be used to provide early detection of technical debt, including duplication of code. Executing static code analysis tools to find duplicate code provides essential information, but it is up to the team to take action on the findings. The following team and organizational practices help to counteract duplication of code as well:

- **Pair programming:** The act of working with others across the team will spread knowledge and improve the competencies of each team member. Pair programming is not as easy as just putting two team members at the same workstation and telling them to work together. The increased interaction between team members using pair programming could lead to conflict. This conflict can be positive or detrimental to the team, depending upon how it is handled. It is important to support team members in their use of pair programming through coaching and periodic reflection.

- **Copy-and-paste "Spidey-sense":**[6] Every time you think about copying and pasting a large section of code, DON'T! There is a reason why the other code looks as if it solves your current need. Refactor the code to a common location for use in both places. Copying code from another project or off the web is another potential pitfall since assumptions about direction of invocation and the necessary parameters could be quite different from your actual needs. It could be best to just remove "Copy" from the "Edit" menu in your integrated development environment (IDE), but learning and practicing copy-and-paste "Spidey-sense" is probably enough.

- **Continually evolving software design:** At a large medical systems company, experienced developers were ordered not to use most "Gang of Four" (GoF)[7] design patterns because they were too complicated for some of the novice developers to comprehend. Instead, nested conditionals and structural programming techniques were used, causing the software to grow beyond five million lines of code. Find ways to continually introduce better design elements and refactor existing code to implement them for the software's evolutionary benefit.

A team that becomes aware of the potential for duplication and takes steps to identify it early will produce code with more flexibility in design and opportunities for reuse. Code reused in multiple locations across an application's features can be changed in one place to meet new business needs quickly.

Get It "Right" the First Time

Getting it "right" the first time is antithetical to duplication. Because duplication in all of its incarnations is thought of as a negligent programming style, getting it "right" attempts to counteract this style with overabundant planning and design. This has been a problematic ideal that creates overly

---

6. "Spidey-sense": an indistinct feeling that something is wrong, dangerous, or suspicious around you.
7. Erich Gamma, Richard Helm, Ralph Johnson, and John M. Vlissides, *Design Patterns: Elements of Reusable Object-Oriented Software* (Addison-Wesley, 1994).

complex solutions with unused functionality that must also be maintained into the future. Designing a perfect solution is a destructive endeavor and is elusive to even the most capable software craftsman.

We must admit to ourselves that software is complex even in its basic form. Turning a user's need into software that a computer is able to execute is daunting. To work with other people in the delivery of that software further complicates the undertaking. Why would we want to believe that it is possible to get the software "right" the first time given these challenges?

First of all, there is pressure to manufacture software solutions to meet operational demands quickly. The belief of those in technical and nontechnical positions that software is a "cookie-cutter" activity similar to manufacturing widgets creates assumptions about how reasonable making exact plans and expectations is. There is also a false belief held by technical folks that the needs of business do not change for extended periods of time. Speculation based on these beliefs from both technical and nontechnical people results in rationalizing the belief in getting the software "right" the first time.

I am sure that some people will read this section and think they have a counter-example of how once they were "right" the first time. I will even admit that I can think of a time when I was involved in designing the technology for a solution "right" in initial plans. It has been my experience that this is the exception rather than the rule. As I have worked with more and more Agile teams, it has occurred to me that

> **We're more likely to get it "right" the third time.**

By realizing that this is closer to the truth than getting it right the first time, I develop software that is easier to change. If I know that what I am initially developing will change at least two more times, it is important that it be malleable. Effective use of scaffolding to support change such as automated unit and regression tests is essential. Identifying design patterns and simplifications that will enhance the structure through refactoring is essential. Ultimately, sustaining the software's internal quality leads to more sustainable software overall.

Acknowledging Technical Debt

There is a cost to not addressing technical debt. Early in its existence the cost is quite small, and it could take just a few seconds to work around it. Dealing with small work-arounds throughout the code becomes part of a team's status quo. Team members think, "We should fix that" and continue working around obvious technical debt.

There is a problem with this attitude toward technical debt. The longer an instance of technical debt exists in the code, the more code will surround and interact with it, thus making the debt more difficult to remove. Even if no more code is added around a piece of code with technical debt, when someone comes back to that code later it will be more difficult to modify the code since the context for why it exists is no longer readily at hand. Therefore . . .

> **No matter what, the cost of addressing technical debt increases with time.**

The first step in addressing technical debt is acknowledging that it exists and is detrimental to the maintenance of the software you are working on. This seems obvious, but I commonly find that teams don't acknowledge the technical debt consequences and only complain about its existence. If teams do not address technical debt as they identify it, they are setting a precedent of ignoring it. Each time they don't acknowledge and take action on technical debt the cost to maintain the software increases. Following are a few ways that technical debt is dealt with effectively:

- Pay off technical debt immediately (otherwise known as "Fix it now").
- Strategically place runtime exceptions where the technical debt is and fix it within a few minutes.
- Write down the location, description, and potential cost of not addressing the technical debt and add it to the Product Backlog for prioritization against future work.

Pay Off Technical Debt Immediately

The most effective method of these three is probably the most controversial. Paying off technical debt immediately goes against the software industry project norms. Teams are used to coding only the feature they are currently working on and leaving technical improvements for a later time, even though that later time never seems to arrive. How could a team possibly justify fixing technical debt as they find it rather than just adding the functionality the customer directly asked for? The mind-set behind this question has at least two flaws, in my opinion.

The first flaw in this mind-set is that the customer did not hire the team to make decisions about how best to develop the software. Customers, either internal or external, employ teams to implement software that meets the needs of users and, in many cases, to continue adding value for those users into the future. This means the software must be maintainable. A project team is responsible for making decisions about the implementation that enhances the software's maintainability so that it continues to be considered valuable to its users.

The second flaw is the assumption that the costs associated with fixing technical debt remain constant over time. There are many examples of technical debt and the potential costs, and all of these examples point to increased cost with age. A simple example is unclear variable names as shown here:

```
PRC p;
```

What is a PRC? Would you immediately know that this refers to a court proceeding? Let's say that you saw the variable p used later in a method and did not see the initialization above. Would you know what this variable is without looking back to the point of instantiation? Maybe with newer tools you could hover over the variable and figure it out, but that is not an excuse for being lazy. It will still take more time than naming the variable appropriately from the start. The amount of effort exerted each time you look at this section of code to figure out what the variable represents adds to the cost of this instance of technical debt.

After one of my presentations on "Managing Software Debt" at the SD West 2009 conference, an attendee described an interesting example of technical debt. The software that he was working on had a section of code that included more than 128 conditions within the same if block. The reason 128 was a significant number had to do with the GCC for C++ compiler limitations on the development platform. When the 129th condition was added to the block, the compiler would fail. Instead of using alternative design methods to rectify the problem, a person on the team decided to game the compiler. In the 128th condition, the result was captured in a variable so that the current block could conclude and a new if block could start with saved Boolean variable state. I cannot imagine how difficult it must be to navigate a conditional block with more than 128 conditions, but it must create significant confusion and frustration for team members.

Customers expect project teams to create valuable and maintainable software. Project teams should not get duped into believing that delivering value while decreasing maintainability is what the customer wants. As technical debt increases in your software, the confidence with which team members

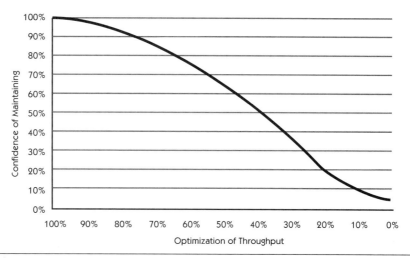

Figure 2.1   The confidence with which a project team approaches maintenance of software directly relates to the optimization of their feature delivery throughput. This curve originated in a conversation between Dan Rawsthorne and me in the San Jose airport. Thanks, Dan.

approach the code decreases. This lack of confidence leads to conservative actions and slower throughput of feature delivery. Removing technical debt enables a team to increase their confidence and slowly increase feature delivery throughput, as shown in Figure 2.1.

Each instance of technical debt, no matter how small, increases in cost over time and leads to additional technical debt on top of it. Teams should not ignore this increase in cost and how it can affect the cost of maintaining the software for the customer in the future. Awareness of a drop in team member confidence in modifying software helps to address decreases in throughput earlier in the project.

Strategically Placed Runtime Exceptions

From time to time, and sometimes more than we would like, we find technical debt in the code we are currently working on. Changing direction to fix the technical debt seems like too much of a distraction from the current thread of thought. What is the protocol in this situation? We know that not paying down the technical debt will increase the cost of maintenance, but we are currently making progress in a different direction.

In the past I have used "cleanup"-focused comments such as TODO or FIXME. Over time I have found these to be less effective. Using the cleanup comments seemed to always lead to reports generated by our continuous integration environment on how many existed in the code. Although our team's intentions were to use these cleanup comments only as temporary placeholders so we could come back to them later, they still somehow found their way into source control. Teams that rack up enough of these "cleanup" comments start using the reports to identify work to be done in the future. This breaks an essential principle of managing work for a team:

Maintain only one list of work.

In the scenario with "cleanup" comments, the customer manages a list of work—features—and the team manages another list of work—technical debt. It is highly recommended that teams do not do this. Instead, apply the techniques in the next section, "Add Technical Debt to the Product Backlog," to manage this situation more effectively.

Instead of using "cleanup" comments, throw strategically placed runtime exceptions into the code so that it is left in a broken state. This way you will not be inclined to check in the code with the existing technical debt you know should be cleaned up. This technique is an improvement in the following ways:

- Feedback is presented in the development environment rather than in generated documentation and reports.
- At least one test is still broken, either manual or automated, and therefore code won't be checked in until it is dealt with.
- The exception message can be used to provide context for the technical debt when you come back later to deal with it.
- The development environment provides a line number where the exception is thrown, and you will be able to click through directly to the location of the technical debt.
- The exceptions will cause you to think about how to decouple the technical debt from the functionality you are working on, and what *is* and *is not* involved in that functionality.

Let's look at an example of using this technique. We've just taken on a task to make showing tool tips configurable in our application. As we are implementing this functionality, we come across the following code:

```
try {
    File toolTipConfigFile = new File("C:/app/tooltip.config");
    FileInputStream fis = new FileInputStream(toolTipConfigFile);
```

```
    Properties toolTipProperties = new Properties(fis);
} catch (IOException ex) {
}

String debugVal = toolTipConfigFile.getProperty("debug");
Boolean debugTurnedOn = Boolean.parseBoolean(debugVal);
```

It seems the tool tip configuration file is getting loaded from a hard-coded location. This is problematic because the location is hidden in the code, and in order to change it we need a new build. On top of that, the exception that is thrown when the configuration file is not found will just get caught and ignored.

Instead of diverting our focus to removing the duplication and improving loading of the tool tip configuration file, we want to finish adding the show_tool_tips configuration property. We don't want to lose sight of the technical debt, so we strategically place a runtime exception:

```
try {
    File toolTipConfigFile = new File("C:/app/tooltip.config");
    FileInputStream fis = new FileInputStream(toolTipConfigFile);
    Properties toolTipProperties = new Properties(fis);
} catch (IOException ex) {
}

String debugVal = toolTipConfigFile.getProperty("debug");
Boolean debugTurnedOn = Boolean.parseBoolean(debugVal);
throw new RuntimeException("Don't load tool tip config from hard
coded file location above");
```

This allows the file to get loaded, as it has been done up to this point, and parse out the properties from the configuration file. This allows us to finish adding our new property to the configuration file and verify that it is used correctly. It also makes all of the unit tests interacting with this part of the code fail at the strategically placed runtime exception. When they all fail at this point in the code, we know it is time to tackle the configuration loading.

The cleaned-up code might look something like the following:

```
void loadToolTipConfigurationProperties() throws IOException {
    File toolTipConfigFile =
      new File(Configurations.getToolTipConfigFileLocation());
    FileInputStream fis = new FileInputStream(toolTipConfigFile);
    Properties toolTipProperties = new Properties(fis);
    parseToolTipProperties(toolTipProperties);
}
```

```
void parseToolTipProperties (Properities toolTipProperties);
    …
    parseShowToolTipsProperty(toolTipProperties);
    …
}
```

I find that this technique is difficult from time to time. The difficulties usually expose the further need to fix the technical debt immediately because the functionality I am adding is more tightly coupled to it than I originally thought. You might find an alternative approach, but make sure that it forces you to deal with the technical debt so that it can't be ignored.

Add Technical Debt to the Product Backlog

Legacy code that more closely resembles a *Big Ball of Mud* will uncover hefty refactoring opportunities. It may not make sense to divert attention from the task at hand to attempt a giant refactoring now. Foote and Yoder define the Big Ball of Mud software architecture as follows:

> *A BIG BALL OF MUD is a casually, even haphazardly, structured system. Its organization, if one can call it that, is dictated more by expediency than design.*[8]

A Big Ball of Mud encompasses components that are thoroughly entangled, leaving the software awkward to work with. A seemingly simple modification tends to have an impact on other parts of the software that you probably wouldn't have believed beforehand. A component within an application can be a Big Ball of Mud yet the rest of the software is not. Teams may avoid making changes to code in this component or areas entangled with it.

When they find components or applications that resemble a Big Ball of Mud, the project team can create a policy by which they capture areas of technical debt and make them visible to the customer for prioritization. In Scrum, a team would write an item to be placed in the Product Backlog for the Product Owner to prioritize, for example.

It is important to note that creating a separate infrastructure improvement list or visible chart on the wall is not a replacement for placing it into the main work stream managed by the customer. It is again highly recommended that you stick with the principle of maintaining only one list of work. Sec-

---

8. Brian Foote and Joseph Yoder, Department of Computer Science, University of Illinois at Urbana-Champaign, "Big Ball of Mud," June 26, 1999, www.laputan.org/mud/mud.html.

ondary lists always take a backseat to primary work streams and are usually forgotten or ignored. Management will tell project teams to manage their workload with a large percentage dedicated to the primary work stream and the rest for the secondary. Team members then make decisions about how to meet commitments on primary and secondary work stream priorities. This always ends with teams not being able to make improvements to the software because it is secondary to feature delivery, which almost always takes more time than initially thought.

Since adding technical debt to the Product Backlog does not fix the problem immediately, there is an increased risk that it will not be taken care of. The following list represents problems to watch out for when using this approach:

- All technical debt items are prioritized as low.
- Too many technical debt items have been captured to be managed effectively.
- The number of technical debt items is used as an excuse to do Big Design Up Front.
- Technical debt items take more than one week to address.

When a customer prioritizes technical debt items as low, the project team is not explaining the importance of the items well enough or there are factors driving the customer to ignore them. Project teams should work with management and the customer to figure out how the technical debt items can be prioritized more effectively.

In software that resembles the Big Ball of Mud architecture, it is common for technical debt to be found around every corner in the code. When too many items are identified, they become overwhelming to deal with. The project team should find ways to filter out the items with the most potential value and lowest cost to implement. By taking on high-value and low-cost items, the project team will alleviate technical debt in the software at a faster rate and improve the effectiveness of subsequent changes in the code.

Technical debt is frustrating to deal with. This frustration could lead team members to focus on designs that fix "all" of the technical debt. This entails rewriting significant portions of the component or application to a new design. Project teams should take a deep breath and tackle the technical debt with patience and diligent refactoring.

Because of the complexity inherent in detangling a Big Ball of Mud, project teams will find fixes to particular technical debt issues that continue further and further into the code. It is common for team members to exhaust their original estimates to fix the technical debt while still staring down many unknowns. Project teams should watch for these situations and call them out immediately. Use the knowledge gained thus far and either get a larger group within the team or bring in a subject matter expert to help.

SUMMARY

Technical debt is

> the decay of component and inter-component behavior when the application functionality meets a minimum standard of satisfaction for its users.

Technical debt tends to follow the use of particular work patterns such as schedule pressure, duplication, and the mentality of getting it "right" the first time. Excessive schedule pressure results in teams taking shortcuts to meet the expectations of management and customers. Duplication with the software because of cut-and-paste coding tactics results in teams making even simple changes in more than one place. The idea of get it "right" the first time is fraught with incorrect assumptions about what we can know about the future. Instead, approach software based on this notion:

> **We get it right the third time.**

Acknowledging the existence of technical debt by finding ways to take action to resolve it incrementally is essential to keeping software maintainable. Approaches that were discussed in this chapter were to pay off technical debt immediately, insert strategically placed runtime exceptions, and add technical debt to the Product Backlog. Paying off technical debt immediately may be beyond the comfort of many teams, but it is the most effective way to resolve technical debt and make software more maintainable. Strategically placed runtime exceptions can be an effective method for ensuring that technical debt is resolved before integrating it into source control. When the technical debt identified is too large, such as in software that resembles a Big Ball of Mud, it may be appropriate to capture it in the Product Backlog alongside features to be delivered in the future.

As teams learn how to combat technical debt, meaning those deferred changes that will impede future development if left undone, they will find maintaining the software to be more consistent and predictable. This enables better planning, increases feature delivery throughput, and makes the code more fun to work on.

Chapter 3

Sustaining Internal Quality

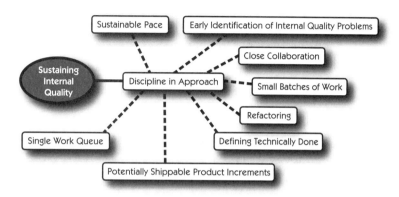

It's not the strongest who survive, nor the most intelligent, but the ones most adaptable to change.

—attributed to Charles Darwin

Discipline in Approach

Code found in the wild comes with different levels of quality. The level of quality necessary depends on the risk profile of the software. One could point to many open-source and commercial software projects where the internal quality could be described as suspect. Yet, in some cases, there is a large following of users for the software because it provides sufficient value to compensate for its perceived internal messiness.

It is not common for the perceived value of software to outweigh high levels of quality issues. In cases where the quality issues become recognizable to users, such as odd behavior and surprising errors, the users' perception of the software can deteriorate to a point where they stop using it. The level of quality has now dropped below the value that the software provides. It is not easy to recover from a perception of low quality, as many software companies, organizations, and teams have found out.

Sustaining adequate quality in the software under development does not just happen. If quality attributes are not discussed and teams haven't described how quality will be assessed, quality will decay as the project progresses. Teams must use disciplined approaches to sustain a minimum level of internal quality. Following is a set of approaches that seem to enable teams to sustain the internal quality of software:

- Sustainable pace
- Early identification of internal quality problems
- Close collaboration
- Refactoring
- Small batches of work
- Defining technically done
- Potentially shippable product increments
- Single work queue

When used together, these approaches create a framework that supports trust building between teams and customers. Teams are able to show progress and have confidence in their feature delivery capabilities. Customers are able to provide feedback on progress and spend less time focusing on whether the team is working on the "right" tasks. The following sections will explore each approach in more detail and how it applies to sustaining internal quality through discipline.

Sustainable Pace

In the 12 principles behind the Agile Manifesto, there is a single principle that refers to sustainable pace directly:

Agile processes promote sustainable development. The sponsors, developers, and users should be able to maintain a constant pace indefinitely.[1]

"Sustainable pace" is sometimes misinterpreted as meaning "Don't work overtime ever" or as an excuse to leave early for personal sustainability. This is not always the appropriate interpretation of sustainable pace. It is not that teams should never work overtime but rather that they be able to sustain their average pace into the foreseeable future. There are situations where working overtime is an appropriate choice that the team is involved in making.

---

1. "Principles behind the Agile Manifesto," http://agilemanifesto.org/principles.html, 2001.

The problem is that many teams are not part of this conversation and find themselves in situations where sustainable pace is not even a possibility. Teams, management, and customers should be aware of the ill effects of taking on too much work. By not working at a sustainable pace, a team will deliver less valuable software and create higher levels of software debt.

Software organizations, and the industry as a whole, have difficulty measuring the value that software currently has or will eventually provide. Our inability to measure software value forces us to measure different aspects of the software delivery process. How accurate are our estimates for constructing the software? How accurate were our release schedule predictions? How close to our budget targets is our project? Are we getting all the features into the release deliverables?

If we were able to measure the value of software delivered, projects would show that continuous pressure to work overtime increases value delivered for only a short period of time but reduces it over the long term, as shown in Figure 3.1.

It is important that business and technical stakeholders in a project understand the effects of schedule pressure over time. Teams are able to accelerate feature delivery for a short period of time, days or weeks. Under continual schedule pressure—for example, a month or more—delivering at an unsustainable rate will result in substantial software debt. Even when a team accelerates for a short period of time to meet a date, such as for showing alpha

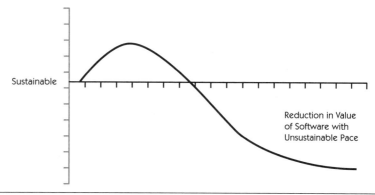

Figure 3.1 If a team is pressured to accelerate software delivery for an extended period of time, its ability to deliver valuable software over time will decrease. The cost to deliver the same amount of value increases because the team has taken on technical debt to meet the schedule pressure and unrealistic expectations.

software at a conference or a start-up launch date, the team must be able to follow up with software debt cleanup activities. There is a cost to putting schedule pressure on a team, and the overall cost is usually more than if the team was to work at a sustainable, but effective, pace.

Early Identification of Internal Quality Problems

Internal quality issues are introduced in small doses. Each dose is software debt that enables entropy to set in more deeply. It is not easy to identify these internal quality issues early without proper tooling because each issue is small and, from an external point of view, seemingly harmless. Because it takes time to identify the internal quality threat, the team continues to deliver on top of the problems, and this intensifies the cost to future delivery.

Agile teams and organizations should find ways to identify internal quality problems early. Whenever a problem arises, a question similar to the following should be asked:

How could this problem have been identified earlier?

There is a plethora of free, open-source, and commercial tools that help identify internal quality issues early. A few major categories of tools used by teams today are

- Unit test frameworks
- Static code analysis
- Continuous integration

These tools help teams find out when their software is decaying in internal quality during development and integration activities. The next few sections will go into more detail about how each of these tools supports early identification of internal quality problems.

Unit Test Frameworks

Unit tests are focused specifications of how an extremely small facet of the software internals should behave. If a unit test fails, a team should easily be able to find the software artifact(s) that did not conform to current unit test specifications from the broken test case. Unit tests are usually automated in the same programming language as the feature implementation code, but this is not a requirement.

Table 3.1 A Simple Pattern System for Writing Unit Tests as Expressed by Kent Beck.

Pattern	Purpose
Fixture	Create a common test fixture.
Test case	Create the stimulus for a test case.
Check	Check the response for a test case.
Test suite	Aggregate test cases.

Many frameworks have been developed to help construct unit tests more quickly and consistently. One category of unit test frameworks is referred to as *xUnit*. These frameworks follow the xUnit naming convention, where the letter *x* is overwritten, which started with SUnit developed for the Smalltalk platform by Kent Beck.[2] Subsequent unit test frameworks were developed with similar design principles for other programming languages, such as Java (JUnit), .NET (NUnit), Python (PyUnit), and C/C++ (CppUnit).

Kent Beck's original paper on "Simple Smalltalk Testing: With Patterns"[3] provided the philosophy and constructs for effective unit testing. The philosophy of xUnit frameworks is that programmers write their own tests in code to check assumptions of self-contained units within the software. When writing these tests, programmers check for expected results. If the unit does not behave in a way that is consistent with the expectations, the framework notifies the programmer of a *failure*. An unexpected condition, as opposed to a failing expectation, that occurs in the testing of a unit is expressed as an *error*. Finally, each unit test sets up just enough test data to support its expected results.

The constructs of unit testing are defined in Kent's paper as shown in Table 3.1.

An example of these patterns in action can be seen in the following JUnit (a Java xUnit library also created by Kent Beck) code sample:

```
public class WhenUserSendsMessageUnitTest {
    private MessageService messageService = new MessageService();

    @Test
    public void shouldSendValidMessage() {
        messageService.send("this is a valid message");
```

2. Kent Beck and Donald G. Firesmith, *Kent Beck's Guide to Better Smalltalk* (Cambridge University Press, 1998).
3. Kent Beck, First Class Software, Inc., "Simple Smalltalk Testing: With Patterns," transcribed to HTML by Ron Jeffries at www.xprogramming.com/testfram.htm.

```
                    assertEquals("this is a valid message",
                    messageService.getLastMessageSent());
        }

        @Test (expected = InvalidMessageException.class)
        public void shouldFailWithNullMessage(){
messageService.send(null);
        }
}
```

This code sample incorporates the first three patterns for unit tests: *fixture*, *test case*, and *check*. In the JUnit code sample, the class WhenUserSendsMessage-UnitTest is the name given to the test fixture. As the name points out, this test fixture has been created to unit test sending a message. Two test cases are identified in this test fixture: shouldSendValidMessage and shouldFailWith-NullMessage. These test cases check the expected behavior when sending a valid and an invalid message. The first test case, shouldSendValidMessage, asserts that a valid message should send successfully through the MessageService and be retrievable after it was sent. In the second test case, shouldFailWith-NullMessage, the test case expects that an InvalidMessageException will be thrown because the MessageService will not send a *null* message.

The last construct of a unit test that is not shown in the preceding example is a *test suite*. The following code example shows how a *fixture* can be included in a test suite alongside other fixtures:

```
@RunWith(Suite.class)
@Suite.SuiteClasses({
 WhenUserSendsMessageUnitTest.class,
    …
})
public class SyncSuite {
}
```

The class SyncSuite is identified as a test suite by using the @RunWith annotation. This test suite takes a list of test fixture classes to be included using the @Suite annotation. All of the fixtures added to this list will be included in the test suite's execution. As the suite runs, each test case will be executed. Nowadays, creating a test suite class is usually necessary. There are numerous tools and frameworks that take care of generating a test suite when you conform to their project structure or provide the location of where the unit tests reside.

For automated unit tests to realize their true value, they must be executed against the code with frequency. With each small modification, a team member executes a test case against the unit he or she is working on within an application. Before checking in the code, a team member executes the project's full test suite and ensures that all of the test cases pass. Next, a team member updates the local project with any changes integrated into the team's source control branch and executes the test suite again to ensure that nothing that will put the project into a broken state is being checked in. After the test suite passes again, the team member checks in the changes to a central repository. Each of these test suite executions can help with early identification of internal quality issues.

It is important that the time frame for gathering feedback at each level of test suite execution be appropriate. In a team member's environment, the test suite should execute within seconds. This means that the test suite a team member executes in the development environment should include only fast-running tests. Michael Feathers's definition can help teams figure out what should *not* be considered a unit test:

> *A test is not a unit test if:*
>
> - *It talks to the database*
> - *It communicates across the network*
> - *It touches the file system*
> - *It can't run at the same time as any of your other unit tests*
> - *You have to do special things to your environment (such as editing [configuration] files) to run it.*[4]

The Extreme Programming practice of Test-Driven Development, also known by its acronym TDD, provides additional benefits on top of automated unit testing. These additional benefits include higher code coverage based on expected application behavior. A more in-depth discussion of TDD is in Chapter 4, "Executable Design."

Static Code Analysis

Static code analysis tools come in many different forms. Their features range from validating code formatting rules to finding design issues in the code. The accuracy and usefulness of static code analysis are questioned by some and praised by others in the software development community. My opinion is that making high-level decisions as a team on coding standards and design as a project progresses makes code easier to work with. Being in a team means making concessions about preferred code formatting ideals so that the team can execute effectively as a group. Static code analysis can help teams

---

4. Michael Feathers, Artima Developer, "A Set of Unit Testing Rules," www.artima.com/weblogs/viewpost.jsp?thread=126923, September 9, 2005.

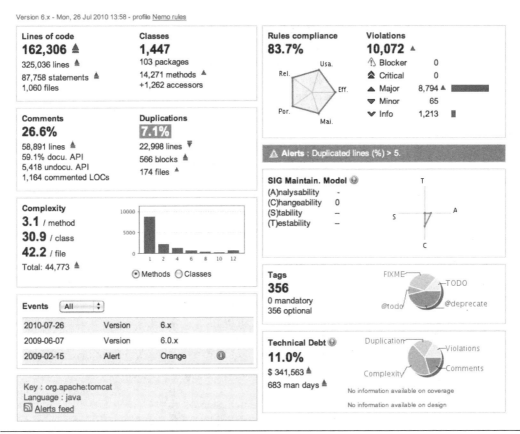

Figure 3.2   Example dashboard with static code analysis metrics using Sonar, a free and open-source internal quality dashboard platform[5]

identify issues in coding standards and areas of design closer to the time the code is modified. If a team has agreed to particular coding standards and design decisions, static code analysis should be easy to automate in a developer's IDE and during the automated build and validation process for the project. If coding standards are broken or areas of the design do not adhere to decisions made by the team, the build should break so the team can fix the issues quickly. An example dashboard showing static code analysis results is shown in Figure 3.2. A principle that I have found useful to support early identification of divergent design aspects is:

Aspects of the software's design that teams agree to should be automated, if possible, and break the build when they are not adhered to.

---

5. Image of the Sonar project dashboard. The Sonar web site is at www.sonarsource.org/.

Static code analysis tools can be dangerous when used in an environment where respect for the team's capabilities is lacking. Team leadership and external management can abuse static code analysis tools to measure a team's effectiveness or, even worse, to evaluate team members' performance. This is abusive and an invalid way to evaluate a team's adherence to standards and its competency. There are many factors that support differences in approach, focus, and design of an application. It is impossible to generalize these factors for enterprise analysis and standardization and provide value in every project's context.

Teams should be empowered to integrate tools that are useful for their software delivery. If teams are forced to execute tools they do not find valuable, they will find ways to minimize the tool's interference in everyday development. The act of executing static code analysis tools against your code base only for reporting purposes seems to me useless because reports are easily ignored or used as a tool to punish teams. Also, project teams may strive to meet the expectations of the enterprise to the detriment of delivering the right software to their customers.

When using static code analysis tools, find ways to automate their execution in team member and integration environments. There are many free and commercial plug-ins for popular IDEs that support static code analysis. If team members can easily execute static code analysis on their changes and use the information to make better decisions in the software, they will be more likely to use the tool. In the application integration build and cross-application integration environments, it is also useful to automate static code analysis to generate reports for teams to review. Look for ways to make the reports easily accessible from the integration build dashboard. The team might also find it useful to post printouts or share the reports on a large video monitor to provide visibility within and outside the team.

Continuous Integration

In traditional software development environments, integration of functionality across application components is usually deferred until each feature is functionally complete. The time from when the software is functionally complete until it is released is the stabilization period. This approach is followed because integration has been shown to be difficult and teams want to optimize their focus, coding features before dealing with integration issues. A big risk is that the duration of the release stabilization period is unpredictable. Teams guess at how long integrating components, testing the integration, fixing found issues, and regression testing existing functionality will take and commonly underestimate it.

Continuous integration differs from the release stabilization approach in that teams integrate small batches of software artifacts frequently, at least every day. All members of the team work from a single common source repository. An automated build and verification process is executed with each update to the source repository. The act of integrating often in small batches enables teams to reduce the risk of unpredictable integration issues found in a traditional release stabilization approach.

Integrating software artifacts late in the release leads to poor development and source code repository practices. To enable team members to work in isolation, complicated branching strategies are put in place, making integration a frustrating and error-prone process for teams. Teams implementing continuous integration should change their source code management approach. The main change is for the entire team to work from a single stream in the source control repository. Depending upon the source control management system in use, this could mean

- Working on a single branch with short-lived branches, less than a week, for experimentation, or
- Frequently integrating streams of work into a single mainline stream

Reducing and managing configuration management debt will be discussed in more detail later in Chapter 6, "Configuration Management Debt."

Close Collaboration

Sustaining internal quality also involves team members interacting on daily activities. Scrum prefers and XP advocates collocating team members. In an interview about the top ten ways to know you're not doing Agile for *Software Quality News*, Alistair Cockburn, a signatory of the Agile Manifesto, said the following:

> *The team is collocated, but people are not sitting within the length of a school bus to each other.*[6]

The length of a bus, which is typically about 40 feet, is a great visual aid to help teams understand how collocated teams situate themselves. There are many benefits that the team can take advantage of when team members are all in close proximity:

---

6. http://searchsoftwarequality.techtarget.com/news/interview/
   0,289202,sid92_gci1255480,00.html.

- Team members can ask for help and get face-to-face support from other team members.
- Conversations within the team area can be overheard by other team members, which allows them to provide critical information.
- Visual aids, sometimes referred to as "information radiators," can be placed on walls around the team area, continually radiating important information such as team working agreements, continuous integration build status, and current iteration statistics.
- This arrangement facilitates the building of trust among team members through frequent interaction and group learning opportunities.
- There are more opportunities for team members to distribute technical and domain knowledge across the team.

People who are used to organizations with functional silos, high-wall cubicles, and secluded offices are likely to get an initial shock when placed in open team areas. It takes time for team norms to be established that balance individual focus and privacy with ad hoc communication. Important feedback about the software internals and domain will move between team members more frequently in collocated and open team areas. Impediments to progress will be resolved in a shorter period of time, and therefore the team's feature delivery throughput will increase.

Small Batches of Work

It is inevitable that the needs of users will change as development progresses. This has been discussed in multiple papers and books. The following quotes are from some of the research into the subject:

> *It is not possible to completely specify an interactive system*
>
> *—Wegner's Lemma, 1995*

> *Uncertainty is inherent and inevitable in software development processes and products.*
>
> *—Ziv's Uncertainty Principle, 1996*

> *For a new software system the requirements will not be completely known until after the users have used it.*
>
> *—Humphrey's Requirements Uncertainty Principle, 2005*

A common approach to requirements is to gather them at the start, elaborate them early, and make them fixed for the entire release. This is done to reduce the uncertainty inherent in software requirements. If we could only elicit *all* of the requirements before construction, the design of the software could be fully understood and optimized to meet those requirements. The problem is that even after the requirements phase of a traditional software development project, users still want to change how the software works once they touch and feel it.

Instead of defining all the requirements before constructing the software, an Agile team begins with just enough to get started and works incrementally on small batch of features. The design of the software is continually evolving as the project team progresses from iteration to iteration. The requirements are continually evolving based upon what is learned each iteration. New requirements are further elaborated when they are raised higher in priority. This continuous cycle of elaboration and design permits the team to address specific attributes of the requirements closer to the time of implementation, when they have the most knowledge.

Working on small batches of features allows teams to get feedback from users earlier in the release. This way, the team is able to respond to the feedback before more software is built around functionality that doesn't meet the user's needs fully. To get this feedback frequently, teams should make a staged environment available to users interested in providing early feedback. The team should also give those users a mechanism to contribute feedback to incorporate back into the software. Gathering this feedback closer to the time functionality is implemented simplifies its incorporation since less functionality has been added around it.

Refactoring

Refactoring supplements the writing of automated unit tests to improve the design of the software's internals without changing how the software functions to the user. When teams work in an iterative and incremental way, they must keep the design flexible to incorporate feedback and new capabilities as development progresses. We will go into more detail about refactoring in Chapter 4, "Executable Design."

The following example code takes an array of messages and sends them to all of the receivers listening for our messages. We are working on a new feature that will send messages to a specified set of receivers rather than all listening receivers. We will use a basic refactoring named *Extract Method* to extract common functionality between sending messages to all or a specified set of receivers. Along the way, we will also look to improve the readability of the code through the naming of our methods.

```
public void sendMessages(Message[] messages) {
    List<Receiver> receivers = ReceiverCache.getReceivers(this);
    for (Receiver receiver in receivers) {
        FaultMap messageSendFaults = new FaultMap();
        for (Message message in messages) {
            try {
                send(message, receiver);
            } catch (Exception ex) {
                messageSendFaults.put(message, ex);
            }
        }
        handleMessageFaults(receiver, messageSendFaults);
    }


}
```

In thinking about how the new feature will affect the current code, it seems that we should be able to reuse the for loop through the receivers. This way we could send messages to a list of receivers, either all or a specific list. After we extract a method for sending to a list of receivers, the code looks like this:

```
public void sendMessages(Message[] messages) {
    List<Receiver> receivers = ReceiverCache.getReceivers(this);
    sendMessagesToReceivers(messages, receivers);
}

private void sendMessagesToReceivers(Message[] messages,
        List<Receiver> receivers) {
    for (Receiver receiver : receivers) {
        FaultMap messageSendFaults = new FaultMap();
        for (Message message : messages) {
            try {
                send(message, receiver);
            } catch (Exception ex) {
                messageSendFaults.put(message, ex);
            }
        }
        handleMessageFaults(receiver, messageSendFaults);
    }
}
```

This section of code is now able to support both features. As team members implement each part of a feature, they should look for ways to refactor the code they are working in to continually improve the design. Upon completion of each refactoring they will have left the code in a better state than when they started. By continually refactoring the code, a team makes the addition of features easier to implement. For older and less factored code, refactoring enhances the design in small, bite-size pieces. Over time these refactorings will add up to code with a better design for changes needed in the future.

Defining Technically Done

Many years ago, a project manager asked if I was done with a feature for our project. I replied, "Yes, as far as I can take it right now." She excitedly responded, "Great, I will get the user acceptance testing going right away." To which I retorted, "Wait, wait, it isn't ready for user acceptance yet. There were some environment issues that stopped me from testing it fully. We must execute a full regression test pass once the environment is up and running." Immediately she looked perplexed and quipped, "But I thought you said you were *done*?"

Reflecting on this experience, I realized that we had a different definition of "done." My original answer of "yes" had a caveat that I assumed was understood: "as far as I can take it." This perspective did not consider the potential interpretation or intentions of the project manager. Our differing interpretations of "done" created frustration and misunderstandings between us that continued through the completion of the project.

Scrum suggests that teams should be cross-functional, meaning that all the skills needed to deliver potentially shippable product increments are represented on the team. This does not mean that all team members are generalists; in fact, Scrum advocates that the diversity in team member skills adds value to development. When cross-functional teams first come together, it is common for each member of the team to have a different focus and perspective on what "done" means. Getting all team members on the same page about what "done" means from a technical perspective for an iteration's worth of work increases focus and reduces confusion about integration and release management concerns. Teams capture the artifacts and procedures that they agree must be delivered each iteration to consider their work "done" in a *Definition of Done*. Teams make their Definition of Done visible in their common team area or team page for dispersed teams.

For teams that are not able to create software that is shippable at the end of each iteration, it is also important to understand what will not be completed at the end of the iteration. These aspects of the software must be finished toward the end of the release cycle and incorporated in release plans. Since these aspects of the software are left undone each iteration, the iteration deliverable still has undone work to be completed. There must be a reason why teams must leave software in an undone state. The reasons are hidden in those aspects of the software that are not completed each iteration. Teams can identify what impediments stop them from completing these aspects each iteration. Over time, the team and supporting management should look for ways to resolve these impediments so that each iteration ends with potentially shippable increments.

As discussed earlier in this chapter, some organizations have enterprise guidelines. Often these guidelines are governed through delivered artifacts, defined processes, and reports. The artifacts, processes, and reports can be added to the Definition of Done so that the team can ensure they are continually updated, completed, and accepted.

The following exercise helps teams create a Definition of Done for their project.

Exercise	**Creating a Team Definition of Done**

Following is an overview of steps a team can use to create its own Definition of Done:

1. Brainstorm release artifacts: Write down all artifacts essential for delivering on a feature, iteration, and release.
2. Identify release stabilization artifacts: Separate artifacts that cannot currently be updated or finished in the iteration.
3. Capture obstacles: Reflect on each artifact that is on the release stabilization list and identify at least one obstacle to delivering that artifact in the iteration.
4. Team commitments: Gain consensus from the whole team on the Definition of Done as a starting point that can be reviewed upon completing upcoming iterations.

Brainstorm Release Artifacts

Ask each team member to write down one artifact per sticky note that is essential for delivering a feature, an iteration, and ultimately a release of the software the team is currently working on. Explain that this exercise will capture those artifacts that constitute a potentially shippable product increment. Also, identify those artifacts the team must finish before the software is released into production.

Here are some examples of artifacts that have gone into a Definition of Done:

- Installation build (golden bits)
- Pass all automated tests in the staging environment
- Signoff
- Pass audit
- Installation guide accepted by operations
- Release notes updated
- Training manuals updated

It is important to note that these are not features of the application but rather the artifacts that are generated for a release.

It is common to find out that some artifacts are not necessary. Asking the following questions will help determine if each artifact is essential to delivering a quality release:

- Who is the target audience for this artifact?
- Is this a transitory artifact for the team or stakeholders?

- Who would pay for this?
- Is it practical and valuable to maintain this artifact?

Identify Release Stabilization Artifacts

On a whiteboard draw a line about one-third of the way from the bottom. Write *iteration* above the line and *release* below the line. Take each artifact from the brainstorming step and decide if that artifact can be updated for the features being delivered in the iteration. If the artifact can be delivered within the iteration, place it above the line. If the team believes the artifact must be finished after the last feature is delivered for the release but not within the iterations, place it below the line. The artifacts below the line represent work to be completed in a release stabilization period between the last feature being added and releasing to users. Your whiteboard should look something like Figure 3.3.

Capture Obstacles

Look at each of the artifacts in the release stabilization period and discuss each obstacle. This is a difficult task for some teams because they hold themselves to the status quo of their role, team, and organization. Inform the team that answers such as "That is just the way it is" or "We can't do anything about that" are not acceptable because they cannot take action on those. Each obstacle, no matter how large the effort to remove it may seem, is essential information for management about how they can support the team in releasing with more predictability. If the artifacts in the release stabilization period take an unknown or variable amount of time to finish, it will be difficult to predict an actual release date.

These are some example obstacles:

- Testing is handled by a different department and nobody from there is assigned to the team.

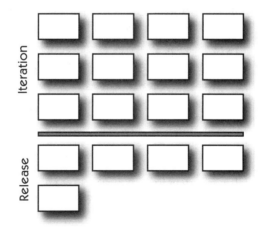

Figure 3.3   Example of separating artifacts in a team's Definition of Done into artifacts delivered each iteration and those that must be finished in a release stabilization period.

- Compliance audits cost too much to do in the iteration.
- Executing the entire regression test suite takes too long to run in the iteration.

Over time, the team may overcome an obstacle, at which point the artifact dependent on that obstacle in the release stabilization period can be completed every iteration.

Team Commitment

It is time for the team to commit to a Definition of Done. The Definition of Done is the list of artifacts above the line in the iteration section of the whiteboard. These artifacts constitute what the team believes is a potentially shippable product increment. Ask all team members if they agree that the Definition of Done is achievable in the iteration. If anyone on the team has reservations, the team should discuss those concerns further before committing to the Definition of Done. The team may decide as a group to move forward with the current Definition of Done for the next iteration and then review how well it worked. It is important that all members of the team agree to the Definition of Done because they will all be accountable to each other for delivering to it.

Figure 3.4 is an example of an actual team's Definition of Done.

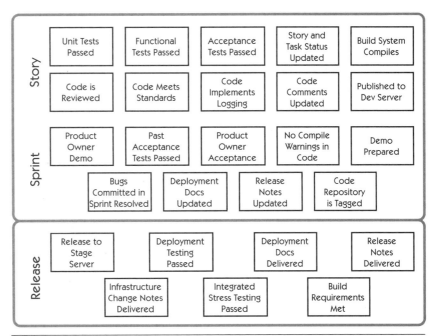

Figure 3.4 An example Definition of Done depicting artifacts that must be finished for each feature (story) and iteration (sprint) in a release. This example also captures those artifacts that are not delivered each sprint and must be resolved in an unpredictable stabilization period before releasing the software to users.

The Definition of Done can have many ramifications, including

- Creating a list of team obstacles for management to resolve so the team has more predictable releases
- Organizational awareness of problems stemming from the current organizational structure
- Better understanding of the expectations of the delivery objectives
- Team awareness of other team member roles and their input to the delivery

It is important that the resulting Definition of Done be made visible in the team area and used to evaluate feature "doneness" a few times so it is tested against the reality of delivery. It may take a couple of reviews by the entire team to identify the appropriate Definition of Done for their context. Review the Definition of Done during iteration planning and apply any changes needed before starting the iteration.

Potentially Shippable Product Increments

Scrum asks that teams create "potentially shippable product increments" each sprint. This means the code is tested, coded, integrated, documented, and whatever else must be finished to ensure the product has internal integrity for the features being delivered. This forces traditional development teams to modify their processes because they do not usually overlap development phases in this way.

Teams that are used to a sequential development process will have difficulty implementing the Scrum framework initially. Their initial sprints look like a miniature waterfall process with design followed by code and finally test. This results in the same issues at the end of a sprint as happen in a traditional project's release. Code is not finished on time and testing cannot be completed given the inadequate time left in the sprint. Also, team members with different functional roles find themselves either with no tasks to work on or with too many tasks assigned to them during the sprint.

This failure to test the functionality adequately inside the sprint leaves unfinished and buggy features to be completed in the next sprint. The unfinished work causes the team to take on less work in the next sprint in order to leave a sufficient buffer in which to fix the bugs. Or even worse, the team tries to take on the same amount of work again and continues not finishing what was signed up for in the sprint. The team is no longer creating potentially shippable product increments each sprint. As the team continues to miss its

Figure 3.5   Teams that take a sequential approach to development within a Scrum sprint do not create potentially shippable product increments that are tested, coded, integrated, and documented. This leaves features that have not been fully tested and an increased chance of bugs to be dealt with later.

commitments each sprint, trust decays between the team and stakeholders. Figure 3.5 shows that a team runs the risk of not completing any of the features committed to in the iteration when taking a traditional sequential approach to development.

In a sequential development process, the risk is that all or most of the features will not be finished at the end of a sprint. This is because all of the features are being worked on at once. Implementing thin, vertical slices of functionality in shorter cycles allows the development team to finish features early in the sprint before moving on to the next feature the team committed to. The risk profile changes from not finishing most or all of the features to not finishing one feature. This allows stakeholders to provide feedback on fully tested, coded, integrated, and documented software during and at the end of each sprint. Figure 3.6 shows how delivering in thin, vertical slices of functionality ensures that most, if not all, of the features committed to are finished at the end of each sprint.

Developing potentially shippable product increments helps align stakeholders and teams through continuous delivery of working software. Stakeholders are able to provide feedback on working software early, and this feedback may be incorporated into the sprint work rather than pushed out as a future enhancement. Development teams create the necessary internal structure to

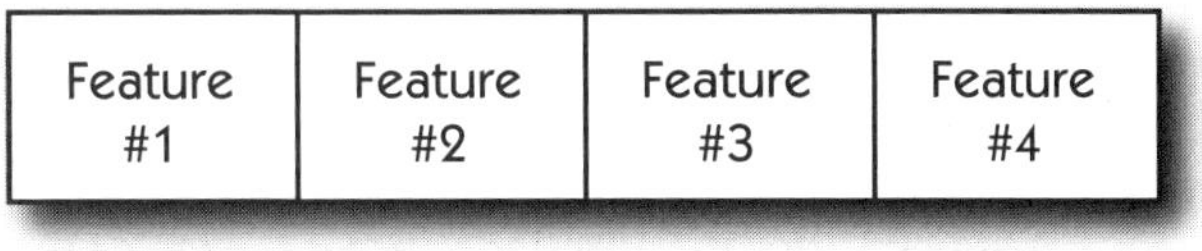

Feature #1	Feature #2	Feature #3	Feature #4

Figure 3.6   Implementing thinner slices of functionality throughout the sprint rather than all at the end allows the development team to deliver potentially shippable product increments that are fully tested, coded, integrated, and documented.

support each feature so that it is potentially shippable. This balance between business needs and working software engenders trust with stakeholders, allowing the development team to focus its efforts on maintaining the overall structure and integrity of the software.

Single Work Queue

In Scrum, the Product Backlog is a list of desired features prioritized by the Product Owner. Prioritization should be focused on optimizing the value of the software delivered to users. Instead of prioritizing by levels of importance such as high, medium, and low, the Product Owner must prioritize in a "stack-rank" order. This means that no Product Backlog item has the same priority as another item in the list. This form of prioritization gives clear directions to teams about what is the most important feature to work on at all times.

A healthy Product Backlog contains not only new features and improvements but also technical requirements to support upcoming functionality. The team is expected to review the Product Backlog frequently and provide estimates for Product Backlog items to help the Product Owner prioritize based on the size of each item and its benefit. During the team's review, team members suggest technical items that are missing from the Product Backlog. These technical Product Backlog items are discussed with the Product Owner so that they can be prioritized effectively. It is essential that the team explain why each technical Product Backlog item is important to the software delivery. If the value of these items is not expressed, the Product Owner will be inclined to demote them in priority.

Another type of item that sometimes falls into a separate list is a bug. When issues are found in the software, they usually come in three varieties:

- **Enhancement:** a suggestion for improving the current state of the software from a user's point of view
- **Defect:** a system fault that occurs while using the software
- **Fire:** a defect that must be fixed immediately because of its impact

Enhancements are requests for improvements to the software based on the perspective of the user. Enhancements and defect issues are hard to distinguish from one another at times. Defects are system faults that users are able to work around but should not occur in a functioning software implementation. Since users are able to work around these defects and the team is able to provide a fix in the next iteration, they are added to the Product Backlog and prioritized. Fires are defects that cannot be worked around and cause serious

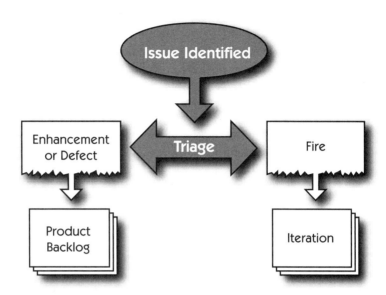

Figure 3.7   How an identified issue is triaged in an iterative and incremental approach such as Scrum. If the issue is an enhancement or defect that can be worked around for now, it goes into the Product Backlog and is prioritized based on its value. If the issue is a "fire" or defect that cannot be worked around, it must be fixed immediately. The development team puts the fire into the current list of work in the iteration and figures out how it affects their commitment to deliver on the current iteration.

problems for users of the software. In healthy software applications, fires should be a rare occurrence. It is important that a fix be implemented right away and deployed even though this interrupts the work that the team committed to in the current iteration. Figure 3.7 depicts a common workflow for enhancements, defects, and fires.

Defects are captured in bug databases at many organizations. Teams using the Scrum process to manage their software development find themselves in a predicament. Do they continue working from two lists, the Product Backlog and a bug database, or do they incorporate items from the bug database into the Product Backlog? Most teams should incorporate defects into the Product Backlog rather than carrying around two lists. There are multiple reasons to do this:

- The development team does not have to make priority decisions about whether to work on defects or Product Backlog items.

- It minimizes the amount of work hidden from the Product Owner. By providing visibility into the defects, the team is providing transparency into the state of the software it is working on.
- It provides the Product Owner with an opportunity to prioritize the defect lower when appropriate. The Product Owner could decide that the defect is not important enough to fix at this time.
- It allows the development team and Product Owner to design a solution for dealing with defects. From time to time the defects provide insight into a design flaw that the Product Owner and team should review.

A Story about Prioritizing Defects

Once, a Product Owner asked, "How do I prioritize defects in the Product Backlog?" The QA Lead leaped up and gave the following example of how they could be prioritized:

"Do you remember the defect that describes a message that tells the user to call our customer support center because a problem has occurred processing their request? That defect gets triaged down in priority every month, yet it is something we could fix very quickly. It would have tremendous value since it would reduce the number of customer support calls by approximately 100 per week based on early analysis. Each of those calls costs between $5 and $13; therefore, the savings would be anywhere from $500 to $1,300 per week."

The Product Owner turned to me and said, "I think I can figure out how to prioritize defects in the Product Backlog now."

A single work queue, such as the Product Backlog, provides visibility to the team about business priorities. The Product Owner should share the Product Backlog with the development team frequently and discuss the direction of the product beyond the next iteration. As the team members gain knowledge about the direction of the product, they will be able to provide input into the Product Backlog. This visibility is important so that Product Backlog items do not surprise the team members and leave them in a situation where they are unable to provide a solution in a timely manner.

SUMMARY

To sustain the internal quality of software, teams must approach development in a disciplined way. Common approaches that teams use to sustain internal quality are the following:

- Sustainable pace
- Early identification of internal quality problems
- Close collaboration
- Refactoring
- Small batches of work
- Defining technically done
- Potentially shippable product increments
- Single work queue

By applying these approaches, teams will enhance their delivery capabilities while delivering high-quality software.

Chapter 4

EXECUTABLE DESIGN

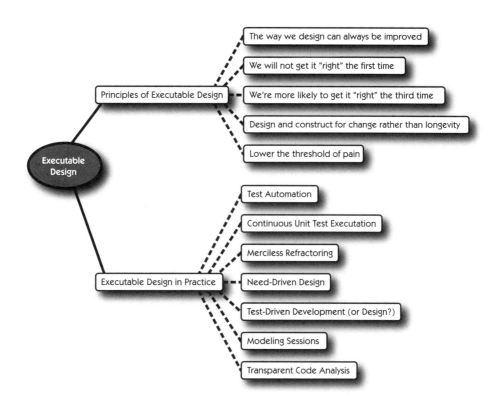

If we are not enhancing the design then we are just writing a bunch of tests.

—An anonymous developer in a meeting about a Test-First development implementation

PRINCIPLES OF EXECUTABLE DESIGN

Executable Design is an approach involving existing well-known practices, helpful principles, and a mind-set shift from traditional views on software design. There have been many projects, conversations, and mistakes involved in defining Executable Design as described in this chapter. There is always room for improvement and perspective. Please take what you can from this chapter and apply it to your own context. In fact, this is an essential principle of Executable Design:

The way we design can always be improved.

This particular principle is not all that controversial. There is a continuous flow of writing about design methods and ideas in our industry. It does, however, suggest the notion that following a single design method is not recommended. By trying multiple methods of design, teams continue to learn and innovate for the sake of their applications.

People in our industry strive for the "best" design methods for software. This has led to many innovations that are in common use today, such as UML and Inversion of Control. In the development of these design methods many ideas were considered and changes were made along the way. In application development, teams also consider ideas and make changes based on their current understanding of the application's design. It is easy sometimes to choose an architectural design style such as Model-View-Controller (MVC), peer-to-peer, and service-oriented. But when these architectural design styles are put into practice to implement a solution of any size, many decisions must be made about specifics in the design. This has led to the following principle of Executable Design:

We will not get it "right" the first time.

This has been shown to be true in my career in the following situations:

- Abstracting web design from application behavior
- Creating a text formatting library for portable devices
- Using model-driven development on a project

Although we will not usually get the design "right" on the first attempt, the design does tend to settle out for most applications. It has come to my attention over the years that

We're more likely to get it "right" the third time.

I am positive that it is not always the third time, but that is not the point of this statement at all. The point is for team members to construct software so that changes can be incorporated at any point in time. If we accept that we're more likely to get the design "right" closer to the third attempt, we will build software to support change. This gets us to our next principle of Executable Design:

Design and construct for change rather than longevity.

If software is designed and constructed for change, it will be technically and economically feasible to change the software for new needs rather than rewriting it. Designing and constructing with such discipline that changes are easily supported at any time is quite difficult. It takes tremendous discipline when patterns of technical debt, such as schedule pressure as discussed in Chapter 2, are introduced to a team. It is my opinion that we cannot rely on disciplined design over a long period of time by every team member. Therefore, our last principle of Executable Design is

Lower the threshold of pain.

At a workshop in Grand Rapids, Michigan, on technical debt, Matt Heusser proposed that technical debt could be an outcome of individual developers not having to deal with the consequences of their actions. The decisions that we make each day in developing software lead to technical debt because of a "moral hazard."

> *Moral hazard* is the view that parties insulated from risk may behave differently from the way they would behave if they were fully exposed to the risk.

This does not mean that team members act in a malicious or dishonest way. It means that if individual team members are insulated from the long-term effects of a decision, they will not take as much care in the short term. Matt's example was that a person may take a shortcut in developing a feature because that person is not going to be working on the code one year from now when it must be changed to support a new feature.

Immediately following Matt's discussion on moral hazard, Chet Hendrickson pointed out that a good way to minimize the moral hazard problem is by "lowering the threshold of pain." For instance, Chet brought up how many people approach doing their taxes in the United States. They could incrementally update their tax information for two hours each month. Instead, many of us wait until two weeks prior to the deadline to complete our tax forms. We push to complete our taxes by the deadline because the potential headache of tax evasion is strong enough that a pain threshold would be crossed.

Teams can agree to a threshold of pain they are willing to tolerate and put in feedback mechanisms to let them know when that threshold is crossed. In XP, there are multiple frequencies of feedback provided. *Pair programming* enables team members to provide feedback within seconds. *Test-Driven Development (TDD)* and *acceptance testing* provide feedback within minutes of the changes. By using *continuous integration* teams are provided feedback within tens of minutes on how all of their code works together. Having an *on-site customer representative* in close proximity can support getting feedback on an implementation detail within hours of starting work on it. Teams working in time-boxed iterations get feedback from stakeholders within weeks. Getting feedback as close to when an action has been taken is critical to the evolutionary nature of software development using XP.

Identifying a threshold for providing feedback to the team is also a critical aspect of Executable Design. Automating the feedback, when possible, enforces the team's threshold. The feedback could be automated in each team member's development environment, the continuous integration server, and promotion of software to servers exposed to stakeholders.

On some legacy development platforms there could be costs that make frequent feedback difficult or even seemingly impractical. Teams should work toward the shortest frequency of feedback at all levels of the software development process that is practical and feasible in their context. The frequency of feedback that a team can attain is probably more than initially thought.

To recap the principles that drive Executable Design:

- The way we design can always be improved.
- We'll get it "right" the third time.
- We will not get it "right" the first time.
- Design and construct for change rather than longevity.
- Lower the threshold of pain.

Taking on the Executable Design mind-set is not easy. I continually use these principles in design discussions for products, technology, code, tests, business models, management, and life. It has been helpful for me to reflect on situations where these principles have caused me to change my position or perspective. From these reflections I have found more success in setting proper expectations, learning from others in the design process, and designing better solutions for the situation.

Teams can tailor their practices and tools and still be in alignment with the Executable Design principles. The rest of this chapter will provide a set of suggestions about practices and tools to support an Executable Design approach. By no means are these suggestions the only ways to apply the principles or the only ways that I have seen them applied. These suggestions are only examples to help clarify their application to the software development process. If they work for your current context, your team has a place to start. But please do not stop once you apply them successfully. Remember the first principle:

The way we design can always be improved.

EXECUTABLE DESIGN IN PRACTICE

Executable Design involves the following practices:

- Test automation
- Continuous unit test execution
- Merciless refactoring
- Need-driven design
- Test-Driven Development (or Design?)
- Modeling sessions
- Transparent code analysis

The rest of this chapter will provide detailed information about all of these practices in terms of Executable Design.

Test Automation

This practice may seem implied by Executable Design, but the approach used for test automation is important to sustainable delivery. Also, teams and organizations sometimes think that automating tests is a job for the test group and not for programmers. The approach to test automation in Executable Design is based on the approach to testing in XP. Taking a *whole team* approach to testing is essential to having a successful and sustainable test automation strategy. This does not mean that all team members are the best test case developers and therefore are generalists. It does mean that all team members are able to understand the test strategy, execute the tests, and contribute to their development when needed, which is quite often. The following principle for automated test accessibility sums up the Executable Design suggested approach:

Everyone on the team should be able to execute any and all automated and manual test cases.

This is an extremely important statement because it expresses the importance of feedback over isolation in teams. If any team member can run the tests, the team member can ensure the integrity of changes closer to the time of implementation. This lessens the amount of time between introducing a defect and when it gets fixed. Defects will exist in the software for a shorter duration on average, thus reducing the defect deficit inherent in traditional test-after approaches.

The focus on how automated tests are used is also important. Automated tests at all levels of execution, such as unit, acceptance, system, and performance, should provide feedback on whether the software meets the needs of users. The focus is not on whether there is coverage, although this may be an outcome of automation, but to ensure that functionality is behaving as expected. This focus is similar to that of Behaviour-Driven Development (BDD), where tests validate that each application change adds value through an expected behavior. An approach to automating tests for Executable Design could be the use of BDD.

In addition to the automating test development approach, understanding how the test infrastructure scales to larger projects is essential for many projects. Structure and feedback cycles for each higher layer of test infrastructure can make or break the effective use of automated tests for frequent feedback. Over time, the number of tests will increase dramatically. This can cause teams to slow down delivery of valuable features if the tests are not continually maintained.

The most frequent reason for this slowdown is that unit tests are intermingled with slower integration test executions. Unit tests should run fast and should not depend on special configurations, installations, or slow-running dependencies. When unit tests are executed alongside integration tests, they run much slower and cause their feedback to be available less frequently. This usually starts with team members no longer running the unit tests in their own environment before integrating a change into source control.

A way to segregate unit tests from integration tests is to create an automated test structure. In 2003, while working on an IBM WebSphere J2EE application with a DB2 on OS/390 database, our team came up with the following naming convention to structure our automated tests:

- *UnitTest.java: These tests executed fast and did not have dependencies on a relational database, JNDI (Java Naming and Directory Interface), EJB, IBM WebSphere container configuration, or any other external connectivity or configurations. In order to support this ideal unit test definition, we needed to isolate business logic from "glue" code that enabled its execution inside the J2EE container.

- *PersistanceTest.java: These tests depended on a running and configured relational database instance to test integration of EJB entity beans and the database. Because our new architecture would be replacing stored procedure calls with an in-memory data cache, we would need these integration test cases for functional, load, performance, and stress testing.
- *ContainerTest.java: These tests were dependent on integrating business logic into a configured IBM WebSphere J2EE container. The tests ran inside the container using a framework called JUnitEE (extension of JUnit for J2EE applications) and would test the container mappings for application controller access to EJB session beans and JNDI.

In our development environments we could run all of the tests whose names ended with "UnitTest.java". Team members would execute these tests each time they saved their code in the IDE. These tests had to run fast or we would be distracted from our work. We kept the full unit test execution time within three to five seconds. The persistence and container tests were executed in a team member's environment before larger code changes—meaning more than a couple of hours of work—were checked in.

The full suite of automated programmer tests was executed on our continuous integration server each time code was checked into our source control management system. These took anywhere from 5 to 12 minutes to run. The build server was configured with a WebSphere Application Server instance and DB2 relational database. After the build and automated unit tests ran successfully, the application was automatically deployed into the container, and the database was dropped and re-created from scratch. Then the automated persistence and container tests were executed. The results of the full build and test execution were reported to the team.

Continuous Unit Test Execution

Automated programmer tests aren't as effective if they are not executed on a regular basis. If there is an extra step or more just to execute programmer tests in your development environment, you will be less likely to run them. Continuous programmer test execution is focused on running fast unit tests for the entire module with each change made in a team member's development environment without adding a step to the development process. Automating unit test execution each time a file is modified in a background process will help team members identify issues quickly before more software debt is created. This goes beyond the execution of a single unit test that tests behavior of the code under development. Team members are continually regressing the entire module at the unit level.

Many platforms can be configured to support continuous unit test execution:

- In Eclipse IDE, a "launcher," similar to a script that can be executed, can be created that runs all of the unit tests for the module. A "launcher" configuration can be saved and added to source control for sharing with the entire team. Another construct in Eclipse IDE called "builders" can then be configured to execute the "launcher" each time a file is saved.
- If you are into programming with Ruby, a gem is available called ZenTest with a component named *autotest* for continuous unit test execution. It also continuously executes unit tests when a file is changed. Autotest is smart about which tests to execute based on changes that were made since the last save.
- Python also has a continuous unit test execution tool named *tdaemon* that provides similar functionality to ZenTest for Ruby.

As you can see, continuous testing works in multiple programming languages. Automating unit test execution with each change lessens the need for adding a manual step to a team member's development process. It is now just part of the environment. Teams should look for ways to make essential elements of their software development process easy and automatic so it does not become or appear to be a burden for team members.

Merciless Refactoring

Refactoring is an essential practice for teams developing solid software and continually evolving the design to meet new customer needs. The web site managed by Martin Fowler, who wrote the original book conveniently called *Refactoring*, says:

> *Refactoring is a disciplined technique for restructuring an existing body of code, altering its internal structure without changing its external behavior.*[1]

It is important to understand that refactoring is not just restructuring code. Refactoring involves taking small, disciplined steps, many of which are docu-

---

1. Martin Fowler, "Refactoring Home Page," www.refactoring.com/.

mented in books and online resources on refactoring, to alter the internal structure of the software. (If you haven't done so already, please read the books and online resources on refactoring to learn how it is applied more effectively. This book will not describe specific refactorings in detail.)

When taking an iterative and incremental approach such as Scrum, it is imperative that the software continue to be changeable. Merciless refactoring is an approach that teams should adopt whether they are working on new or legacy software.

> *merciless*—adj.: having or showing no [mercy—show of kindness toward the distressed]

To refactor *mercilessly* means that the team will

Relieve distressed code through kindness and disciplined restructuring.

Some teams wonder if they will be allowed to apply merciless refactoring in their project. It is important to understand that teams are not asked to develop software that does not allow for new changes to be easily added. Stakeholders do tend to want features quickly, but that is their role. Teams should understand that their role is to create quality software that does not accrue abnormal costs with each change. Robert C. Martin wrote in his book *Clean Code: A Handbook of Agile Software Craftsmanship* about a simple rule that the Boy Scouts of America have:

> *Leave the campground cleaner than you found it.*[2]

Teams that I work with use a variant of this simple rule in their own working agreements:

Always leave the code in better shape than when you started.

Teams demonstrating this mind-set will continually improve the software's design. This leads to acceleration in feature delivery because the code will be easier to work with and express its intent more concisely. On a project that is well tended in terms of its design and structure, the act of refactoring can be elegant and liberating. It allows teams to continually inspect and adapt their understanding of the code to meet the customer's current needs.

---

2. Robert C. Martin, *Clean Code: A Handbook for Agile Software Craftsmanship* (Prentice Hall, 2009); www.informit.com/articles/article.aspx?p=1235624&seqNum=6.

On a legacy application or component, the act of refactoring can seem overwhelming. Although refactoring involves making small, incremental improvements that will lead to improvement in the software's design, figuring out where to start and stop in a legacy system is often unclear. How much refactoring is sufficient in this piece of code? The following questions should help you decide whether to start refactoring when you see an opportunity for it:

1. Does this change directly affect the feature I am working on?
2. Would the change add clarity for the feature implementation?
3. Will the change provide automated tests where there currently are none?
4. Does the refactoring look like a large endeavor involving significant portions of the application components?

If the answer to the first three questions is yes, I lean toward refactoring the code. The only caveat to this answer is when the answer to the fourth question, Does the refactoring look like a large endeavor?, is yes. Then I use experience as a guide to help me produce a relative size estimate of the effort involved in this refactoring compared to the initial estimate of size for the feature implementation. If the size of the refactoring is significantly larger than the original estimate given to the Product Owner, I will bring the refactoring up to the team for discussion. Bringing up a large refactoring to the rest of the team will result in one of the following general outcomes:

- The team thinks it is good idea to start the large refactoring because its estimated size does not adversely affect delivery of what the team committed to during this iteration.
- The team decides that the refactoring is large enough that it should be brought up to the Product Owner. The Product Owner could add it to the Product Backlog or decide to drop scope for the current iteration to accommodate the refactoring.
- Another team member has information that will make this refactoring smaller or not necessary. Sometimes other team members have worked in this area of code or on a similar situation in the past and have knowledge of other ways to implement the changes needed.

After starting a refactoring, how do we know when to stop? When working on legacy code, it is difficult to know when we have refactored enough. Here are some questions to ask yourself to figure out when you have refactored enough:

- Is the code I am refactoring a crucial part of the feature I was working on?
- Will refactoring the code result in crucial improvements?

Adopting a *merciless refactoring* mind-set will lead to small, incremental software design improvements. Refactoring should be identified in the course of implementing a feature. Once the need for a refactoring is identified, decide if it is valuable enough to do at this point in time, considering its potential cost in effort. If it meets the criteria for starting a refactoring, use disciplined refactoring steps to make incremental improvements to the design without affecting the software's external behavior.

Need-Driven Design

A common approach to designing application integrations is to first identify what the provider will present through its interface. If the application integration provider already exists, consumers tend to focus on how they can use all that the provider presents. This happens when integrating services, libraries, storage, appliances, containers, and more.

In contrast, *Need-Driven Design* approaches integration based on emergence and need. The approach can be summarized in the following statement:

> **Ask not what the integration provider gives us; ask what the consumer needs.**

Need-Driven Design, in its basic form, is based on the *Adapter* design pattern[3] as shown in Figure 4.1. There are two perspectives for integration in Need-Driven Design:

- **Consumer:** Ask what the consumer needs from the interface contract.
- **Provider:** A provider's interface emerges from needs expressed by more than one consumer.

From the consumer perspective, the idea is to depend only on what the software actually needs and no more. Instead of coupling the application to a web service directly, create an interface in between that defines only what the software needs, then implement the interface to integrate with the web service. This way, dependency on the web service is limited to the implementation of the interface and can be modified or replaced if the need arises in a single place. In the case of integrating a library, creating too much dependence on the library could make the application less changeable for new user needs. Wrapping the specific aspects of a library that the application uses could be an approach worth pursuing.

---

3. Erich Gamma, Richard Helm, Ralph Johnson, and John M. Vlissides, *Design Patterns: Elements of Reusable Object-Oriented Software* (Addison-Wesley, 1994).

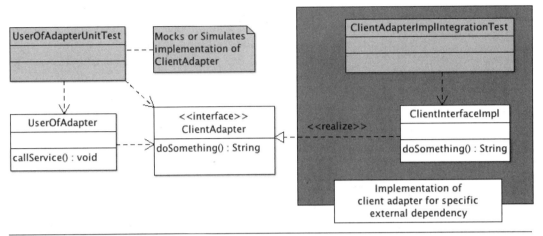

Figure 4.1   Example implementation of the Need-Driven Design approach for exploiting an external component using the Adapter design pattern

From a provider perspective, generalizing an interface should be done only after there is more than one consumer of the provider's capabilities. This contrasts with how many organizations approach application integration. They might have a governance program that identifies services before construction of software begins. The Need-Driven Design approach is to wait for more than one consumer to need access to a particular capability. Once the need to create a provider interface is identified, it is promoted to a reusable asset.

The Need-Driven Design approach is best applied in conjunction with automated unit tests. The automated unit tests describe what each side of the adapter, the consumer interface and provider interface, will be responsible for. The application using the adapter should handle general usage of the client interface and should not care about specialized concerns of the provider interface. This can be explained with the following real-world example where Need-Driven Design was applied.

Instead of designing software toward what an external dependency can provide, decide what the application needs. This need-driven approach focuses on adding only what is necessary rather than creating dependence on the external component. Need-Driven Design has the following steps:

1. **Assess the need:** Add external dependencies to your project only when the value outweighs the integration costs.
2. **Define the interface:** Create an interface that will provide your application with the capabilities that it needs.

Container Trucks and RFID

The application we were working on tracked containers on trucks being loaded on and off of ships in the port. Radio-frequency identification device (RFID) was becoming the way containers were tracked coming in and out of port. Ports in the United States were finding ways to support reading these RFID tags on the containers.

Our team was employed to implement the software that would take an RFID tag identified on a container and relay that information to port workers. A separate vendor was hired to create the RFID-reading hardware since none existed to our knowledge that could handle the corrosive nature of being near salt water.

Since the hardware did not exist, we asked the other vendor for an example of what the message would look like so that we could implement a parser for it. When we got the example message, we found that the XML it contained was malformed. This was mentioned to the hardware vendor, but we still had to make progress because of our contractual obligations. We were all supposed to be finished with our application changes, integrated with the RFID hardware, in three months.

Our team decided to figure out what the application needed rather than what it would receive from the other vendor's hardware. In one of the integration scenarios, the application needed an RFID tag and a timestamp, so we created an interface to access these pieces of information. To ensure that the application was able to handle implementations of this interface, we wrote automated unit tests that used mock objects to run scenarios through the interface. For instance, what if the RFID could not be read?

After understanding how the application would use the interface, we created an initial implementation of the interface for the vendor's hardware based on what we thought would be close to the actual message. Since the hardware was providing the XML through a web service, the interface implementation caught any web-service-specific errors and exceptions so that the application did not have to be coupled to even the technical aspects of it. Automated unit tests validated that the interface implementation handled such conditions.

It turned out that the hardware vendor was more than three months late. Our team created a simulator that would send multiple versions of an example XML message with random RFID tags and random exception conditions. One item was still needed for release when we finished our work: integration with the actual hardware through the interface implementation.

As an epilogue, our clients sent us a note on the day they got the hardware. They modified the interface implementation to accommodate the actual XML message from the working hardware in only one hour and ran all of the automated tests. It worked! They put it into production that same day.

3. **Develop executable criteria:** Write automated unit tests for expected scenarios your application should handle through the defined interface; mock up and/or simulate the various scenarios.

4. **Develop the interface implementation:** Create automated unit tests and the interface implementation to integrate external components, and make sure to handle conditions that the application does not need to be aware of.

By driving integration strategies through the steps defined in Need-Driven Design, we can decrease integration costs, reduce coupling to external dependencies, and implement business-driven intentions in our applications.

Test-Driven Development (or Design?)

Test-Driven Development (TDD) is a disciplined practice in which a team member writes a failing test, writes the code that makes the test pass, and then refactors the code to an acceptable design. Effective use of TDD has been shown to reduce defects and increase confidence in the quality of code. This increase in confidence enables teams to make necessary changes faster, thus accelerating feature implementation throughput.

It is unfortunate that TDD has not been adopted by the software development industry more broadly. The TDD technique has been widely misunderstood by teams and management. Many programmers hear the name and are instantly turned off because it contains the word *test*. Teams that start using TDD sometimes misinterpret the basics or have difficulty making the mindset shift inherent in its use. Using tests to drive software design in an executable fashion is not easy to grasp. It takes tremendous discipline to make the change in approach to design through micro-sized tests.

The following statement summarizes how I describe TDD to teams that are having difficulty adopting the approach in their development process:

TDD is about creating a supportable structure for imminent change.

Applications and their components change to meet new business needs. These changes are effected by modifying the implementation, improving the design, replacing aspects of the design, or adding more functionality to it. Taking a TDD approach enables teams to create the structure to support the changes that occur as an application changes. Teams using a TDD approach should maintain this structure of unit tests, keeping the unit tests supportable as the application grows in size and complexity. Focusing on TDD in this manner helps teams understand how they can apply it to start practicing a design-through-tests approach.

Automated unit tests are added through a test-driven approach and tell us if aspects of each component within an application are behaving as expected. These tests should be repeatable and specific so they can be executed with the same expected results each time. Although the tests are important, teams should not lose focus on how these tests drive the software design incrementally.

A basic way to think about TDD is through a popular phrase in the TDD community:

Red, Green, Refactor.

This simple phrase describes the basic steps of TDD. First, write a failing test that describes the scenario that should work at a micro level of the application component. Then write just enough code to make it pass, and no more. Finally, refactor the implementation code and tests to an acceptable design so they can be maintained over time. It is important to emphasize once again to write only enough code to make the current failing test pass so no untested code is written. Untested code is less safe to change when it's time to make necessary refactorings. Figure 4.2 shows the basic steps involved in the TDD approach.

These three basic steps are not always sufficient to do TDD effectively. Uncle Bob Martin wrote "The Three Laws" of TDD as follows:

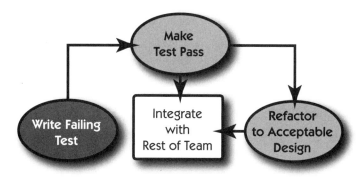

Figure 4.2   The basic steps of Test-Driven Development are to write a failing test, write only the code that makes the test pass, and refactor to an acceptable design.

Test-Driven Development is defined by three simple laws.

- ▪ *You must write a failing unit test before you write production code.*
- ▪ *You must stop writing that unit test as soon as it fails; and not compiling is failing.*
- ▪ *You must stop writing production code as soon as the currently failing test passes.*[4]

He goes on to say that software developers should do TDD as a matter of professionalism. If, as software developers, we do TDD effectively, we will get better at our craft. Uncle Bob Martin provides an initial list of things we could improve by doing TDD:

If you follow the three laws that seem so silly, you will:

- ▪ *Reduce your debug time dramatically.*
- ▪ *Significantly increase the flexibility of your system, allowing you to keep it clean.*
- ▪ *Create a suite of documents that fully describe the low level behavior of the system.*
- ▪ *Create a system design that has extremely low coupling.*[5]

Difficulty in Introducing Test-Driven Development

TDD is a highly disciplined approach. The discipline involved is difficult for some people to apply each day. Following is a list of team environmental issues that lower the chances for effective use or adoption of TDD:

- Pressure from management and stakeholders to release based on an unreasonable plan: Integrity of the software is always sacrificed when the plan is inflexible and does not incorporate reality.

- When there is a lack of passion for learning and implementing effective TDD practices on the team: The high degree of discipline required in TDD makes passion for working in this way extremely helpful.

- Not enough people on the team with experience doing TDD in practice: Without any experience on the team, success in adoption is lower.

- On an existing code base, if the software's design is poor, low cohesion, and high coupling, or is implemented in a way that is difficult to test, then finding a starting point could seem nearly impossible.

---

4. Robert C. Martin, "Are You a Professional?" *NDC Magazine*, Norwegian Developers Conference 2009, Telenor Arena, Oslo, June 17–19, p. 14. Reprinted with permission.
5. Ibid.

- If the existing code base is large and contains no or minimal test coverage, disciplined TDD will not show valuable results for some time.

- Managers tell team members they don't believe TDD is effective or directly prohibit its use on projects.

To successfully adopt a TDD approach, it is important to manage these environmental issues for the team. This could include managing expectations, providing the team with support from a coach, and allowing sufficient learning time to understand the tools and techniques.

Modeling Sessions

When team members get together and discuss software design elements, they sometimes use visual modeling approaches. This usually happens at a whiteboard for collocated team members. While the team names model elements and their interactions, the conversation revolves around how the model enables desired functionality. The points discussed can be thought of as scenarios that the solution should support. These scenarios are validated against the model throughout the design conversation and can be easily translated into one or more test cases.

As the modeling session continues, it becomes more difficult to verify the number of scenarios, or test cases, that have already been discussed. When an interesting scenario emerges in conversation and causes the model to change, the group must verify the model against all the scenarios again. This is a volatile and error-prone approach to modeling because it involves manual verification and memorization. Even so, modeling is a valuable step since it helps team members arrive at a common understanding of a solution for the desired functionality. Minimizing the volatile and error-prone aspects of this technique improves the activity and provides more predictable results. Using TDD to capture the test cases in these scenarios will eventually make them repeatable, specific, and executable. It also helps to ensure that the test cases providing structure to the solution's design are not lost. Without the test cases it is difficult to verify the implementation and demonstrate correct and complete functionality.

By no means would I prescribe that teams eliminate quick modeling sessions. Modeling sessions can provide a holistic view of a feature or module. Modeling only becomes an issue when it lasts too long and delays implementation. The act of designing should not only be theoretical in nature. It is good to timebox modeling sessions. I have found that 30 minutes is sufficient for conducting a modeling session. If a team finds this amount of time insufficient, they should take a slice of a potential solution(s) and attempt to implement it before discussing the rest of the design. The act of implementing a portion of the design provides a solid foundation for further exploration and modeling.

Modeling Constraints with Unit Tests

To reduce duplication and rigidity of the unit test structure's relationship to implementation code, teams should change the way they define a "unit." Instead of class and method defined as the only types of "unit," use the following question to drive the scenario and test cases:

What should the software do next for the intended user?

The approach for writing unit tests I follow is that of Behaviour-Driven Development (BDD).[6] Thinking in terms of the following BDD template about how to model constraints in unit tests helps me stay closer to creating only the code that supports the desired functionality:

```
Given <some initial context>
When <an event occurs>
Then <ensure some outcomes>.
```

By filling in this template I can generate a list of tests that should be implemented to supply the structure that ensures the desired functionality. The following coding session provides an example of applying this approach. The fictitious application is a micro-blogging tool named "Jitter." The functionality I am working on is this:

> **So that it is easier to keep up with their child's messages, parents want shorthand in the messages to be automatically expanded.**

The acceptance criteria for this functionality are:

- LOL, AFAIK, and TTYL are expanded for a parent.
- It should be able to expand lower- and uppercase versions of the shorthand.

The existing code is written in Java and already includes a `JitterSession` class that users obtain when they authenticate into Jitter. Parents can see their child's messages in their session. The following unit test expects to expand "LOL" to "laughing out loud":

---

6. An introduction to Behaviour-Driven Development (BDD) can be found at http://blog.dannorth.net/introducing-bdd/, and the Given, When, Then template is shown in the article in a section named "BDD Provides a 'Ubiquitous Language' for Analysis."

```
public class WhenParentsWantToExpandMessagesWithShorthandTest {

    @Test
    public void shouldExpandLOLToLaughingOutLoud() {
        JitterSession session = mock(JitterSession.class);
        when(session.getNextMessage()).thenReturn("Expand LOL");
        MessageExpander expander = new MessageExpander(session);
        assertThat(expander.getNextMessage(),
            equalTo("Expand laughing out loud"));
    }

}
```

Before we continue with the unit test code example, let's look more closely at how it is written. Notice the name of the programmer test class: WhenParentsWantToExpandMessagesWithShorthandTest.

For some programmers, this long name might seem foreign. It has been my experience that it is easier to understand what a programmer test has been created for when the name is descriptive. An initial reaction that programmers have to long names for classes and methods is the fear they will have to type them into their editor. There are two reasons why this is not an issue:

- Because this is a unit test, other classes should not be using this class.
- Modern integrated development environments have code expansion built in.

Also notice that the name of the test method is shouldExpandLOLToLaughing-OutLoud. This naming convention supports how we drive design through our unit tests by answering the question "What should the software do next for the intended user?" By starting the method name with the word *should*, we are focusing on what the software should do for the user identified in the unit test class name. This is not the only way to write unit tests. People have a wide variety of preferences about how to write their tests, so please find the way that fits your team's intended design strategy best.

The MessageExpander class does not exist, so I create a skeleton of this class to make the code compile. Once the assertion at the end of the unit test is failing, I make the test pass with the following implementation code inside the MessageExpander class:

```
public String getNextMessage() {
    String msg = session.getNextMessage();
    return msg.replaceAll("LOL", "laughing out loud");
}
```

This is the most basic message expansion I could do for only one instance of shorthand text. I notice that there are different variations of the message that I want to handle. What if LOL is written in lowercase? What if it is written as "Lol"? Should it be expanded? Also, what if some variation of LOL is inside a word? The shorthand probably should not be expanded in that case except if the characters surrounding it are symbols, not letters. I write all of this down in the unit test class as comments so I don't forget about it:

```
// shouldExpandLOLIfLowerCase
// shouldNotExpandLOLIfMixedCase
// shouldNotExpandLOLIfInsideWord
// shouldExpandIfSurroundingCharactersAreNotLetters
```

I then start working through this list of test cases to enhance the message expansion capabilities in Jitter:

```
@Test
public void shouldExpandLOLIfLowerCase() {
    when(session.getNextMessage()).thenReturn("Expand lol please");
    MessageExpander expander = new MessageExpander(session);
    assertThat(expander.getNextMessage(),
        equalTo("Expand laughing out loud please"));
}
```

At this point, I find the need for a minor design change. The java.lang .String class does not have a method to match case insensitivity. The unit test forces me to find an alternative, and I decide to use the java.util.regex.Pattern class:

```
public String getNextMessage() {
    String msg = session.getNextMessage();
    Pattern p = Pattern.compile("LOL", Pattern.CASE_INSENSITIVE);
    Return p.matcher(msg).replaceAll("laughing out loud");
}
```

Now I make it so that mixed-case versions of "LOL" are not expanded:

```
@Test
public void shouldNotExpandLOLIfMixedCase() {
    String msg = "Do not expand Lol please";
    when(session.getNextMessage()).thenReturn(msg);
    MessageExpander expander = new MessageExpander(session);
    assertThat(expander.getNextMessage(), equalTo(msg));
}
```

This forces me to use the Pattern.CASE_INSENSITIVE flag in the pattern compilation. To ensure that only the code necessary to make the test pass is created, I match only "LOL" or "lol" for replacement:

```
public String getNextMessage() {
    String msg = session.getNextMessage();
    Pattern p = Pattern.compile("LOL|lol");
    return p.matcher(msg).replaceAll("laughing out loud");
}
```

Next, I make sure that if "LOL" is inside a word it is not expanded:

```
@Test
public void shouldNotExpandLOLIfInsideWord() {
    String msg = "Do not expand PLOL or LOLP or PLOLP please";
    when(session.getNextMessage()).thenReturn(msg);
    MessageExpander expander = new MessageExpander(session);
    assertThat(expander.getNextMessage(), equalTo(msg));
}
```

The pattern matching is now modified to use spaces around each variation of valid "LOL" shorthand:

```
return Pattern.compile("\\sLOL\\s|\\slol\\s").matcher(msg)
    .replaceAll("laughing out loud");
```

Finally, it is important that if the characters around LOL are not letters, such as a space, it still expands:

```
@Test
public void shouldExpandIfSurroundingCharactersAreNotLetters() {
    when(session.getNextMessage()).thenReturn("Expand .lol!
please");
    MessageExpander expander = new MessageExpander(session);
    assertThat(expander.getNextMessage(),
        equalTo("Expand .laughing out loud! please"));
}
```

The final implementation of the pattern-matching code looks like this:

```
return Pattern.compile("\\bLOL\\b|\\blol\\b").matcher(msg)
    .replaceAll("laughing out loud");
```

I will not continue with more of the implementation that would expand other shorthand instances. However, I do want to discuss how the focus on "What should the software do next?" drove the design of this functionality. Driving the code using TDD guides us to implement only what is needed. It also helps us approach 100% code coverage for all lines of code. For programmers who have experience writing object-oriented code, the modules will likely have high cohesion, focused on specific responsibilities, and maintain low coupling to other code. The failing unit test represents something that the software does not do yet. We focus on modifying the software with the simplest implementation we can think of that will make the unit test pass. Then we focus on enhancing the software's design with the refactoring step. It has been my experience that refactoring takes most of the effort when applying TDD effectively. This does not mean refactoring is used with each TDD cycle. It means that overall, programmers spend more time refactoring to enhance the design.

Software Design beyond TDD

Most software design approaches are concerned with documenting design artifacts. Agile teams look for ways to reduce documentation to only what is necessary. Because of this statement, many teams and organizations mistakenly think Agile means no documentation. This is an inappropriate interpretation of Agile software development and is not corroborated by thought leaders and books from the Agile community.

To better enable cost-effective and high levels of support for applications deployed in production, teams ought to be aware of artifacts that assist ongoing maintenance. Software development goes beyond just writing code. It also includes demonstrating the integrity of component integration, alignment to business objectives, and communication of the software's structure for continued maintenance. Some of these aspects can be validated through integration tests. As pointed out in the section on test automation earlier in this chapter, integration tests are not executed as frequently as fast unit tests, such as in each team member's environment. Instead, they are executed in an integration environment when changes are integrated into a common stream of work in source control.

Teams that must consider some or all of the aspects listed above should have processes and tools that support effective maintenance. On top of automated integration testing, they might also benefit from

- Frequent and enhanced compliance auditing
- A team member with specific knowledge or appropriate training and practice
- Push-button deployment and rollback capability to all associated environments
- Production-like staging and test environments for more realistic integration testing

As a team, think about which aspects of software design you should be concerned with and then figure out how you will manage them in the software development process.

Transparent Code Analysis

Code coverage tools measure whether all discernible paths through the code have been tested. It is impossible, except in the most basic instances of code, to validate that all paths through the code have been tested with every potential input. On the other hand, it is possible to ascertain whether each line of code in a module has been tested. This involves measuring test coverage by some basic metrics:

- **Statement coverage** checks how many lines of code have been executed.
- **Decision coverage** checks if each path through a control structure is executed (i.e., "if/else if/else" structures).
- **Condition coverage** checks if each Boolean expression is evaluated to both true and false.
- **Path coverage** checks if combinations of logical code constructs are covered, including sufficient loop evaluation (i.e., executing a loop 0, 1, and more than 1 time).
- **Relational operator coverage** checks if inputs in relational operator evaluation are sufficiently verified (i.e., executing $a < 2$ with $a = 1$, $a = 2$, $a = 3$).

Executing code coverage tools inside each development and continuous integration environment can be helpful feedback to identify lapses in test-driven discipline. As a programmer gains more experience with TDD, it becomes practical to approach 100% coverage in most instances. Tools can provide feedback about code coverage, as shown in Figure 4.3.

It is a common belief that striving for 100% code coverage is too expensive and does not provide enough value to offset its costs. In my experience, approaching 100% code coverage increases confidence and accelerates delivery

Element	Coverage	Covered Instructions	Total Instructions
▽ 📁 TisUgly	97.3 %	729	749
▽ 🗀 src/main/java	97.3 %	729	749
▽ ⊞ com.gettingagile.tisugly	100.0 %	106	106
▸ Ⓙ DesignAssertion.java	100.0 %	58	58
▸ Ⓙ MessageConsole.java	100.0 %	25	25
▸ Ⓙ Module.java	100.0 %	23	23
▽ ⊞ com.gettingagile.tisugly.analyzer	99.6 %	284	285
▸ Ⓙ ASMAnalyzer.java	99.6 %	284	285
▽ ⊞ org.objectweb.asm.depend	94.7 %	339	358
▸ Ⓙ DependencyVisitor.java	94.7 %	339	358

Figure 4.3 The Eclipse IDE plug-in, EclEmma, showing a view of the project's code coverage inside the Eclipse IDE

of working software. There are some factors that inhibit teams from approaching 100% code coverage:

- Working with an existing code base that has significantly less than 100% code coverage: If this is the case, track increases in code coverage rather than whether it approaches 100%.
- A brittle component or application where finding a place to put a valid unit test is difficult, or nearly impossible: In this case, using a black-box testing tool that executes the code in its packaged or installable form could be a better option until the code is less tangled. The packaged or installed application could be instrumented sometimes so that code coverage is evaluated during the black-box test execution.
- When code is generated: Teams should look for ways to isolate generated code from code implemented by team members and evaluate code coverage only for the latter. In some circumstances, our team has been able to generate the unit and integration tests for generated code when we had access to the code generation templates.
- When code integrates with third-party components: Although the third-party component probably will not have 100% code coverage, integration tests can be developed that verify how the code is expected to integrate. Evaluate code coverage on only code that your team created. See the Need-Driven Design section earlier in this chapter.

When working with an existing code base, approachiìng 100% is probably not attainable. In this case, make sure that the current code coverage does not deteriorate. Teams should look for ways to slowly increase code coverage of the existing software over time.

Tools to determine code coverage are not the only code analysis tools available. There are many tools in the static code analysis arena as well. Static code analysis tools can provide feedback through a dashboard, such as in Figure 4.4, on aspects of the software such as

- Team's preferred coding rules
- Lines of code
- Cyclomatic complexity
- Duplicated code
- Lack of cohesion
- Maintainability
- Dependencies
- Design
- Architecture
- Technical debt

Name	Lines of code	Technical Debt ratio	Coverage	Duplicated lines (%)	Build time
MasterProject	6,055,141	16.7%	18.7%	6.1%	2010-04-26

Name	Lines of code	Technical Debt ratio	Coverage	Duplicated lines (%)	Build time
AisLib application framework	12,187	9.6%	38.6%	1.1%	2010-04-24
Tapestry 5 Project	58,156 ▲	6.7%	51.4%	0.2%	2010-04-26
Commons Collections	20,901	10.1%	79.8%	3.3%	2010-04-25
MicroEmulator	28,344	11.7%		2.3%	2010-04-25
Apache Jackrabbit	208,413 ▲	16.7%	26.4%	4.6%	2010-04-25
Unitils	18,636 ▲	15.0%	2.8%	3.9%	2010-04-26
javagit	6,127	11.1%	61.2%	0.3%	2010-04-26
Wicket Parent	104,679 ▼	9.5%	36.9%	1.0%	2010-04-26
Commons Chain	3,901	14.4%	64.5%	21.9%	2010-04-25
Commons IO	6,827 ▲	5.5%	82.3%	3.1% ▲	2010-04-25
Commons SCXML	7,331	9.8%	69.8%	7.2%	2010-04-25
Sonar	33,879 ▲	6.5%	67.3%	0.0%	2010-04-26
Apache Velocity	29,086 ▲	11.1%		5.1%	2010-04-26
Apache Abdera	52,670 ▲	8.8%		2.9%	2010-04-24
Castor	112,202 ▲	9.2%		7.0%	2010-04-25
Commons BeanUtils	11,374	15.0%	62.8%	6.8%	2010-04-25
JEuclid	12,664	4.1%		0.5%	2010-04-19

Figure 4.4 The Sonar dashboard showing metrics for lines of code, technical debt ratio, code coverage, duplicated lines of code, and build time[7]

I do not suggest that the metrics generated for all of these aspects of the software are exact. They do provide feedback about our software internals and can help guide our development efforts. Also, it is sometimes easier to drill down into the static code analysis dashboard for an area of code that will be involved in changes for the next feature. Looking at higher-level metrics for the code can provide useful information to guide implementation and opportunities for code improvement.

SUMMARY

Executable Design is a method for driving the implementation of software functionality. It focuses on the following principles:

- The way we design can always be improved.
- We'll get it "right" the third time.
- We will not get it "right" the first time.
- Design and construct for change rather than longevity.
- Lower the threshold of pain.

Going beyond how we write automated tests, Executable Design also involves how they are structured inside projects, how they are executed in different

---

7. Sonar is an open platform to manage code quality available at www.sonarsource.org/. The picture is from their demo web site at http://nemo.sonarsource.org/.

environments, and a way to think about what the next test should be. When we answer the question "What should the software do next for the intended user?" our programmer tests will be more directly focused on delivery of value to the user. Using transparent code analysis, team members can get feedback on the health of the code as they implement in an incremental fashion.

Chapter 5

QUALITY DEBT

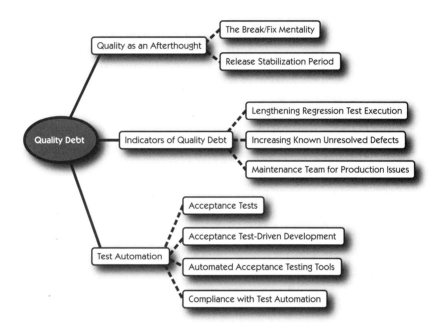

Promises make debt, and debt makes promises.

—Dutch proverb

QUALITY AS AN AFTERTHOUGHT

In traditional projects, quality is assessed late in the software delivery cycle. The idea is to focus on defining requirements, and both code and tests can be separately developed based on those requirements. The problem is that team members implementing code and test artifacts interpret requirements documents, no matter how well they are written, differently.

Executing the tests after the code has been written makes quality an afterthought. Quality is validated only after the code is feature complete, meaning that all features have been implemented but not fully tested. This lack of focus on quality makes releases unpredictable, builds in flaws and defects, and results in teams racing to the release date. All of these problems stemming from quality as an afterthought result in debt. Over time this debt becomes too costly to even think of paying back, and so development teams reduce checking for defects to only risky areas of the software. This debt piles up in a catalog of inadequacies called the *bug tracker*.

The Break/Fix Mentality

An organization that had a list of over 5,000 open issues on a single product was looking to add capabilities to the product. I innocently posed a question to the development manager for this product team: "Are you going to fix all 5,000 of these issues?" She responded quickly, with a slight chuckle, with a firm "No." Then I asked, "What do you do with all of these issues?" She went on to describe a process that I had plenty of experience with, bug triage.

Each month the team leads, project managers, and business analysts got together and identified the top 20% priority issues. This exercise took anywhere from one to three days each month. "So you are going to fix 1,000 of the issues?" I asked. Again she promptly answered, "No," and looked at me somewhat puzzled. Didn't I understand the bug triage process and why it's necessary to address issues our customers have with the product?

The 5,000 issues in that software did not happen overnight. The quality debt accrued over many years of development. The organization's threshold for open issues in its bug tracker kept rising as each release went by. At the end of each release decisions were made to deploy into production with defects still unresolved. The reasons ranged from the defects not being high enough in priority to fix, all the way to just having to get the software out the door because it was late and over budget. Figure 5.1 shows the slow accrual of quality debt represented by captured and unresolved defects over time.

However the quality debt accrued, it was hampering delivery of new features. The development team had grown from 10 to 27 members, and approximately 75% of the team's capacity was dedicated to fixing defects. This meant that even with a 270% increase in costs, the organization was getting only 67.5% of the value originally delivered. Management probably did not have this in mind when decisions were made to cut quality and get the software out to users.

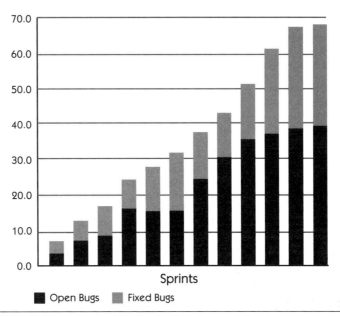

Figure 5.1   Defects accumulate faster than they get fixed on many projects.

Ken Schwaber made the following statement at Agile 2006 on the subject of cutting quality:

> *For every [dollar] of competitive advantage gained by cutting quality, it costs $4 to restore it; and software is an organizational asset and decisions to cut quality must be made by executive management and reflected in the financial statements.*[1]

Software is a business asset. Software automates business processes, increases productivity, enables organizations to collaborate at all hours, and expands the marketplace for more products and services. As costs to maintain software rise and the value of delivered functionality decreases, software accrues debt and eventually becomes a liability unless something changes.

The break/fix mentality leads to increased costs for feature maintenance. Over time, the total cost to maintain software with increased quality debt will include the need for additional testers, more operational support hours, and time wasted working around poorly maintained features. Teams that decide

---

1. Ken Schwaber, "Cutting Quality Should Be an Executive Management Decision," presentation at Agile 2006 in Minneapolis, MN.

to take a break/fix approach will find quality diminishing quickly during and, even more, after each release.

Release Stabilization Period

In traditional sequential software development processes, such as the waterfall[2] approach shown in Figure 5.2, software components are specified, designed, and constructed before they are validated and integrated as a full solution. A release stabilization period in waterfall starts on the "code freeze" or "feature complete" date. This date indicates that all new functionality has

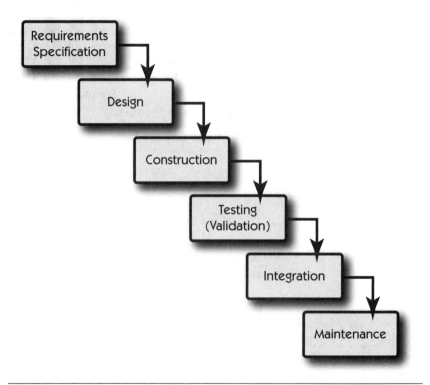

Figure 5.2   The waterfall sequential development process model used in many software development organizations. Winston W. Royce presented this model as an example of a flawed model for large systems development in 1970.

---

2. Winston Royce, "Managing the Development of Large Software Systems," *Proceedings of IEEE WESCON* 26 (August 1970): 1–9.

been coded with nominal unit testing performed and that it is now time to test it. There is work left to stabilize the release such as resolving conflicts in component integration, executing detailed tests, and performing a successful deployment of the software to appropriate platforms.

The release stabilization phase is unpredictable. Continuing to stabilize the release at the end will take its toll on the software over time. The first release is manageable, in some cases, because the amount of code to integrate during the stabilization phase is still relatively small. The subsequent release has defects that were left from the previous release, and the team works around these to add new functionality. The amount of code to manage and sift through has increased since the previous release. The confluence of more defects and work-around code leads to longer release stabilization periods. This leads to additional staff on the project, more planned time to execute the release stabilization phase, and a decrease in the delivery of new functionality over time.

INDICATORS OF QUALITY DEBT

Although many in the software industry do not correlate quality issues with architecture, the direct impact of quality debt on the structure and integrity of an application is indisputable. The longer it takes to validate an application's build, the more likely it is that quality will decay because of lack of feedback. Decay of the internal software quality leads to poor tactics being used to maintain the software. Teams decide to run regression tests for only portions instead of the whole application. Inadequate regression testing results in increased production issues that distract teams while they are developing the next release of the application. These distractions reduce the amount of time teams have to deliver the new features.

Quality debt in an application is detectable. The following is a list of quality debt indicators:

- Lengthening regression test execution
- Increasing known unresolved defects
- Creating a maintenance team for production issues

The upcoming sections will go into more detail about each quality debt indicator and ways to track and identify problems earlier. Also, they will include processes, practices, and tools that can be used to help manage each effectively.

Lengthening Regression Test Execution

The amount of time it takes to execute all of the regression tests for an application tends to increase as more code is added to the software. If teams are not automating system, unit, acceptance, integration, performance, load, and stress tests, regression test execution will continually increase in duration. There are many reasons why teams don't automate regression tests:

- Teams don't think the customer wants to pay them for creating automated tests.
- There are compliance processes that seem to make automation impractical.
- The software has complex areas of functionality that are difficult to test.
- The teams lack the experience to implement automation effectively.

Each of these issues can be overcome. Keep track of how long it takes to execute the full regression test suite. If the duration is lengthening, ask what is causing it. When working with legacy code, find ways to reduce the time needed to execute the full regression suite. This may start out as weeks and slowly reduce to days, hours, and maybe even minutes. This enables the team to have exceptional feedback about existing expected behavior as the software is changed over time.

Performance, Stress, and Load Testing

This book will not go into great detail on how to implement performance, stress, and load testing. There are other books on this topic. Instead, we will focus on the characteristics of performance, stress, and load testing for frequent feedback:

- Find performance, stress, and load testing tools that can be executed through a script. This enables team members to execute these tests from their own machines. Also, these types of tests may need to be executed from multiple nodes at once, so remote script execution will make them much easier to run.
- Do not wait to execute performance, stress, and load tests. Once the team has information about the type of performance the customer expects, they should begin developing these tests and executing them. It is common to run these tests three or more times per iteration, and in some cases I have seen them run many times per day.
- Create performance, stress, and load testing environments that resemble production as closely as possible. Small variations in environment setup or configuration can cause test results to be invalid.

- Automatically promote functionally validated builds to performance, stress, and load testing environments. After the functional tests have been successfully executed against the changes, deploy and execute these tests in an automated fashion.

Again, there are a lot of tools out there that can support these effective performance, stress, and load testing characteristics. It is important to continually find better ways to execute all types of tests so they can provide effective feedback as code and technology evolve.

Increasing Known Unresolved Defects

This might be the most prevalent indicator of quality debt and also the most obvious. If a software development team creates more defects than they are able to fix, the number of defects being tracked increases. Figure 5.3 shows how the number of known defects to track increases over time.

If defects are outpacing the ability of your software development team to fix them, the first thing to do is reduce the velocity of delivery per iteration. The team is attempting to implement more functionality than it is able to do with

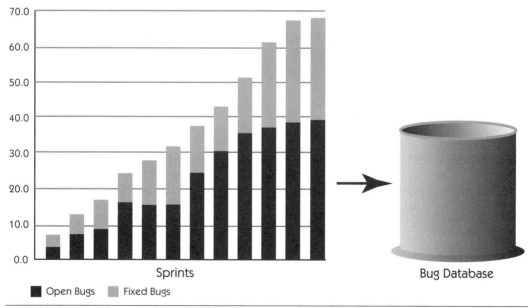

Figure 5.3 If teams are not able to fix defects as quickly as they accrue, the number of defects to track will increase.

sufficient quality. This will lead to increases in production issues and will eventually contaminate the end user's perceptions of the software. As defects increase past a certain point, management will find that the development team is spending too much time on production issues and is not able to focus on delivering new functionality. This leads to increasing the operational costs by separating out a maintenance team to handle production issues specifically.

Maintenance Team for Production Issues

When production issues outpace the team's ability to fix issues, a conflict is realized. Production issues are highly important, but they distract the team from implementing requested features that the business stakeholders want. In most software development organizations, this is a candidate situation for creating a maintenance team. One of the biggest problems with a maintenance team solution is this:

The team creating the defects is not responsible for fixing them.

Therefore, the maintenance team is kept busy fixing existing defects while the accumulation of new defects continues to accelerate. This acceleration occurs because

- The feature team does not learn as fast how to avoid activities that produce serial defect creation.
- The feature team continues to have schedule pressures and is expected to deliver the same amount of functionality.
- Maintenance teams tend to work off a separate branch of code and the feature team does not pay the cost to integrate defect fixes.

Although creating a maintenance team for production issues is an indicator of quality debt, I do not suggest that the maintenance team should be disbanded to begin quality debt reduction. There are a few courses of action that can bring about healthy change for handling production issues while delivering requested functionality:

- Cycle feature team members through the maintenance team and vice versa.
- Reduce the velocity of feature delivery.
- Automate tests on defect fixes.
- Create a production issue workflow for handling different severities.
- Maintain one list of work.

Cycle Feature Team Members through the Maintenance Team

One of the simplest changes that can be made is cycling feature team members through the maintenance team. This means that maintenance team members also cycle through the feature team. This gives the entire group opportunities to work on both activities and learn how to avoid defect-creating activities more effectively by working on maintenance.

Reduce the Velocity of Feature Delivery

When teams are accelerating accrual of quality debt, an obvious choice is to reduce feature delivery so the team is able to incrementally reduce the quality debt. This is much easier said than done. There is a dilemma for management when it comes to reducing feature delivery.

The Development Manager's Dilemma

A supportive ScrumMaster said to a manager, "The team continues to complain about working with that legacy code base because it has so much debt. The debt slows them down in their feature delivery. They are asking if we can raise the priority of fixing it."

The manager looked distraught about the request. She knew that paying back some of the debt would be a valuable effort, but what would the business say about the priorities? "Tell the team that we'll start paying back some of the debt in the next release. We must get the current release out the door, and a change in priorities won't allow us to get there," the manager responded.

Given the environment in which most development managers work, it is not surprising that a decision is made to push paying back debt to the next release. A typical development manager understandably has many influences on his or her decision making, such as

- Business pressures for having a set of features on a certain date at a specific cost
- Expectations of feature delivery based on past software releases
- Unreasonable deadlines due to business issues such as lapsing support contracts and executive management promises
- Perception of the organization's capabilities
- A compensation plan that does not reward managing software assets for future capability

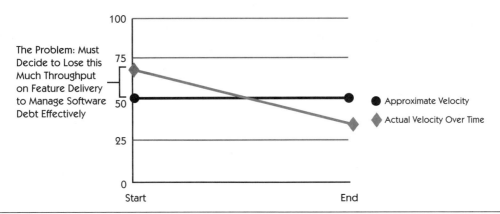

Figure 5.4   The problem development managers have in deciding whether or not to manage software debt effectively on existing software

The development team will have to slow its current feature delivery in order to achieve consistent velocity while managing the software debt, as shown in Figure 5.4. Managing the software debt effectively is the best decision for maintaining the value of the software for the business. Development teams and associated management should find ways to make incremental changes in feature delivery expectations so they can make progress toward better software debt management.

Automate Tests on Defect Fixes

On projects where the number of defects is growing, there are many recurring or similar defects. Significant progress can be made on reducing the number of defects by automating tests for defect fixes. These tests establish how the software should behave and are executed frequently to make sure it still behaves as such.

Teams should automate the tests at the smallest unit of behavior so the tests run fast and are more durable. This means that unit tests, like those discussed in Chapter 4, "Executable Design," are best to automate for defect fixes. If it is too difficult to create unit tests because of tangled legacy code, the next option for test automation is creating automated acceptance tests. Automating tests through the user interface should be done only as a last resort because these are the slowest and most brittle tests to execute. Automating tests for defects could also lead to performance, stress, and load test automation. Please review the section "Performance, Stress, and Load Testing" earlier in this chapter for more details.

Development teams that find recurring or similar defects getting logged against the software should find ways to reduce rework in the infected areas. Test automation for defect fixes will incrementally supply tests to be frequently executed to validate that previously expected behavior is still correct.

Create a Production Issue Workflow

As production issues become visible, business stakeholders ask for them to be fixed. Not all production issues must be fixed immediately. Those that must be fixed immediately will interrupt planned work. A balance must be struck to fix immediate needs now and fix not-so-immediate needs at another appropriate time. Production issues fall into these two categories:

- **Fires** that must be fixed right away
- **Issues** that must be prioritized

Fires are issues that get prioritized ahead of all current work of the team. These are handled best in one of the following ways:

- The entire team designates a buffer to handle fires as they crop up. Teams set this up because production issues are a regular occurrence for them, and until the software debt is paid back sufficiently, this will continue to be the case.
- One or more members of the team are designated to handle production issues as they crop up. This allows most of the team to focus on feature delivery. The team members assigned to production issues don't make feature delivery commitments. If there are no production issues, these team members help with paying off software debt or additional feature delivery.
- The least preferred method is to create a separate maintenance team. When choosing this option, consider the suggestions in "Cycle Feature Team Members through the Maintenance Team" earlier in this chapter.

Issues that are not fires must be prioritized along with other work so the team knows what is most important to work on next. In Scrum, the Product Backlog should include these issues in its stack-ranked list of prioritized work. If issues are insignificant enhancements or probably will not get worked on in a reasonable amount of time (three to six months), they might just get resolved so the Product Backlog size does not get out of control. Anytime an issue is closed without being fixed, the requestor should be notified why it was not prioritized. This workflow is represented in Figure 5.5.

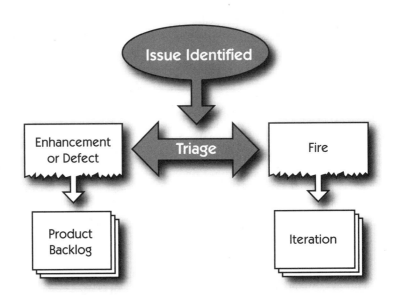

Figure 5.5 The basic workflow for handling production issues on a Scrum team. If the issue is a "fire," it interrupts the current iteration. If it is not a fire, it gets prioritized against other work in the Product Backlog in preparation for a future iteration.

What is most difficult about putting a production issues workflow process into practice, as described, is defining a "fire." It is important to get a good cross section of the project stakeholders in the decision-making process to define a fire. When working with the stakeholder group on defining a fire, it is good to facilitate decision making with thoughts about impact on services or revenue and whether work-arounds exist. Not all of the production issues identified will be easy to triage, but a definition that can take care of more than 90% is a great workflow.

Maintain One List of Work

One certain way to increase software debt in your systems development is to have multiple master lists from which to work. Clear direction is difficult to maintain through multiple lists such as bug tracking systems, desired features, and technical infrastructure enhancements. Which list does a team member choose from? If the bug tracker includes bugs in the higher-priority levels, such as priority 1 and 2, this may be an obvious choice, right? Well, the problem is that influential stakeholders want their new features so that they can show progress to management and customers. Also, if we don't enhance our infrastructure, we will never improve our delivery capabilities and will

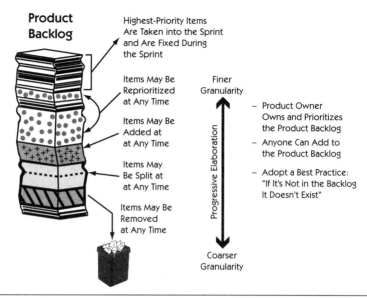

Product Backlog

Highest-Priority Items Are Taken into the Sprint and Are Fixed During the Sprint

Items May Be Reprioritized at Any Time

Items May Be Added at at Any Time

Items May Be Split at at Any Time

Items May Be Removed at Any Time

Finer Granularity

Progressive Elaboration

Coarser Granularity

– Product Owner Owns and Prioritizes the Product Backlog

– Anyone Can Add to the Product Backlog

– Adopt a Best Practice: "If It's Not in the Backlog It Doesn't Exist"

Figure 5.6   The Scrum Product Backlog is a tool that was created to meet the objective of maintaining only one list of work. This shows how a Product Backlog works; it is best used with the practice of "If it's not in the backlog, it doesn't exist."

continue to endure frustrating issues between our development, test, staging, and production environments.

Deployed and appropriately used software is a business asset. Modifications to a business asset should be driven by business needs. Bugs, features, and infrastructure desires for the software should be pitted against features and defects in one list from which the team can pull work. Business stakeholders must prioritize across varying descriptions of value for each type of work. The focus gained with one prioritized list of work will more than make up for the continued management of the one list from a business perspective. Figure 5.6 shows how the Product Backlog is managed in Scrum, including a good practice of "If it's not in the backlog, it doesn't exist."

TEST AUTOMATION

Although test automation approaches could include unit tests with xUnit-type libraries, this section will focus more on functional and integration test execution. For more detailed information on unit tests, check out Chapter 4, "Executable Design." A way to differentiate unit testing from functional and integration testing is to think of the granularity of each type of test. Unit tests are employed to execute one specific capability of a component of the software. Functional and integration tests execute the interactions between multiple components within an application from an end user perspective. Therefore, unit tests are finer in granularity than functional and integration tests.

The question of when it is appropriate to automate tests has been around for some time now. Points of view range from "Test automation should be constrained to unit testing" all the way to "Automate all test cases." Neither extreme is an optimal approach for all software projects. It is becoming apparent that some automation should be present in all software projects of any measurable size. Automation is best used for test cases that are repeatable and specific. This does not represent all of the highest-value tests to be executed on a software solution. Brian Marick, an Agile Manifesto signatory, wrote a wonderful paper "When Should a Test Be Automated?" in which he described his own insights into test automation:

> . . . two insights that took me a long time to grasp—and that I still find somewhat slippery—but which seem to be broadly true:
>
> 1. The cost of automating a test is best measured by the number of manual tests it prevents you from running and the bugs it will therefore cause you to miss.
>
> 2. A test is designed for a particular purpose: to see if some aspects of one or more features work. When an automated test that's rerun finds bugs, you should expect it to find ones that seem to have nothing to do with the test's original purpose. Much of the value of an automated test lies in how well it can do that.[3]

Brian's insights seem to take two perspectives on test automation. The first insight provides a negative perspective on automated tests because a human being does not physically execute them. If we rely too much on test automation to find all defects in the software, we will miss quality attributes that are not easily automated. Usability is an example of a software quality attribute that could be overlooked by teams with extreme reliance on test automation. Not only will quality attributes get overlooked, but also alternative and valuable usage scenarios could be missed. The second insight describes how automated tests can be evaluated in terms of value to the software delivery. Since automation is best for repeatable and specific test cases, defects found after successful execution are usually the effects of changes made for purposes

---

3. Brian Marick, "When Should a Test Be Automated?" *Testing Foundations*, 1998. This paper was originally presented at Software Quality Engineering's STAR*EAST* 1999 conference.

other than what the original test was created for. The ability to execute appropriate automated test cases against a software solution often allows the team to get feedback on their changes quickly and modify the behavior before it gets tangled with other features. In my opinion, both perspectives on a team's automation approach are important and should guide us to appropriate automation techniques for our domain and technology choices.

Acceptance testing has become a popular mechanism for incremental development and testing. The past few years have given rise to many great open-source tools to support team development of functional and integration tests using automated acceptance testing tools. The next few sections will go into more detail about acceptance tests, acceptance test automation, acceptance testing tools, and maintaining compliance effectively using automation.

Acceptance Tests

Acceptance tests are created by anyone on the team in response to the acceptance criteria confirmed with the customer. They are edited by anyone on the team, including the customer or subject matter experts who feel comfortable with the test case syntax, to provide more detail about the acceptance criteria for specific functionality. Every team member should know how to execute the acceptance tests for the project. Acceptance tests should be automated so they can run in the continuous integration environment against integrated changes.

The acceptance tests for desired functionality are started before construction. Team members work with the customer around a whiteboard, or other collaboration tool, to describe and clarify the expected behavior of the functionality. When the team members believe they have enough information to get started, they write automated acceptance tests that focus the implementation of the functionality to only what is needed.

Acceptance tests are not sufficient as the entire test suite for ensuring quality. Teams still need unit tests, integration tests, more detailed functional tests, and manual exploratory testing to provide a safety net for the implementation. All of these tests together give confidence to the team that changes are not breaking existing functionality.

Acceptance Test-Driven Development

Acceptance Test-Driven Development (ATDD) is a technique that teams use to capture the acceptance tests before implementing the functionality. Initially, the automated acceptance test fails because the application does not currently include the functionality being requested. The team implements the

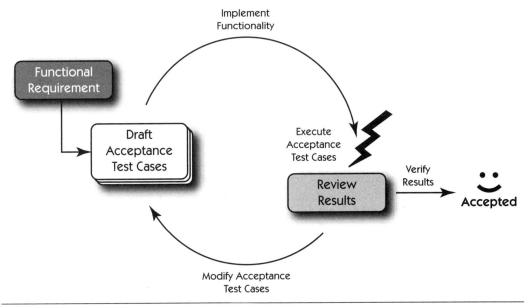

Figure 5.7   High-level flow diagram of the Acceptance Test-Driven Development process for functional and integration regression test automation

requested feature, using additional technical test practices, until the automated acceptance test passes. Once it has passed, the automated test is added to the regression test suite for the continuous integration environment to execute. Figure 5.7 shows the basic flow of ATDD.

The ATDD approach is a "test first" and incremental technique. Acceptance tests specify desired logic that allows implementation to start from an understanding of acceptability for particular scenarios. Initial acceptance tests are not fully fleshed out and allow for emergence of understanding to be included as the implementation proves ideas and unfolds the unknowns about the feature. In order to clarify the feature, close collaboration with users, customers, and subject matter experts is essential.

Automated Acceptance Testing Tools

Acceptance tests are developed using many different types of tools. Some customer testing tools execute against the graphical user interface (GUI). Some act as if they are the GUI calling into the integrated application components. In some cases, the automated acceptance tests are implemented using a unit test framework with a different naming convention or some way to differentiate them from the faster-running tests. The idea is to create automated acceptance tests that can be executed by all team members to ensure that previously developed functionality is not broken by new changes. This continuous execution of acceptance tests provides more confidence that existing functionality still works as expected.

Tools in the acceptance testing arena take in HTML, spreadsheets, textual, and programming language formats. A team should decide what type of automated acceptance test tool will work best for their development style and customer collaboration needs. If the customer is highly involved in defining specific behavior, a tool that is approachable, such as HTML or spreadsheets, could be more appropriate. If the team is defining more of the specific behavior and reviewing it with the customer, using the same programming language as the implementation may be more appropriate.

Software development using an ATDD approach puts pressure on the test automation tools and frameworks that teams use. Some tools support the approach better than others. The functionality in test automation tools and frameworks that enable ATDD comprises

- **Modularity:** the ability to encapsulate test components for use in bigger regression test cases. Rather than using a large script to execute many test scenarios, a modular testing framework allows for the inclusion of test components that encapsulate parts of a scenario and are reusable across test cases. In a tool such as StoryTestIQ,[4] this is accomplished with the !include function as shown in the following example:

  ```
  !include loginAsAdministrator
  !include navigateToUserAdministrationScreen
  !include addReadOnlyUser

  | clickAndWait | removeUser_readonlyuser | |
  | clickAndWait | yes_i_am_sure | |
  | assertValue | console_message | readonlyuser has been removed. |

  !include navigateToReadOnlyUsersScreen

  | assertTextNotPresent | readonlyuser | |

  !include logoutOfAdministrationSite
  ```

  When the !include directive is used, StoryTestIQ knows that it should load the script with the following name to be run as part of a larger test case.

---

4. StoryTestIQ is an open-source automated acceptance testing tool that can be found at http://storytestiq.sourceforge.net/.

Keyword	Action	Argument	Argument
Search For Term	[Arguments]	${term}	
	Open Browser	http://localhost	
	Input Text	search_box	${term}

Figure 5.8   A keyword-driven test using an open-source tool called Robot Framework.[5] This example describes a keyword that can be used in other tests called "Search For Term" that takes one argument, which is the term you want to search on.

- **Keyword-based:** tools that use keywords to support creation of automated tests based on a domain-specific language (DSL) for the application under test. Each keyword can be used in test cases, like a programming language function, to encapsulate a test component. Keywords can take arguments that fill in information for a specific usage scenario in a test case. Figure 5.8 shows an example of a keyword-based tool.
- **Behavior-driven:** acceptance test cases expressed in the language of users and that are also executable. There is specific focus on how the team and customer use language to better understand the behavior of software under development. The acceptance test scenarios are expressed using a Given, When, Then statement. Following is an example of a test scenario before it is put into an automated test:

```
Given I have valid username and password
When I login to payroll system
Then I should see time entry screen for current week
```

Some tools that support a Behaviour-Driven Development (BDD) approach are able to take these statements and execute them against the software. Here is an example using Cucumber:[6]

```
Feature: Authentication
  In order to enter my time
  As an employee
  I want to authenticate into our payroll system

Scenario: Successful Login
  Given I have valid username and password
  When I login to payroll system
  Then I should see time entry screen for current week
```

---

5. Robot Framework is an open-source keyword-driven automated acceptance testing tool that can be found at www.robotframework.org/.

6. Cucumber is an open-source BDD automated acceptance testing tool that can be found at http://cukes.info/.

The feature scenario is then translated into a test fixture written in the Ruby programming language:

```
Given "I have valid username and password" do
  @user = User.find(1)
end

When "I login to payroll system" do
  visit '/login'
  fills_in 'user_login', :with => @user.username
  fills_in 'user_password', :with => @user.password
  clicks_button 'login'
end

Then "I should see time entry screen for current week" do
  assert_select 'title', 'Time Entry'
  // more code to verify current week here…
end
```

- **Visual playback:** allows the test executor to watch the user interface (UI) interactions while the test case runs. This is helpful for some exploratory testing activities and is also more approachable for users and non-developer stakeholders to understand. Watching automated acceptance tests executing against the software through a GUI can help team members see odd problems as screens pass by. Figure 5.9 shows an example of a visual playback automated acceptance test tool.

Although each of the test automation features described above is supportive of an ATDD approach, teams should not always look for a tool that does all of them. Test tools and frameworks that support modularity are generally preferable. Using tools that support keywords and DSLs explicitly may not be necessary but could be helpful to some teams. Behavior-driven tools are becoming popular and are helpful for getting business and technical project team members to use the same language. Visual playback is not necessary and can represent the most brittle types of tests since they are coupled to highly volatile user interfaces. Teams should find tools that meet their specific needs and that they are able to use effectively after overcoming the tools' learning curve.

The following techniques have helped teams write effective and maintainable automated acceptance tests:

- **Create test components:** Create small test components and tie them together to create larger tests. Test components are best when they do one thing well. This may be filling out a form and submitting it,

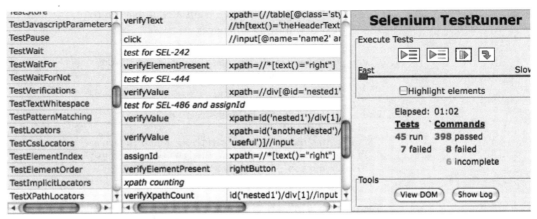

Figure 5.9   The Selenium[7] test runner for visual playback of automated acceptance tests inside a web browser. In the upper left frame is the test suite. The upper middle frame contains the test case currently being executed. The upper right frame has the controls to run the whole suite, a single test case, and interactions with the currently executing test. The web application under test is loaded in the bottom frame. As actions are executed, their execution is shown on the actual web application in real time.

navigating from one section of an application to another, or validating a system's current context for executing the rest of a test case.

- **Extract test data from scripts:** It is important to keep test data outside of the test scripts to prevent duplication. Duplication creates most of the maintenance headaches for aging software and tests. Maintainability of test scripts is reliant on continued removal of duplication, including usage of test data across multiple scripts. Use references from the current test case to other scripts that contain the test data used.

- **Reference interface controls abstractly:** A big reason that automated functional tests are brittle is that they reference components that change location. For instance, when the text on a button is changed

---

7. Selenium is an open-source automated acceptance testing tool that can be found at http://seleniumhq.org/.

from "Log in" to "Sign on," the test script referencing the original text will break because the text no longer exists on the screen. Most current interface libraries and standards allow controls to have abstract names through an `id` attribute. In HTML most elements allow for the attribute `id` to be defined for components, and each identifier must be unique per page. Referencing the unique identifier of the "Log in" button as `authenticateUserButton` would allow the automated test script to continue working.

- **Execute automated test scripts often:** Automated tests are best used to find problems with existing functionality. Running automated tests often allows teams to know quickly when they are breaking existing functionality and to fix it before the problem lingers and becomes embedded within other functionality. The faster automated tests can be executed against changes, the better. Some teams start by running automated regression test scripts once per day. This usually occurs overnight and provides results that the team looks over the next morning. More ambitious teams execute regression tests every time they check code into their source code management system. Small changes are scrutinized multiple times a day and provide frequent feedback to the team.

This list only contains techniques to create more value and increase the maintainability of your recorded automated test scripts. It does not describe ways to create better tests for your applications. These techniques revolve around how to encapsulate, organize, and execute your automated test scripts. It is up to your team members to create good test cases and incorporate these techniques for managing them.

Automation with Fit: A Case Study

An insurance company decided to migrate an application to a new platform. A team that had recently adopted Scrum was assigned to the migration project. The team initially started testing functionality using manual test case execution and found out quickly that the manual regression testing was taking too much time and would start impacting their ability to write as much functionality as they had been doing so far.

The team decided to adopt Fit[8] for automating acceptance tests to verify conversion of legacy data to the new platform. Fit is a tool that allows teams to verify customer expectations to actual results using HTML tables to describe

---

8. Fit is an open-source table-driven acceptance testing tool that can be found at http://fit.c2.com/.

test conditions. After eight two-week iterations using Fit the team was extremely happy with the progress and stability of the data migration.

There was anecdotal evidence that substantial time and money were being saved, but they could not provide exact details of how much. A member of the team was tasked with extracting quantitative results to share with the organization.

The team calculated the cost of manual regression test execution before the introduction of Fit. It was found that the team had been executing two full regression test runs lasting 75 person hours per two-week iteration. These full regression test runs incorporated comprehensive manual regression testing and data conversion and validation. The overall cost for executing manual test regression per iteration was $17,000.

After the introduction of Fit there was a significant reduction of cost per iteration for testing. The team had developed a healthy amount of Fit test fixtures and automated tests. This reduced the 70-plus-hour test runtime to 6 hours, and the cost for regression test execution per iteration went from $17,000 down to $7,000. Because of this change in cost per iteration, the team was able to focus more of its time on design and validation tasks rather than repetitive manual regression test execution.

This case study shows that significant time and cost reduction can be realized with test automation. Within 16 weeks this team was able to reduce testing costs per iteration from $17,000 to $7,000 and test execution runtime from more than 70 hours to 6 hours.

Compliance with Test Automation

Software compliance has become a concern for many software development organizations. Not keeping software in compliance could result in substantial penalties and regulatory ramifications. The potential risk of being out of compliance has led these organizations to identify ways to govern compliance such as independent verification and validation (IV&V). IV&V is a way to check what the software a team delivers from an independent perspective. Robert O. Lewis defines verification and validation this way:

> Verification *is an iterative process aimed at determining whether the product of each step in the development cycle fulfills all the requirements levied on it by the previous step and is internally complete, consistent, and correct to support the next phase.*
>
> Validation *is the process of executing the software to exercise the hardware and comparing the test results to the required performance.*[9]

---

9. Robert O. Lewis, *Independent Verification and Validation: A Life Cycle Engineering Process for Quality Software* (Wiley-IEEE, 1992).

IV&V is especially used in highly regulated industries such as medical systems, health care, and banking. Entire departments are dedicated to executing IV&V for software development teams to check requirements, design, code, and test phases of a traditional system development life cycle (SDLC). When automated testing is introduced into this environment, it is difficult for the organization to see how IV&V fits into the development life cycle without eliminating most of the gains they hoped to achieve. There are some essential practices that support effective integration of automated testing while sustaining an IV&V process:

- Delivering potentially shippable product increments each iteration
- Favoring high-level design documentation over detailed design while providing automated programmer tests
- Small test components that are put together to form larger test cases
- Iterative delivery to the IV&V group for per-iteration verification and validation
- Ability to provide a list of artifacts that have been modified since the last iteration

Test Automation, IV&V, and Agile

A QA manager at a medical systems company said that test automation was too difficult to implement because of the company's IV&V process. The problem was that IV&V had to manually verify all of the test scripts that were created during the release at the end. Because a manual verification was executed against the entire product, it made less sense to pay for test automation along the way. The automated tests would not be executed to validate the release build anyway.

After some discussion, I asked him why the IV&V group couldn't verify and validate after each iteration. He said that the record-and-playback scripts were too large, and the IV&V team had to manually verify the entire script even if only a small part was modified. Next, I asked him if the development team could create smaller scripts that were more focused and then piece them together to create larger test scripts. He responded, "Yes, in fact we started doing this and it seems to be a better way to automate for the team, as well."

It seemed we were getting to a solution, but as he thought more in depth about it he asked, "How would we know what scripts have been modified since the last iteration?" Because they were using a source control management system to house their code, we could easily run a diff between each sprint tag and provide a listing to IV&V of which artifacts changed. He left our conversation and immediately worked with the team and the IV&V group to set up this solution. The development team was able to take advantage of test automation from that point forward.

Teams should look for creative ways to work with the IV&V group when necessary. Automated testing techniques may have to be modified to work with the IV&V group in an iterative and incremental fashion. Also, the IV&V group must be included in any process to work with Agile software development teams so that their needs are met.

SUMMARY

Although code is what teams deliver to users, there are other aspects of the software development process that must be managed effectively. When quality is maintained only through manual testing, as the application grows the tests take longer and longer to run. This puts more pressure on the team to meet feature complete dates and on testers to squeeze test execution into an unreasonable fixed time frame. Teams can automate the repeatable and specific tests to reduce the time needed for regression testing an application. This does not remove the need for exploratory testing, but it allows testers to focus on more important aspects of testing.

Automation of tests after feature implementation is also problematic. It is common for test automation to fall well behind feature development and not get completed at a later point in time. Taking a "test-first" approach with automation, even for functional tests, allows teams to drive the design and implementation from the acceptance tests. An approach to automating acceptance tests in a test-first manner is Acceptance Test-Driven Development (ATDD). Conversations involving the team and customer about lightweight requirements lead to the development of draft automated acceptance tests. These automated acceptance tests of what the customer wants the software to do guide feature implementation. The tests start out failing because the functionality is not implemented yet, and the team focuses on getting the acceptance tests to pass.

The initial automated acceptance tests are incomplete. During the implementation process, more information is learned about the desired functionality. As needed, the team modifies the automated acceptance tests to reflect new knowledge. Sometimes the team needs to collaborate with the customer to clarify the needs of users. As the team members continually iterate on the feature implementation, they converge on a more complete understanding of the functionality and solidify the automated acceptance tests. They can use these tests to quickly evaluate current work and future regressions. Once the automated acceptance tests pass, the team has completed the feature implementation, and the customer can do a final review to accept the work.

ATDD changes the traditional user acceptance and regression testing activities. Traditionally, the activities happen too late in the release cycle to act on the feedback and findings. This information is usually placed into a tool for capturing issues and only the most pressing problems are addressed. This leads to quality debt, both external and internal quality, in the software as more and more issues are deferred. Rather than waiting until it is too late to act on the feedback and findings, a team using an ATDD approach iterates with the customer to incorporate feedback throughout the release. Therefore, teams continually focus on creating *working software* for the users.

Chapter 6

CONFIGURATION MANAGEMENT DEBT

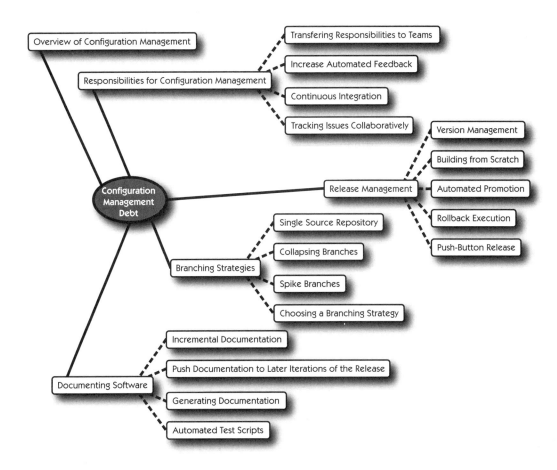

If releases are like giving birth, then you must be doing something wrong.

—Robert Benefield[1]

---

1. Robert Benefield, from a conversation at Agile 2008 in Toronto, ON, Canada.

OVERVIEW OF CONFIGURATION MANAGEMENT

As software development organizations grow, if automation of builds, versioning, and deployments are not well tended to they become difficult for teams to manage. To deal with the complicated nature of managing builds, versioning, and deployments, it is common for teams to hire a "build" person to focus on scripting these activities to automate them. A team becomes dependent on the build person for incorporating configuration and build monitoring so the rest of the team can focus on other activities like developing software functionality. If the team has test automation, the build person figures out how to script the execution of automated tests in preproduction deployment environments. Sometimes the build person finds ways to script and run more complex activities such as load, stress, and performance testing.

If the organization has multiple teams and strict phased processes, a department focused on *configuration management* (CM) can take on many of these activities, including additional responsibilities such as source control repository management, multiple environment configuration, and monitoring production deployments. It is not uncommon for CM folks to have or share a pager so that they can monitor environments beyond their normal workday hours.

A big problem with separating CM activities is that the people who implement software that has issues are not the same as those who deal with their ramifications. The thought is that development teams should focus on feature delivery and not be bothered by CM activities. When this separation of responsibilities is perpetuated, configuration management debt builds up. The following is a list of items that constitute configuration management debt:

- Inability to re-create deployment environments
- Slow and error-prone manual build processes
- Complicated and excessive branching in the source control repository
- Production problems that make feature delivery unpredictable
- Unpredictable and lengthy integration stabilization periods
- Anemic application deployment, management, and monitoring tools
- Application releases piling up waiting for deployment to production
- Conflict between the CM group and project teams

The rest of this chapter will go into more detail about CM responsibilities, release management, source control branching strategies, and documenting software. The focus will be on how teams can limit separation of CM responsibilities and continue to execute effectively on feature delivery.

RESPONSIBILITIES FOR CONFIGURATION MANAGEMENT

Agile teams tend to deliver more frequently to their users than teams using traditional approaches. This focus on delivery is captured in the "Principles behind the Agile Manifesto" in the following principle:

Deliver working software frequently, from a couple of weeks to a couple of months, with a preference to the shorter timescale.[2]

Delivering frequently can put a strain, at least initially, on parts of an organization beyond the project team. For build, release, and production management, this strain can cause current processes to become overly bureaucratic and ineffective. To keep pace with frequent deliveries, some CM responsibilities must be delegated to teams. Teams must understand these responsibilities and deal with competing priorities at times. Configuration management teams deal with at least the following competing priorities:

- **Fires:** Production problems can make an application unusable.
- **Deployment requests:** As more teams start delivering functionality more frequently, the volume of deployment requests increases.
- **Maintenance:** Keeping applications up and running is a significant effort.
- **Test infrastructure:** So that teams are able to deliver more frequently, additional test environments must be maintained to allow testing efforts to run in parallel.

If all of these responsibilities fall to a single group, the work will become overwhelming and cause the group to make more mistakes and/or delay completion. Either of these outcomes is costly to the organization in perception, trust, and finances. CM groups start to be perceived as slow and incompetent because they are not responsive to service requests. Project stakeholders begin to question whether the CM activities are essential for delivering their software applications, and distrust of the CM group increases. As the CM group becomes less responsive to requests, project teams are made to wait for CM activities to complete. This results in reduced productivity and delayed return on investment for the software.

---

2. "Principles behind the Agile Manifesto," http://agilemanifesto.org/principles.html, 2001.

There are three areas that organizations can work on to improve CM performance:

- Transfer some CM responsibilities to teams.
- Increase automated feedback.
- Track issues in a collaborative manner.

Organizations should find ways to invest in these areas to reduce delays, decrease the cost of handoffs, and take a more proactive stance on CM issues. The following sections will discuss ways to manage changes in these three areas to attain additional value.

Transferring Responsibilities to Teams

CM activities are separated from feature delivery because they are not simple and require considerable care with the details. This means that CM activities cannot just be transitioned over to project teams without some careful planning. The activities of CM that are commonly transitioned to project teams are non-production-related activities and deploy/rollback automation.

Non-Production-Related Activities

As CM groups take on responsibility for application build and deployment activities, there is a tendency to take these responsibilities beyond production to staging, test, and even development environments. There are a couple of good reasons for the CM group's involvement in these non-production-related activities. First, because of the detail orientation of the CM role, the deployment processes assumed to work from the project team's perspective are validated. Second, all of the non-production environments can be kept in sync with infrastructure upgrades.

The good that results from this centralized ownership is quickly outweighed by the need to support frequent delivery and the flexibility Agile teams need in their environments. Not only do Agile teams deliver more frequently to production, they also deploy to development, testing, and staging environments more often. This quickly drives too much work to the CM group and cripples its ability to be responsive. In organizations with non-production responsibilities under a centralized CM group's control, there are times when teams wait anywhere from hours to days and even weeks for environment requests to be completed. This paralyzes the organization's ability to deliver.

Transferring non-production-related activities to teams is not a simple endeavor. There is a need for training and automation to enable teams to take on these activities without adversely affecting their delivery. CM team members should keep only limited involvement in non-production environment configuration activities and allow teams to have increased control of and responsibility for these environments. Involvement could include participating in deployments and configuration in testing and staging environments and providing feedback and guidance. Also, if there are infrastructure changes in production environments, helping the team implement needed changes and configurations is useful.

Install and Rollback Procedures

Anyone who has performed deployments to production over a period of time knows the importance of being able to roll back changes. During feature development, installation activities usually do not take rollback into consideration. Giving responsibility for rollback procedures to teams supports a couple of good behaviors. It gives teams an appreciation for the intricacies of application deployment, such as server configuration and network topology. Also, the teams will consider production deployment issues when designing their applications, so changes can be better understood and managed.

The CM group's support of a team's initial efforts to automate install and rollback procedures is important. The team may not know all of the problems inherent in deployment and rollback procedures. Installation could be as easy as switching an IP address on the Domain Name System (DNS) with a rollback plan of switching back to the original IP address if there is a problem. In a highly transactional application with usage 24 hours a day, seven days a week, the installation and rollback procedures could be deployment to a range of machines while monitoring closely for any issues and rolling those changes back on those machines at any sign of an issue.

Increase Automated Feedback

Team members probably won't become legendary configuration management stars tomorrow. Therefore, it is important to automate important configuration management activities as much as possible. It is also important that the amount of feedback from the resulting automated monitoring tools does not inundate the team with too much information. Software configuration management is focused on understanding what each node in an environment has on it and being able to audit the configurations. CM teams can then allow partial control with specific application audit capabilities such as

- Constraining the access of credentials that teams use to access nodes
- Automating build and deployment procedures
- A strategy for versioning releases and builds from the source control repository

When compared to programming and testing that are mostly about delivering software, CM activities in software development are predominantly about management using controls. Even though CM is focused on controls, teams should negotiate and work closely with CM groups to identify essential activities to automate and audit during the delivery process. It is important to incorporate into the delivery process the ability to re-create environments and audit the configuration of environments, and the process doesn't have to be overly bureaucratic. Problems in production and other environments occur for reasons other than application defects, and therefore being able to take an application through the entire build and deployment process ensures recovery when things go wrong.

Tools such as Maven make versioning, release, and deployment activities are a part of the application development life cycle. Information can be placed into a project descriptor file with configurations for

- Issue management
- Continuous integration server
- Project mailing lists
- Source control management (SCM) access
- Deployment environments
- Reporting tools

Using Maven as an example, creating a release version of an application could be as easy as putting the following information into the project descriptor:

```
<project>
  ...
  <build>
    ...
<project>
  ...
  <build>
    ...
    <plugins>
      <plugin>
        <groupId>org.apache.maven.plugins</groupId>
        <artifactId>maven-release-plugin</artifactId>
        <configuration>
          <tagBase>
            https://svn[…]/tags/releases
          </tagBase>
        </configuration>
      </plugin>
    </plugins>
```

```
    ...
  </build>
    ...
</project>
```

and then running the following command to execute the release procedures that include building an installable version of the application and tagging the source control repository:

```
mvn release:perform
```

Project teams might also find it useful to create scripts that launch the release commands for their projects and include additional parameters and execution procedures, such as

```
./release_application.sh
```

This further specifies what is performed during the application's release and does not force the team to delve too far into the use of specific configuration management tools.

Continuous Integration

Continuous integration (CI) is a practice from Extreme Programming (XP). The practice of CI requires that team members integrate their local changes often, at least daily, with the rest of their team's changes. Every developer on the team is expected to integrate his or her code into a common location at least once per day. Integrating with the rest of the team involves building, packaging, and executing all automated tests so that integration problems are found as early as possible. The cost of integration for large code bases is greater than the aggregate cost of integration in small, frequent increments.

It is common for teams practicing CI to use applications such as Hudson and CruiseControl to automate their CI activities. CI servers update local copies from the source control repository. Every time changes are identified, the CI server executes configurations or build scripts against the updated code base. Once the build and other validation activities have completed, the status of the CI server execution against the code updates is made visible to the team. If the CI server execution fails, teams should stop their current work and figure out how to fix the issue.

After the CI server has executed the build and validation processes, status should be made visible to the entire team and anyone interested in the current state of the build. Teams can put up monitors in their team areas with the CI server status showing so that everyone can see it. Some creative teams have attached lava lamps or streetlights that change color from green to red when the build fails and then back to green when it is successful. Some teams have a build "bunny" that yells at the team when the build breaks. Providing this transparency can help to build trust with project stakeholders and keeps the team focused on delivering quality, integrated software.

Tracking Issues Collaboratively

Incident management is a difficult issue in many software development organizations. Questions such as "How do we manage production issues?" when starting to use Scrum or other Agile methods are commonplace. There is no one-size-fits-all strategy for incident management, but some are particularly problematic.

One particular strategy that is problematic for teams and organizations applying an Agile approach to software development is the *single point of failure*. This involves having a single person in charge of triaging all incoming incidents and assigning them to individuals for fixing. This organizational construct is problematic in at least two ways. First, because it allows a single person to decide which person is best to work on an incident, certain staff members are isolated to work on those particular applications. These staff members are not able to transfer knowledge about managing incidents on these applications and therefore get stuck in the role because they're "the best person to work on that." Second, once the organization grows beyond one team, having a single person in this role makes incident allocation management opaque to the organization. Teams and stakeholders do not have to deal with incident management, which leads them to neglect taking care of issues before they leak into production.

Rather than isolating incident management entirely, look for ways to manage it effectively with the team. If a team is using Scrum, having the ScrumMaster as a point of contact who can deflect some incidents to the Product Backlog and bring others that are more severe to the team as necessary is an option. Some teams have identified a person on the team to take responsibility for communications about production issues. In a scaled Agile adoption, forming a cross-team group that works together to help direct issues to teams can be helpful. The basic idea is to get team members involved in managing issues so they share knowledge and have to deal with their impacts.

RELEASE MANAGEMENT

Releasing can be a difficult endeavor for some applications, platforms, teams, and organizations. If releasing software becomes too complex and is not managed effectively, decay of release timeliness can affect all upstream development and product planning activities. Releasing a software application should be as simple as it can possibly be or else significant costs will result. The cost of waiting for one application to be released increases based on the number of dependencies waiting to release afterward.

Managing releases effectively involves working on the following:

- Version management
- Building from scratch
- Automated promotion
- Rollback execution
- Push-button release

Management of these aspects of an application's release should not happen only in the last week or month before the release date. Involving operations and configuration management early in product planning is essential to being proactive and effective at delivering software to production with the least amount of delay and fewest quality problems. Larger organizations may have a release management team that is responsible for being involved in the product planning activities. Creating clear communication channels between product definition and release management groups is essential to keeping this involvement.

Version Management

Version management activities have become increasingly complex for companies that maintain multiple versions of an application for their customers. Making version management even more complex is the need for component-level versioning to address reuse across multiple applications. As organizations look for more agility, they should take another look at the value of multiple versions of an application in production versus the costs associated with maintaining many versions. If a product is being versioned to excess across a large customer base, the maintenance costs for each version delivered to a customer increases exponentially, not just linearly. It's not long before there is a need to have teams focus on specific product versions and customer segments. Now the organization must pay the costs for the current version of the product and all of the costs to maintain custom versions of the product.

Although having custom versions of an application comes with additional costs, if those costs are visible to product and technology management the organization can make better decisions about product direction. There are times when the total cost of ownership for an application is outweighed by the increase in value being delivered to customers and the revenue growth that can be achieved. Release management teams can be helpful in brokering these decisions because they are usually closest to the costs. A basic principle of version management is:

Reduce the number of versions being maintained.

The theoretical best versioning scheme is to have only one current version that all customers use. This is not only a software development decision and responsibility. To make version management effective, good communication among sales, product management, customer service, and technology groups is essential. A sales strategy that promotes the value of updating customers to the current version can make or break a versioning strategy.

Breaking down complex applications into modular components is a valuable tool to help manage complex software versioning. The breakdown of applications into components supports more effective communication of the technology stack and isolates functionality to reduce duplication of capability. Versioning the components of an application's architecture has some positive outcomes:

- Teams that work on the component are able to focus on making changes without impacting existing functionality that relies on the component.
- Teams dependent on the component are able to decide how often they incorporate a new version.
- The quality attributes of a component are more easily focused on since they are isolated and contained.

These positive outcomes are sometimes taken to excess. Making a team responsible for changes to a specific component and version of the component for use by other teams creates challenges. The team's goals are no longer aligned directly to delivering value to customers. A focus on versioning components without focusing on delivering products to customers leads to the following problems:

- Functionality is created in the component that is never used in the application delivered to users.

- A silo of knowledge about a part of the architecture is created and reduces efficient interfacing with the component.
- Product delivery becomes throttled for applications dependent on the component.
- As new requests are made on the component from dependent teams, the implementation becomes less able to support existing and new interfaces.
- If different versions are simultaneously in use across instances of products, maintenance becomes more complex and slower to meet the desires of each instance.

Rather than versioning components to isolate the work for a team, version management should be focused on delivering more value inside a product. Achieving competency with each component in your architecture to deliver direct value to customers with a cross-functional team will reduce unused functionality, increase feedback across component implementations, and mitigate the slowing of application delivery to users. Chapter 11, "Platform Experience Debt," will go into more detail about configuration of feature teams to support scaled delivery to customers.

Deciding to have only one version of an application is not the only step necessary. In order to keep your customers on the most current version whenever they upgrade, flexible infrastructure, feature visibility, and validation of quality must be at an appropriate level of maturity. It takes time to build these capabilities, but having them will enable more nimble decision making for the business and technology groups.

Building from Scratch

A common practice has emerged in many organizations that always becomes a problem: *copy-and-paste environments*. Copy-and-paste environments are a method of keeping any particular environment up-to-date with current build versions without conducting a full installation of the application. At some point, the development, QA, staging, and even production systems become too fragile to mess with, so the developers and/or release team tend to make the fewest changes possible. Instead of doing a clean installation or automating the installation process, they copy and paste changes from one environment to another.

At first, the copy-and-paste approach seems fast and convenient. Before long, however, verification of the environment takes two days, then one week, two weeks, and so on. The verifications entail identifying the module versions, updating relational databases from a cleansed production export, and assuring that configurations are set up correctly. It is important that teams adopt the following principle to combat copy-and-paste environments:

> **Have at least one environment that is built from scratch frequently, preferably daily, and fix issues with that environment immediately.**

By building from scratch frequently, the team is able to ensure that production deployments are more successful. There are still other reasons why deployment issues could occur because it is nearly impossible to create an exact copy of the production environment such as network topology, rack location, and monitoring tools. Still, building from scratch often will greatly reduce the risk of production deployment issues.

Automated Promotion

Customer involvement is critical to successful software delivery. Reviewing functionality with customers so they can provide feedback will enhance the product when the feedback is gathered earlier in the release cycle. Incorporating feedback and still meeting release expectations can be difficult if feedback is not gathered early enough. Automated promotion is a way to get software in front of stakeholders frequently to gather valuable feedback on current progress. Upon successful builds and tests in a continuous integration environment, the build is automatically promoted to another environment that includes more extensive validation procedures. For instance, upon completion of automated functional tests, a build could be deployed into three more environments: load/stress/performance lab, exploratory testing, and staging for user feedback. Figure 6.1 shows a basic continuous integration environment that includes automated test execution for validating before automated promotion.

Automated promotion also helps functional integration testing when scaling to multiple teams across a diverse feature set and multiple platforms. A continuous integration server builds from the mainline of SCM for a particular module of the application. If the build is successful, it is promoted to a higher-level continuous integration environment that incorporates functionality from multiple modules and executes functional integration tests to verify the integration. Figure 6.2 shows how automated promotion across integrated modules looks logically.

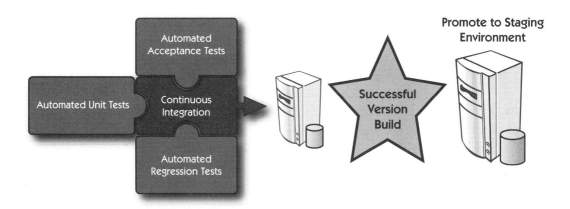

Figure 6.1 After the successful build, test, and deployment of an application in the continuous integration environment, it can be automatically promoted to a staging environment to get frequent feedback from the customer or to perform exploratory testing.

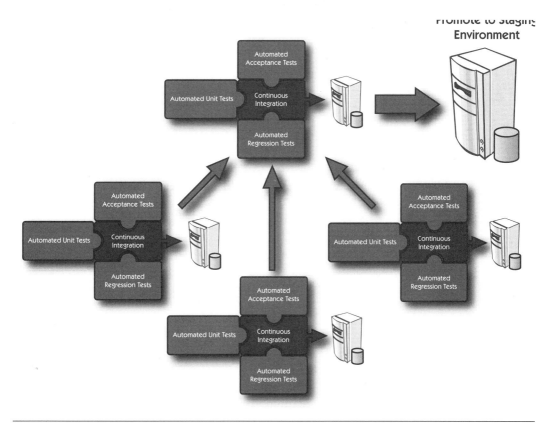

Figure 6.2 Successful continuous integration builds can lead to automated promotion to execute integration activities across a larger set of modules.

Rollback Execution

When looking at deployment, it is important not just to look at how to update environments to the next build. It is also important to understand how to restore the existing version if there are any hiccups during the deployment. Creating a rollback strategy, automating it, and testing whether it works on a regular basis can minimize pain when releasing an application. If there are steps that currently must be done manually, documenting a step-by-step approach to executing deployment and rollback together is a good option.

The basic strategy for creating a rollback strategy is

1. **Capture the current state:** Back up the application, environment configurations, and database to an archive or other applicable backup artifact.
2. **Install the new version of the application.** Run an automated script and, if needed, follow documented manual procedures to install the application.
3. **Validate the installation.** Run an automated script and, if needed, conduct manual verification checks to make sure the application is up and running.
4. **On error, roll back to the previous state.** Run an automated script and, if needed, follow documented manual procedures to roll back the application.

An example of rollback procedures could be on a web site with a load balancer pointed at the current deployed instances of an application. For deployment, you could take an instance offline and deploy the new application build to it. Then you could switch the load balancer to point at the server instance running the new application version. In this scenario, the rollback procedure is to switch the load balancer back to the still-running previous version instances.

If there are updates to central server environments, such as relational database instances, it is important that any changes to those environments be successfully rolled back as well. Running the rollback procedures frequently helps teams and operations groups manage deployments more effectively. Rollback procedures should be executed during the iteration. Teams can then deal with any issues with configuration or installation changes. If multiple versions of software are running in many environments, deploy and rollback procedures should include stepwise updates to safely upgrade the software installation from any version to the one being installed.

Push-Button Release

All right, all of the previous release management sections set us up for this specific technique, *push-button release*. We've discussed automated version management, building release environments, promotion of builds to different environments, and rollback procedures. Now it is time to make releasing software to production a non-event.

The reason why push-button release is important is that agility includes increasing the flexibility of businesses to make decisions about the direction of their software assets. At the end of the iteration, if a team is building potentially shippable product increments, the Product Owner can decide to deploy the increment to production when he or she sees fit. If releasing the application is more difficult than pushing a button, there is a cost for it. The less cost there is for releasing an application, the more flexibility a business has to make a deploy decision. Of course, the business will consider the impact to users, servicing the application, and marketing, but the decision whether to deploy or not should be a business decision.

When working on an application, I look for ways to automate all deployment and rollback procedures to where there are only two commands to execute, one for deployment of the new version:

```
$ ./deploy.sh
```

and another for rollback:

```
$ ./rollback.sh
```

This has led to great flexibility for customers. In one particular instance, a team I worked with was able to release 33 out of 36 iterations to production, which from a business perspective greatly enhanced the value of the software application. A feature in production earlier provides more value than a feature waiting to deploy. Be relentless in automating deployment and rollback procedures. Teams should work with operations and configuration management groups to enable the push-button release capability.

If a release for your software application means generating a physical product, such as a DVD or appliance, push-button release is still applicable. While I was working with a team that created installation discs for a product, we discussed the meaning of potentially shippable product increments. Almost immediately the conversation devolved into statements such as "Well, we deliver a physical CD and we don't create the image until it's almost time to release." I asked,

"Do you ever have trouble with file system structure, missing files, or installer defects?" The team members responded, "Of course, and it has definitely been difficult to debug the problems because they could have happened anytime during the release." After some more discussion, the team decided they would generate a disc at least once per iteration and install the software from scratch into a test environment they already had. This allowed them to validate their installation disc as potentially shippable on a frequent basis and made debugging a more focused effort on small changes since the last validation.

Continuous Deployment

If your organization and team want to really harness the advantages that come with push-button release, continuous deployment may be of interest to you. Timothy Fitz wrote a thought-provoking blog entry[3] in which he discusses the approach taken at a company called IMVU, which develops a virtual world product. Timothy has been kind enough to give me permission to pull some text from his blog entry here:

Continuous Deployment at IMVU

Our tests suite takes nine minutes to run (distributed across 30–40 machines). Our code pushes take another six minutes. Since these two steps are pipelined that means at peak we're pushing a new revision of the code to the website every nine minutes. That's 6 deploys an hour. Even at that pace we're often batching multiple commits into a single test/push cycle. On average we deploy new code fifty times a day.

. . .

Great test coverage is not enough. Continuous Deployment requires much more than that. Continuous Deployment means running all your tests, all the time. That means tests must be reliable. We've made a science out of debugging and fixing intermittently failing tests. When I say reliable, I don't mean "they can fail once in a thousand test runs." I mean "they must not fail more often than once in a million test runs." We have around 15k test cases, and they're run around 70 times a day. That's a million test cases a day. Even with a literally one in a million chance of an intermittent failure per test case we would still expect to see an intermittent test failure every day. It may be hard to imagine writing rock solid one-in-a-million-or-better tests that drive Internet Explorer to click ajax frontend buttons executing backend apache, php, memcache, mysql, java and solr.

---

3. Timothy Fitz, "Continuous Deployment at IMVU: Doing the Impossible Fifty Times a Day," February 10, 2009, http://timothyfitz.wordpress.com/2009/02/10/continuous-deployment-at-imvu-doing-the-impossible-fifty-times-a-day/.

. . . nine minutes have elapsed and a commit has been greenlit for the web-site. The programmer runs the imvu_push script. The code is rsync'd out to the hundreds of machines in our cluster. Load average, cpu usage, php errors and dies and more are sampled by the push script, as a basis line. A symlink is switched on a small subset of the machines throwing the code live to its first few customers. A minute later the push script again samples data across the cluster and if there has been a statistically significant regression then the revision is automatically rolled back. If not, then it gets pushed to 100% of the cluster and monitored in the same way for another five minutes. The code is now live and fully pushed. This whole process is simple enough that it's implemented by a handful of shell scripts.

Continuous deployment is not right for every software development context. In fact, most situations are not ready, nor would it be a good idea yet, to take a continuous deployment approach. I do believe that in the near future the use of continuous deployment will increase and teams will have to execute using this approach.

BRANCHING STRATEGIES

Talking about SCM and branching strategies in the software industry is a potential minefield for the instigator. Depending on your point of view, strategies can vary from "Lock all files and branch for each individual developer and environment" to "Everyone uses one mainline branch." If you were to ask me, I would tell you that I believe an approach that continually integrates code is preferred. The "mainline branch for everyone on the project" is closest to my opinion, although even I can think of situations where a team may pull from multiple branches. So, of course, there is no silver bullet to SCM.

There are entire books written on SCM and how to do effective branching across projects, teams, and individuals. Also, there are many different SCM systems in use by organizations, such as CVS, Perforce, ClearCase, Subversion, and Git. This section of the chapter on branching strategies will talk about the base principles that combat configuration management debt. It will not be an in-depth discussion of SCM principles and practices but will give a team enough information to apply in their context.

Single Source Repository

Getting to a "single source of truth" for an application is important to making potentially shippable product increments. In traditional SCM, teams, and sometimes team members, are asked to delay merging their branches in order to keep the mainline branch in a "pristine" state. This delay causes complex, problematic, and unpredictable integrations of one branch with another branch. This is caused by many factors, including

- Number of changes to merge in both branches
- Diverging implementation in design, structure, and naming
- Not knowing how much needs to be integrated
- Merge tools leaving much of the process to interpretation

Instead of delaying integration, forcing frequent integration helps alleviate these issues:

- A smaller number of changes are integrated.
- There is less time to diverge in design, structure, and naming.
- Integrations happen nearer to the time of implementation.
- Merges are less likely to be needed.

At scale, getting to a single source repository could seem impossible. If multiple teams are working off the single source repository, it could be a common occurrence for changes from one team to affect another team's progress. The frequency of one team impacting another is directly related to the amount of time it takes to validate any snapshot of the single source repository. If validating a snapshot involves execution of manual testing that takes a couple of weeks to complete, there could be many changes during this time frame that are not getting validated. Automating the validation process, using principles, practices, and tools described in earlier chapters, will reduce the number of times one team's changes impact another team.

Because of the issues inherent in multiple teams working off a single source repository without automated validation of changes, I recommend that teams in this situation do not immediately go to a single source repository. Instead, read on to the next section about collapsing branches to make incremental steps toward a single source repository while balancing validation concerns.

Collapsing Branches

If the project team is working off of multiple branches today but would like to transition to a more Agile approach, collapsing branches could be a starting point. Instead of moving to a single mainline branch immediately, teams should discuss the goal of a single source repository and how to make decisions about collapsing some branches now.

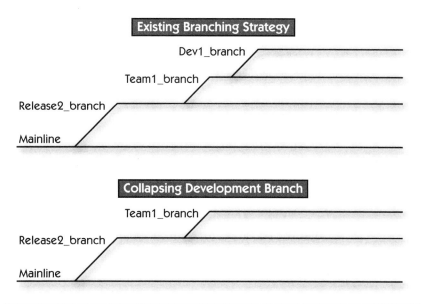

Figure 6.3   Making progress toward a single source repository by collapsing two branches into one branch in the SCM system for the application under development. In this example, it would be expected that the team negotiated a strategy that allows them to integrate more often on the single team branch rather than creating development branches to delay integration.

The basic approach is as follows: Within each of your teams on the project, discuss how many branches you work on. If there is more than one branch related to a specific module, ask yourselves if the two branches are necessary for reasons other than trying to delay integration. If the team finds that there are no other reasons, decide how to collapse the two branches into one branch. Continue to do this until you have the minimum number of branches that your team believes they need to do development but still integrate on a daily basis.

Figure 6.3 shows how a team might approach collapsing multiple branches into a single branch.

Spike Branches

From time to time, a group or individual on the team will want to try something out that should not go into the mainline or release branch. This could be for some experimentation purposes, also known as a "spike," which is explained in Chapter 10, "Technology Evaluation Styles." Spikes are conducted to figure out how something works, such as integrating a library or trying out an algorithm, and should be thrown away upon gaining enough knowledge from the experiment. Some teams find it to be a good practice to save spikes on a separate branch for later review. For this, it helps to have an SCM system that is able to branch part of the source tree at a snapshot point in time.

Choosing a Branching Strategy

The previous sections give only high-level principles and practices for generating a branching strategy to be used by an Agile team. Each SCM system, whether open-source or commercial, has different capabilities, approaches, and language that teams should become somewhat familiar with. Look for ways to get those who manage the SCM system to mentor teams on usage scenarios that can help them move toward potentially shippable product increments more frequently.

DOCUMENTING SOFTWARE

Traditional software projects involve the creation of many documentation artifacts. These include requirements specifications, functional analysis, high-level design, detailed design, test plans, manual test scripts, and more. As the software is implemented, it is common for many of these documentation artifacts to be out of sync with the code. This makes the documentation less useful for maintaining the software after its construction. It could even be detrimental to maintainers of the software if the gap between what is documented and what is actually implemented is too large, leading them down incorrect paths when trying to resolve issues.

In a defined process like waterfall, it is necessary to make multiple handoffs on the way to implementing the code. Documentation plays a critical role in the progression of handoffs through the requirements, analysis, design, code, integration, and maintenance phases. When using an Agile approach, frequent communication between cross-functional team members on small batches of work can alleviate the need for the amount of documentation needed in waterfall projects. It is important to note:

> Just because a team takes an Agile approach does not mean they throw out the need for documentation. Instead, the team focuses on the documentation that will support effective delivery of working software to the users and maintainability of that software into the future.

Some forms of documentation that I have seen Agile teams continue to generate are

- Installation guide
- User manual
- Training materials
- Traceability matrix
- Test execution reports
- High-level design
- Data dictionaries
- Compliance artifacts

Teams use different methods for delivering documentation artifacts. Some teams update a document incrementally with additions based on features being delivered in the current iteration. There are also teams that put off some documentation until later iterations of a multi-iteration release. Other teams generate as much of the documentation as they can from the source code artifacts. Also, as will be further detailed later in this chapter, some teams use test automation tools where the test scripts tend to supplant traditional documentation elements.

Incremental Documentation

As teams implement new functionality, it is common for artifacts to be updated with specific information about that functionality. This could include

- Configuration changes in the installation guide
- Release notes
- High-level design artifacts

The most common way that this approach is determined and tracked by teams is through their Definition of Done. By adding documentation artifacts that must be updated incrementally before the end of the iteration, the team is able to keep the software closer to shippable. This approach is preferable to pushing documentation tasks until later in the release cycle, which will be discussed in the next section.

Push Documentation to Later Iterations of the Release

There are a few reasons why teams might not incrementally update documentation artifacts in early iterations of a multi-iteration release. First, the cost to create the documentation could be too great. Getting localization performed, for example, is sometimes too expensive to be done iteratively. Second, getting people onto the team who are focused 100% on supporting the deliverables could be an organizational challenge. Technical writers are sometimes asked to work on multiple products at a time. Finally, a team may not have enough information yet to deliver documentation. A team may be researching alternatives or gathering feedback from prototypes and still not have clarity on what will be in the end product.

Delaying documentation until later in a release should be only a last resort. By delaying any release deliverables until later, the team is building up a queue of work that must be completed before the release. The further the documentation tasks are worked on from the time functionality is implemented, the more likely it is that the documentation will be incomplete and error-prone.

Generating Documentation

There are plenty of tools that generate documentation and visuals from software artifacts. A commonly used form of generated documentation is API documentation in XML or HTML formats such as Javadoc, NDoc, and RDoc. Other tools exist for generating documentation on domain models, database schemas, UML diagrams, and help documentation. Some of these document generation tools are for end user information, and others support maintenance of the software. Teams should generate documentation anytime it is possible and when the cost of maintaining the tools is low.

Automated Test Scripts

Some test automation tools allow decorating test scripts with documentation. The language used to implement test scripts is also sometimes easily read as specification documentation. For the documentation inside of automated test scripts to be useful, it must be easy to search through and identify what behavior in the application it is associated to. Teams should maintain the documentation as they do the executable parts of the scripts; otherwise they will get out of sync with the actual implementation just as traditional documentation does.

SUMMARY

In an organization gaining more agility in its software development capabilities, configuration management, and especially release management, can become a bottleneck to teams delivering to production. The teams are able to deliver more frequently, but the software to be deployed sits in line waiting for release management teams to catch up. Organizations must find ways to identify and eliminate this problem.

A first step toward alleviating the release management issue is to look at departmental responsibilities and how they can be rearranged for better throughput. Transferring responsibilities to the team for managing its own releases, as much as is appropriate, will decrease effort spent by configuration or release management teams. When the team is responsible for its own releases, team members will figure out ways to make releasing have less impact on their daily activities. This will result in automation of release processes that can be frequently executed in the continuous integration environment. If there are problems, the continuous integration server will notify team members of it and the team should fix the problem immediately, thus never getting too far from being able to successfully release software with few to no problems. When transitioning responsibilities, don't underestimate the need for automation so that teams are able to take on the responsibility without creating problems in their test environments. Automate as much of the release process as possible, and make manual steps easy to understand and execute.

To support frequent releases to production, organizations must take care of their release management process. Automating version management and the deployment of specific versions to test environments will reduce the overhead of managing environments manually. Manual management of these environments is error-prone and time-consuming. Teams should be able to build their software from scratch and deploy to re-created environments at all times. By doing this, teams reduce the risk associated with creating or modifying test and production environments. As an application's development scales to multiple teams, getting modular builds and automated promotion from a successful build environment to a higher-level integration environment will provide continuous feedback across the software development team. Being able to install the application is important, but it is also important to have the ability to roll back a deployment when it is not going well. Getting the deployment and rollback procedures to a point of push-button release will make their execution easy for many members of the project team to make environmental changes and reduce the risks around manual steps.

SCM systems are an essential part of the software development process. Branches in SCM are often used to delay integration across people, teams, and departments. This delaying of integration is opposed to the Agile method of frequent integration that allows teams to find problems earlier before they become merge nightmares. Theoretically, the ultimate SCM branching strategy is to not create branches. When there is a single source repository for the entire project team, team members continually integrate their changes with all other changes. If project teams are dealing with an existing code base, changing to a single source repository immediately could be difficult. An incremental approach toward a single source repository that works is beginning the process of collapsing branches within a team, between teams, and finally for the entire application source tree. Never branching is not a practical approach for most software development projects. Teams need the ability to experiment from time to time, and capturing these experiments on the mainline branch is not a good idea. Instead, team members should create branches to capture these experiments in the appropriate manner for their SCM system.

Keeping software maintainable over time is another aspect of configuration management processes. Going Agile does not mean documentation is thrown out, but different approaches may be used compared to traditional software development processes. Finding ways to create documentation incrementally or at specific points during the release will increase the quality of the documentation artifacts and reduce problems around people having to remember something they implemented too far in the past. Some documentation could be generated in the software development process. Generating documentation is preferred if a team is able because this keeps the artifacts closest to the code, which is the most detailed specification of what the software does. Test automation can be a source of generating documentation and can help teams understand the software for maintainability.

Agile teams should not forget that software development involves more than code and test. The act of releasing software is essential, and teams can help to make the act almost a non-event. Use the suggestions in this chapter to make changes toward more effective integration and release management procedures.

Chapter 7

DESIGN DEBT

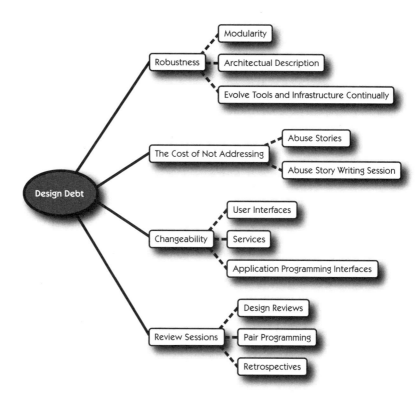

Technical features that involve improving software quality attributes can be prioritized based on the cost of not addressing them.

—Author

ROBUSTNESS

One way to look at design is from the perspective of robustness. The ability of software to be resilient in the face of iterative and incremental change is a measure of how well the design meets business demand. This goes well beyond the code's design into the structural integrity of the supporting infrastructure.

The robustness of a component, application, or enterprise is determined by how quickly it can be acted upon with new knowledge. This has become more important across most industries in the twenty-first century. Strategic plans change more frequently and force companies to respond to competitive pressures, public perception, and regulatory standards. The frequency of reaction puts pressure on software development organizations to stay nimble in meeting the demands of business. This translates into decreasing the time from inception of an idea to delivering it into a customer's hands. Enabling agility in the component, application, and enterprise layers of the software development organization is essential to satisfying these demands.

To meet these recent challenges, we must find ways to reduce the time needed for architectural changes. This involves continuing to develop software with appropriate levels of modularity. Thus, creating an architectural description that the team agrees with helps to guide team member decisions. Because this architectural description is a team artifact, there is still flexibility to evolve it over time to meet new business needs. Evolution involves tools and infrastructure, not just the code, so teams must find ways to identify needs earlier and reduce the potential for reactive and costly changes that have to be made when problems are found too late. Teams must adopt a mind-set of improving the design always throughout the project.

Modularity

When discussing modularity in software design, there is so much left to judgment, subjectivity, and preference. This book will not attempt to profess the ultimate ways to modularize your applications and enterprise. Instead, I will conjecture that there are many appropriate ways to modularize software systems based on the platform, domain, organizational structure, and third-party integrations. This belief is fundamental for organizations to understand and apply so that software can better align to their specific business needs.

First, let's look at the root of the word *modularity* and its definition:

> *module*—noun: each of a set of standardized parts or independent units that can be used to construct a more complex structure

Within this definition, there are the independent parts that support the construction of complex structures. If we apply this to software, the independent parts could be sections of code, libraries, services, agents, classes, functions, or any number of internal structures within an application. In this book I have been referring to these independent parts as *components*. Components are a way to isolate related functionality within an application to reduce duplication, provide appropriate abstractions of the application's complexity, and ultimately provide the ability to restructure the application through isolated changes to internal components. My opinion is this: Modularity is sufficient when teams are able to identify components in a timely manner and make changes that support new business needs in the application or enterprise infrastructure.

The problem lies in the potential for slow degradation as discussed in Chapter 1, "Managing Software Debt." Because design is a higher-level construct and contains much subjectivity and dependence on the environment, there is great potential for *design debt* to creep in. Therefore, teams should keep an eye on the design of an application or enterprise infrastructure. One way to approach design in terms of modularity is making the architectural description explicit as a team.

Architectural Description

Making an application's architectural design explicit and continuing to validate their understanding of the design is a way for teams to manage design debt. They can ask questions like these:

- Are the components within the application well understood?
- Is there inappropriate coupling among components of the application?
- Can the entire team describe the major components of the application?
- Are the interactions between components still appropriate for upcoming features on the product roadmap?
- Is the enterprise infrastructure that the application is to be deployed onto still sufficient to meet quality attribute requirements?
- How easy is identifying components to change in support of new functionality?
- What are the components and interactions between components that are decaying and necessitate some care?

Each software development team can create a list of questions that make sense in their context. I have found this to be an essential element of being aware of design issues as a team. If teams continue to be too myopic in their approach to software development, they will drive design debt into their applications and infrastructure. As a team, try coming up with a list of questions that work for you and then generate an artifact that describes your current architecture, the potential for decay, and areas to work on. This is called an *architectural description*.

An architectural description can take many forms. It could be a diagram plus some Product Backlog items representing the work needed in the near future on the design. Another form could be an architectural roadmap that is a result of the design understanding of an entire team or multiple teams. It could be documentation residing alongside code in source control with frequent meetings to validate existing design decisions and make modifications where appropriate. Whatever the form of the project team's architectural description, it should be explicit and allow frequent visibility into it to align it with new application knowledge or upcoming needs identified on the product roadmap.

Evolve Tools and Infrastructure Continually

Software evolution has been defined as the creation of software followed by continued maintenance. It focuses on adaptation and migration of software systems during maintenance. Lehman's "Laws of Software Evolution" describe a set of behaviors of software evolution found on monolithic proprietary software:

- *Continuing Change—systems must be continually adapted else they become progressively less satisfactory in use*
- *Increasing Complexity—as a system is evolved its complexity increases unless work is done to maintain or reduce it*
- *Large Program Evolution—global system evolution processes are self-regulating*
- *Invariant Work-Rate—average global activity rate tends to remain constant over periods or segments of system evolution over its lifetime*
- *Conservation of Familiarity—in general, the average incremental growth (longterm growth rate) of systems tends to decline*
- *Continuing Growth—the functional capability of systems must be continually enhanced to maintain user satisfaction over the system lifetime*
- *Declining Quality—unless rigorously adapted to take into account changes in the operational environment, the quality of systems will appear to be declining*
- *Feedback System—evolution processes are multi-level, multi-loop, multi-agent feedback systems*[1]

---

1. Meir Manny Lehman, "Programs, Life Cycles, and Laws of Software Evolution," *Proceedings of the IEEE* (September 1980): 1060–76.

Ineffective management of this set of behaviors leads to software asset liabilities in systems. Because of these behaviors in traditionally evolving software systems, a substantial amount of focus has been put on maintenance activities. The International Organization for Standardization (ISO) standardized on four basic categories of software maintenance in ISO/IEC 14764. These basic categories are

- *Corrective maintenance—Reactive modification of a software product performed after delivery to correct discovered problems*
- *Adaptive maintenance—Modification of a software product performed after delivery to keep a software product usable in a changed or changing environment*
- *Perfective maintenance—Modification of a software product after delivery to improve performance or maintainability*
- *Preventive maintenance—Modification of a software product after delivery to detect and correct latent faults in the software product before they become effective faults*[2]

The problem with most maintenance efforts is that their purpose is to prolong the life of the system rather than increase its maintainability. Maintenance efforts tend to be reactive to end user issues. This allows design debt to take hold while teams build on top of decaying application components and infrastructure. This promotes a vicious cycle that sustains and many times grows the need for maintenance activities.

To combat this decay, attention must be given to all four categories of maintenance with every release. Budgets for software projects often ignore costs for adaptive, perfective, and preventive maintenance, and they increase suffering from software debt at a faster rate than can be managed effectively. Understanding that corrective maintenance is only part of the full maintenance picture can help an organization manage its software assets to optimize return on investment over time.

THE COST OF NOT ADDRESSING

I was sitting in a session on user stories run by Mike Cohn[3] many years ago, and someone from the audience asked a question about technical items and

---

2. International Organization for Standardization (ISO), "ISO/IEC 14764: Software Engineering—Software Life Cycle Processes—Maintenance," revised 2006.
3. Mike Cohn, "User Stories for Agile Requirements," session presented at Agile 2006, www.mountaingoatsoftware.com/presentations/5--user-stories-for-agile-requirements.

user stories. I don't remember the exact question, but Mike did provide information that influenced me from that day forward. His response included a topic that was not in his slide deck but that was an important construct for describing the value of software quality attributes. Mike described a special type of user story called an *abuse story*. The idea is to generate a user story that describes how a user will abuse the application or infrastructure it is deployed on in order to capture the need to implement technical changes. By focusing on the abuse that could occur, the abuse story captures what can happen if technical changes are not made to prevent it:

> **The value of technical aspects in an application or its surrounding infrastructure is the cost of not addressing them.**

Abuse Stories

Rather than trying to describe technical changes that must be made, teams describe the value of technical changes in terms of what the cost of not addressing them would be. For instance, if we were creating an e-commerce web site and needed to allow credit card payments, we might tell the customer that we must encrypt the transaction and ensure the data is not accessible beyond the application's context. If we were to describe the need for security to support these needs, the customer might not understand how important it is to make this a high priority in the Product Backlog. Here is what the Product Backlog item might look like:

> **Implement security for payment information.**

When compared with the user-viewable features to be put in this release, this feature will be prioritized as low. Now, if the team were to write this as an abuse story, it might look like this:

> **As a malicious hacker, I want to steal credit card information so that I can make fraudulent charges.**

Reading this item, the customer sees the value of implementing security around a payment transaction in terms of the cost of not addressing the issue. If it is not addressed, we could be put into a bad situation for allowing access to information that leads to fraud. The acceptance criteria for this abuse story would be how the malicious hacker can be stopped. Because this item identifies the value to the business, it is easier to evaluate its importance and priority.

Now, some of you might have established tremendous trust with your customer. And when your team says that an item must be prioritized high on the Product Backlog, the customer tends to listen. Writing abuse stories could be overkill in this case, but generating them anyway could also be valuable for the team to assess potential impacts of new functionality. This can be done in an abuse story writing session.

Abuse Story Writing Session

Generating abuse stories can help a team identify work that needs to be completed on the technical aspects of an application and provide the cost and value of these changes to the customer for prioritization purposes. To generate abuse stories a team might hold an abuse story writing session. This is a time-boxed meeting where a specific abuser or set of abusers is used to support the abuse story generation process. Here are the steps:

1. Identify a user role who will try to abuse the application.
2. Set a time box of 30 minutes to one hour for generating abuse stories.
3. As pairs or individually, assume the persona of the abuser role and brainstorm as many abuse stories as possible. Try not to think too much about whether it is a good abuse story; just write anything that comes to mind. This should take 5 to 10 minutes.
4. Have each person or pair read off their abuse stories and as a team identify abuse stories that are not valid or are duplicates and remove them. This should take 10 to 20 minutes.
5. Prioritize the abuse stories left over in terms of impact or value to the customer as a team. Do this as fast as possible because a small prioritization conflict is not worth continued discussion in most cases.
6. Give all of the abuse stories in priority order to the customer so they can be prioritized in the Product Backlog. Provide clarification on abuse stories that the customer does not understand well.

Thinking of abusers beyond just a malicious hacker might be difficult at first, so here is a list of abusers I have used in the past:

- Mass of users
- SQL injector
- Disgruntled employee
- Naïve API user
- Impatient clicker
- Denial-of-service (DoS) attacker
- Sleazy user

After I start a list like this with teams, they seem to come up with other interesting abusers. Use these as inspiration in your own domain.

Sometimes user roles are found when looking for abusers who don't necessarily fit the abuser profile. For instance, an application team I was working on had to meet certain regulatory standards. A user role they thought of was the "compliance auditor." In the past, the project team would spend a couple of weeks with the compliance auditor whenever they were about to release the application. By identifying the compliance auditor user role, the project team thought they could come up with user stories that would allow them to finish much faster through traceability, centralized logging, and report generation. This could lead to enabling more frequent releases to their users. When a user role doesn't necessarily meet the abuser perspective, just write regular user stories for it.

CHANGEABILITY

One of the major design factors supporting effective iterative and incremental software development is the ability to change. Since the project team does not have all of the information up front, the chances for new understandings to emerge around the user requirements are even higher. Because of the evolutionary nature of user requirements during software construction, teams must find ways to make the software embrace frequent change.

Frequent change is something that software development organizations have traditionally avoided because it causes painful rework on upstream artifacts. If Agile teams work toward the principle of *Travel Light*,[4] they can reduce the pain of reworking existing artifacts. Traveling light reduces the cost of change, in most cases, and therefore enables teams to make larger changes and negotiate impact on release scope or date. This idea is captured in the "Principles behind the Agile Manifesto" in at least two principles:

> *Welcome changing requirements, even late in development. Agile processes harness change for the customer's competitive advantage.*

> *Simplicity—the art of maximizing the amount of work not done—is essential.*[5]

---

4. Scott Ambler, "The Principles of Agile Modeling," www.agilemodeling.com/principles .htm#TravelLight.

5. "Principles behind the Agile Manifesto," http://agilemanifesto.org/principles.html, 2001.

Welcoming changing requirements and simplicity do not come easy. I work with many teams new to Agile software development that have difficulty applying these principles to their deliverables. The next few sections will describe aspects of current software development projects and how these principles can be applied.

User Interfaces

It seems that changes are easier to make when there are no users of the software. This is, of course, not the goal of software. Software is not valuable until it has users using it. So, how does a team keep the UI changeable when there are existing users?

There are many methods of UI design that allow for change, but a lot has to do with the platform and tools that are being used. The number of methods out there could warrant a whole book on their own (and there probably is one that I haven't read yet), so I will only attempt to cover some areas.

Turn On/Off Features

Some UI frameworks allow for turning on and off screens or portions of a screen. This can be done through setting visibility flags, removing menu choices, and setting configurations to remove them from workflows.

In recent years, I have seen this technique used more and more to allow for partial concepts to be developed in development and test environments while other features are being released to production environments. While the partial concepts are still in development, they are not turned "on" for production in terms of visibility or as the installation package is built. This enables releasing off a single source repository across a number of teams at almost any time without interrupting current development cycles.

This technique is not simple and requires quite a bit of maturity in the build and configuration management capabilities of a product development team. I recommend that project team members figure out what their current platform and tools enable in this area and attempt small experiments, maybe spikes, to see if they are able to implement this in the small without production impacts. If a team is successful in implementing this, the business benefit could be delivery of features to production on a feature-by-feature basis rather than wrapping up a releasable feature set. There are other ways to achieve this, but this technique could be helpful in finding what works for your project team.

Automated UI Tests

Automated tests are known for validating expected behavior at the unit and acceptance levels of testing. Although automated UI tests can be more costly to build and maintain, mostly because of the immaturity of tools in this space, they can enable change in UI while still verifying the behavior. In order to get both of these, the whole team must be disciplined in their UI development and test automation.

One basic UI building discipline that the team must adhere to is the naming of UI elements. Elements on the screen must be available to test automation tools via unique identifiers and not location on the screen. If a team is developing a web application, the use of an id attribute on HTML elements can be an application of this:

```
<input type="text" name="account_name" id="AccountName".../>
```

Many automated testing frameworks that can work through a web application UI are able to find this element anywhere on the screen. If your team is not working on a web application, do some research to find out if there are ways of identifying elements on the screen without knowing their location with automated test frameworks for your platform.

Being able to find any element on a screen does not help if a workflow is changed and the element is now on another screen. In this case, a test automation method should be closely followed to isolate the number of places to change for the updated UI. Use of encapsulation in the test automation artifacts can help to keep the changes isolated to one spot. For instance, if most automated UI tests log out of the application to place it into a known state and the logout workflow changes, it is important to include the logout workflow in those tests and not duplicate the script in all UI tests. In StoryTestIQ, an automated acceptance testing framework for web applications, test cases can be built by including other test scripts:

```
!include .TestRoot.TestComponents.Logout
!include .TestRoot.TestComponents.LogInAsAdmin
!include .TestRoot.TestComponents.GoToMonitorHome
... [conduct some tests]
!include .TestRoot.TestComponents.GoToAdminConsole
... [conduct more tests]
```

Each included test script contains UI navigation and also test conditions for that specific area of functionality. If the logout workflow were to change, the team would just modify the .TestRoot.TestComponents.Logout test script and it would be propagated to all places that include it. Encapsulation of test scripts and inclusion into larger test cases is not natural for all UI testing frameworks. Teams can do research on the automated test framework they are using to find out how they can apply this technique.

Applying both the unique identifier for UI elements and encapsulation of test scripts to fulfill larger test cases will make automated UI tests more maintainable. Beware: Automated UI tests will never be as easy to maintain as automated unit tests, so keep their usage to an appropriate level based on your project's context.

Duplicate UI Flows

Even with the involvement of user experience and usability engineers on a development team there are cases where the UI does not meet the needs of its users well after it goes to production. In this case, a team can generate a new version of the UI that duplicates the function but with improved usability alongside the current version. The new version of the UI should be available only in development and test environments. Linking to the existing UI flow through any navigation component of the application until the new version is well understood and tested can do this. By duplicating the UI flow, the team is able to work on improvements without interrupting the current implementation and its usage in production. But please, when the new UI flow is suitable, don't forget to remove the old UI flow from the mainline in source control.

Services

Service-oriented architecture (SOA) can be an effective way to decouple application components, reuse existing capabilities, and leverage the competencies of a company with focus on the target domain. SOA is implemented on many platforms including web services, service provisioning, and interface adapters to expose existing applications. Whether making services available or consuming services, building for inevitable change will enable an application to continue evolving as the business needs evolve.

There are a few main ways that debt builds around service implementations and consumers:

- They do too much.
- Consumers couple themselves.
- There is insufficient instrumentation for monitoring.
- They are not removed when no longer used.

Again, if the information provided here is not sufficient, because this subject fills entire books, please explore books that go into more detail. For those of you who are developing services already and want to assess the design debt in their usage, these four areas will be a good focus for your endeavor.

Services That Do Too Much

Most services start out with simple interfaces and objectives. Those services that become extremely useful to consumers are at risk of growing into services that do too much. Service popularity can lead to consumers requesting additional interface definitions and behaviors that were not in the original designs. As these changes are made, the service interface gets more difficult for consumers to use and for teams to maintain.

Teams that find services growing out of control have a few options. First of all, they should stop all development that will further complicate the interface. From there, a team can

- Add separate interfaces for functionality that is not focused on the original service interface's objectives
- Refactor the service into smaller and more understandable interfaces
- Start a deprecation plan for the complicated service interface to be carried out over a long enough period of time for consumers of the service to make adequate changes

Making changes to service interfaces is much slower than changing internal application component class structures because there are dependencies on them. Creating a plan to refactor a service interface over a period of time, executing that plan in stages, and querying consumers about their experience with the changes will allow for needed change to happen at a rate that does not break the service's usage.

Consumers Coupling to Services

As a consumer of a service, it is important to isolate the direct consumption of the service in an application under development from what the application needs from the service. Encapsulation of the integration to a service behind an interface that can be reused and modified as a single point of contact allows the implementation to change. As discussed in Chapter 4, "Executable Design," taking a Need-Driven Design approach sets proper expectations and interface for using a service.

Insufficient Instrumentation for Monitoring

Developing loosely coupled and highly distributable service-oriented applications enables incredible flexibility. As services are increasingly distributed, the need to monitor their health becomes more essential. Many, many years ago I found the "Eight Fallacies of Distributed Computing":

Eight Fallacies of Distributed Computing[6]

Essentially everyone, when they first build a distributed application, makes the following eight assumptions. All prove to be false in the long run and all cause big trouble and painful learning experiences.

1. The network is reliable.
2. Latency is zero.
3. Bandwidth is infinite.
4. The network is secure.
5. Topology doesn't change.
6. There is one administrator.
7. Transport cost is zero.
8. The network is homogeneous.

At the time, I was developing applications using Jini and JavaSpaces. Understanding these eight fallacies became more and more essential in my development efforts. I continually found new ways that these fallacies would creep into autonomous services and agents. Building instrumentation into these services and agents for monitoring across the network topology became the way that the application's health was assessed, fixes were automatically deployed by the application, and issues that were not automatically fixed were identified. Teams should continually discuss how these eight fallacies of distributed computing are found in their highly distributed application deployments.

Not Removing Services When No Longer Used

Lingering functionality and artifacts are common on aging software development projects. When they are not removed when they are no longer used, the owner of the software is continually paying to maintain their existence. When the lingering functionality is contained in a distributed service, it can cause even more issues:

- The deployment is bloated.
- Time to validate the installation is increased.

---

6. Peter Deutsch, "The Eight Fallacies of Distributed Computing," http://blogs.sun.com/jag/resource/Fallacies.html.

- Unused services become out of date with current business objectives.
- They don't evolve with underlying components and errors creep into responses.

If the project is providing services or is built in a service-oriented way, establishing processes for identifying and removing unused services will enable products and their integrations to be as light as possible. This will support appropriate changeability of application integrations as new business configurations and needs emerge.

Application Programming Interfaces

Application programming interface (API) is an approach to delivering services through a specified set of functions, protocols, and data structures. An API is useful in that it establishes consistent access and hides specific functionality from consumers so they can focus on their own application-specific development needs. Developing an API that lasts over an extended period of time and remains useful to its consumers is a difficult task. It is almost impossible to establish an API with these characteristics without first understanding how it is going to be used.

Many teams fall into the trap of making too many component interfaces into an API. It may even be an organizational norm to create an API before implementing a component that will be consumed by others. Just to be sure, I will not suggest that having an API development focus is wrong. Actually, it is my opinion that identifying opportunities for reusable API is a powerful practice for development teams. The potential for design debt in API development really lies in the decision to establish an API before it is used or to allow it to emerge from real-world usage.

In *Patterns of Software*,[7] Richard Gabriel discusses his view on the work of Christopher Alexander on patterns[8] and how it relates to software development. Gabriel focuses on three particular concepts that relate to emergent design: compression, habitability, and piecemeal growth:

- **Compression:** writing software artifacts with text that is succinct and fully describes the context. An example of this is subclassing in object-

---

7. Richard P. Gabriel, *Patterns of Software: Tales from the Software Community* (Oxford University Press, 1996).
8. Christopher Alexander, *The Timeless Way of Building* (Oxford University Press, 1979).

oriented programming languages. A subclass assumes all the characteristics of its parent.

- **Habitability:** the degree to which software artifacts enable change with ease, comfort, and confidence. Ward Cunningham says, "You know you are working on clean code when each routine you read turns out to be pretty much what you expected."[9] This characterization of clean code defines how to recognize habitable software artifacts.
- **Piecemeal growth:** building software through small, incremental changes.

As a team develops software, its ability to maintain a level of compression appropriate to the domain and technology at the time supports habitability and piecemeal growth. The software parts should provide clarity about what they do so that changes can be made with confidence. As we know, establishing the skill and discipline to do this each day is incredibly difficult. Some basic principles can help in the creation of an API based on Gabriel's concepts:

- *Be careful when using terms that are too technical.* If the technical terminology for a domain is used, be sure to reflect its definition in the associated documentation.
- *Each interface definition should be specific and as small as it can be.* As interface definitions grow too large, they become difficult to use. Look for ways to break up large interface definitions so they are more succinct.
- *Avoid or minimize function overloading.* Interfaces that have the same function call with multiple variations with different parameter lists pollute the definition. Look for ways to consolidate the functionality into a single function.
- *Functions should describe what a developer wants to do.* An API should focus on the fact that other developers will be using it. Naming and accessibility to functionality should be developed from their point of view.
- *Make sure to document each public interface and function.* Developers who are looking to use the API will want to understand quickly how a function behaves. Documentation that is close to the function helps.
- *Assess interfaces for parts that will be difficult to version going forward.* Support for backward and forward compatibility will enable the API to incorporate change over time. An example is the use of configura-

---

9. Quoted in Robert C. Martin, *Clean Code: A Handbook of Agile Software Craftsmanship* (Prentice Hall, 2008).

tion files where older versions use only those configurations they know and ignore newer additions.

Neither defining the API up front nor allowing its definition to emerge will balance focus on the parts with keeping an eye on the whole. When developing an API, defining a skeleton of main functions gives guidance to the construction. Write some pseudo code that describes what a developer would want to see, for instance:

```
ShoppingCart
  addItem(ItemID, Quantity)
  removeItem(ItemID)
  updateItemQuantity(ItemID, Quantity)
  List getItemsInCart()
```

Establishing a basic structure for the initial API development enables the team to implement with a focus on the developer expectations. As the API is constructed, changes to the original structure of the API will emerge as the usage scenarios are better understood.

REVIEW SESSIONS

With changeability comes the need to transfer knowledge quickly to those who are impacted by the change. If changes are occurring and a team member is not able to understand or incorporate them, the team member will become confused and less confident in development activities. There are two aspects of transferring knowledge quickly that are important to keep in mind:

- The habitability of the software artifacts is important for enabling others to understand how to work with them.
- Transference of knowledge should be continuously attended to and therefore built into the team's processes.

Habitability has already been discussed in the previous section on API development but continuous transference of knowledge has not. A number of practices have been implemented by Agile teams that support continuous transference of knowledge, including

- Design reviews
- Pair programming
- Retrospectives

Each of these practices allows for knowledge to disseminate among multiple parties. How they are implemented can have a significant effect on their resulting value. The upcoming sections on each of these practices will go into more detail about some effective techniques to use.

Design Reviews

Continuous attention to technical excellence and good design enhances agility.[10]

In an Agile environment, attention to design enhances the ability of an application to change with time. Giving proper attention to design can be difficult with all of the schedule pressures inherent in most software organizations. Design review sessions are periodic meetings where team members are able to share and get feedback on design decisions.

Effective design reviews involve the development team members. If teams are to take responsibility for the software construction, they must be in control of design decisions. At the same time, it is important to set up communication channels for development teams to obtain support from more senior people in the organization when needed. The design review provides a forum for the team to converge on common design decisions and ultimately clarity in the application's structure.

The typical design review session involves all development team members. The agenda for the meeting is sent out to the team beforehand and includes the one or more design decisions that will be discussed. At the meeting, each design decision is presented while the rest of the team asks questions and discusses the merits and challenges they see. Through this discussion the development team captures action items to take into the software construction process. This cross-fertilizing and feedback allow the entire team to be kept up-to-date on design decisions that could impact their work, whether they focus on code, test, or design during the iteration.

Pair Programming

The practice of *pair programming* from XP has been one of the most controversial practices in the Agile space. The thought of two people sitting at the

---

10. "Principles behind the Agile Manifesto," http://agilemanifesto.org/principles.html, 2001.

keyboard working on the same thing seems to reek of people being allowed to do about half the amount of work they would if working individually. This perception stems from the idea that the busier a person is with tasks, the more output that person will deliver.

In practice, teams I have been part of, coached, and been around that do pair programming tend to deliver more on average than teams that don't. This is only anecdotal evidence but there has been research into the subject.[11] I won't go into detail here about the research. The anecdotal evidence and my observations take into account the quality of the work, the reduction in rework as a result, and the amount of focus a pair has on the work at hand during a day. Although it was shown that it took two team members more time to implement in most of the research conducted, the knowledge sharing, quality, and satisfaction of pairing team members outweighed the additional time spent in terms of value to the project.

Pair programming can be done in many different configurations, such as

2 programmers

2 testers

1 tester and 1 programmer

1 programmer and 1 business analyst

1 tester and 1 business analyst

Beyond these pairing configurations, there are some pairing behaviors that are interesting from a design perspective. A myth about Agile software development is that teams no longer spend time designing. Actually, I have found that Agile teams that I am part of design all of the time. The designs may be more informal than traditional approaches, but they occur when people have more information and with the people who will implement the design. When a pair of team members get together, if there is a need for them to agree on a higher-level design, they should stop and do pair design. This can be done at a whiteboard or on a small piece of paper. If the resulting design is important enough to capture for sharing with other team members, the pair has a responsibility to capture it into an artifact, maybe onto their wiki or in a document.

---

11. Laurie Williams, Robert R. Kessler, Ward Cunningham, and Ron Jeffries, "Strengthening the Case for Pair-Programming," *IEEE Software* 17, no. 4 (July/August 2000): 19–25.

The use of pairing has been shown in research to result in better design deci-sions.[12] This makes sense because the collaboration on a design causes each person to provide a reason for his or her design choices. This forces a person to further explore the validity of the design.

Although pair programming can increase the overall caliber of design in an application or component, it has been shown to be a difficult practice to implement. Some team members with whom I have been in contact had dif-ficulty working with another team member. The difficulty may have been a result of poor social interaction skills or lack of confidence in their own abil-ities. Whatever the reason, it may be difficult for some team members to apply this practice. I recommend that if your team values pair programming, ensure that people joining the team are well aware of this practice and its potential ramifications.

Retrospectives

An Agile retrospective allows the development team to review the processes they have used to deliver a potentially shippable product increment at the end of the iteration or release. The focus is on the processes used, not the people involved. This is captured in the *prime directive* for project retrospectives:

> *Regardless of what we discover, we understand and truly believe that everyone did the best job they could, given what they knew at the time, their skills and abilities, the resources available, and the situation at hand.*
>
> —*Norm Kerth*[13]

Development teams, after they have performed iterations and are starting to become comfortable, should start to think beyond tactical process changes toward software development life-cycle enhancements. Some topics of inter-est may be

- How do we get closer to a push-button release?
- Will pair programming enhance the quality of our delivery?
- What would it take to incorporate performance testing into the iteration?

---

12. N. V. Flor and E. L. Hutchins, "Analyzing Distributed Cognition in Software Teams: A Case Study of Team Programming during Perfective Software Maintenance," pre-sented at Empirical Studies of Programmers: Fourth Workshop, 1991.
13. Norman L. Kerth, *Project Retrospectives: A Handbook for Team Reviews* (Dorset House Publishing Company, 2001).

- Could we automate the promotion of builds from one environment to another?
- What changes should we make to keep our builds at less than ten minutes?
- Are we focusing on the right software quality attributes?

When asking these questions, the development team must capture any decisions made. The decisions could be captured in the working agreement if it deals with how the team approaches a problem, such as pair programming. Other decisions might be captured in the Definition of Done when they deal with deliverables to sustain internal quality, such as builds in less than ten minutes. For those decisions that are about the design, if they can be codified into code, such as "This module should not contact this module," they could actually be put into a unit test that breaks the build if the design decision is not upheld.

The development team should use Agile retrospectives to enhance its technical processes along with interpersonal and workflow processes. Teams should look at what they want to achieve and then create action items that take them a step in that direction. If the team wants performance testing to occur multiple times per iteration and this seems too large an effort to do right away, the first step could be to reduce the overhead in deploying into the performance testing environment. Do whatever it takes to get a step closer to better software delivery and potentially shippable product increments.

SUMMARY

The way a system is designed can have massive effects on its long-term maintenance costs. Whether the system has a multitude of small, interdependent components, crucial point-to-point integration dependencies, heavy duplication of business logic, or does not satisfy new user expectations, a design that does not evolve or is not easily modified may give rise to significant costs that catch management off guard. We must continually implement and evolve our system design to be ready for unforeseen changes so that we can minimize these surprise costs for our business.

Maintaining robustness in the software's design helps support imminent future changes. Proper modularization makes finding the software artifacts that need to change for meeting new business demands easier. Taking a view beyond the next iteration at a high level by creating an architectural description provides guidance as the team delivers increments of work. Software development tools evolve quickly. If teams do not continually evolve with the tools, their progress can be hampered as the software functionality grows. Considering more than just corrective maintenance in the infrastructure is essential as systems age. Remember that adaptive, perfective, and preventive maintenance is also needed to sustain it on an ongoing basis. And just because a design exists today does not mean that it should not change when new business needs don't fit the same design picture. Evolve the design continually, thus keeping it supple in the face of changing needs.

The value of infrastructure and design changes is usually the *cost to be incurred if the underlying issues are not addressed*. Write abuse stories when the customer is not prioritizing software debt effectively. Describing how the software could be abused and the cost associated with that abuse will make it easier for a customer to prioritize the changes needed to prevent it. Get the entire team together, along with any subject matter experts for the technical area to be discussed, and conduct writing sessions to generate a list of abuse and user stories.

Enabling appropriate change is the cornerstone of any good software architecture. There are software constructs that are particularly difficult to support change in: user interfaces (UI), services, and application programming interfaces (APIs). Use the tactics for UI, automated functional tests, allowing features to be turned on and off, and duplicate UI flows to improve confidence that changes do not affect existing functionality. Ensure that services do not incur design debt by doing too much, coupling themselves to consumers, having insufficient monitoring, and lingering in production far beyond their usefulness to the business.

Chapter 8

Designing Software

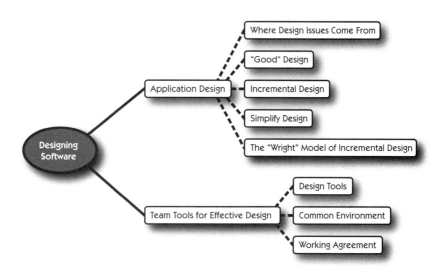

Implement solutions not features.

—"User Interface Design for iPhone Applications" in iPhone Getting Started Videos at the Apple Development Center web site

Application Design

Application design is sometimes thought to be a documentation effort. If we can come up with the "right" design and document it, then it will feed the development team and enable the software construction. Development teams commonly distrust the designs they are given, don't understand them, find them too abstract and ambiguous to be valuable, or find problems with them during implementation that they must work around. No matter if any or all of these are correct, the resulting software does not meet the documented design, and feedback between the designers and the development team usually gets lost.

Instead of thinking about application design as only a thought and documentation process, Agile teams think of design as a process that occurs throughout the software development cycle. It is proven with good tests and the implementation. When necessary, Agile teams spend time thinking about the design of an application beyond a single feature or component so as to get a holistic view and a common understanding across the team about how to proceed without designing themselves into a corner. Here are a few principles of application design in an Agile team:

- *Application design is about changeability, not locking down the right design.* If an application's design is not able to change as the needs of the business change, the application will eventually become a liability.
- *Those who are closest to the implementation details, with external support as necessary, should make application design decisions.* If someone other than those who are implementing the solution is making application design decisions, important information will be lost in the translation of the design to the team. If someone is integral to making good design choices with the team, that person should be put on the team.
- *Application design is about not only the ability to design a new solution, but also knowing what components, applications, and solutions already exist that provide the solution.* Continuous gathering of knowledge about new and existing tools and infrastructure will enable teams to implement solutions faster and will keep people motivated and innovative.

To apply these principles, teams should be equipped with information about design issues to watch out for, how to assess their own designs incrementally, and what tools are available for effective design. The following sections will provide information on each of these topics.

Where Design Issues Come From

There are many reasons that design decays as software ages. Here is a partial list:

- **Pressure of a deadline:** If the team has built software with integrity problems, they will have difficulty removing those problems as a deadline approaches.
- **Inexperience:** Teams lack the experience that comes from working on software from multiple domains and platforms.
- **Lack of automation:** If it takes too long to validate existing functionality of the software as changes are made, the functionality will be validated less often.

- **Premature design decisions:** Laying out an architecture based on a pattern without proving its viability or with insufficient knowledge about the context for the pattern could lead to problematic designs.
- **Developing features that are hard to test:** Features of an application that are implemented but are difficult to test because of the way they are constructed will lead to less frequent validation of those features over time.
- **Ambiguous functional requirements:** Customers do not know exactly what they need and documented requirements are not able to capture their ideal functionality perfectly. Therefore, applications that are developed too long without feedback from customers have built-in assumptions about what customers wanted in the requirements, leading to software that does not meet their desires.

Each of these reasons is correctable but not without costly change. These issues cannot be resolved across an organization overnight. An organization must identify and communicate goals that produce positive change over time and apply principles for good design decision making across teams.

"Good" Design

After working on many applications over the years, I consider some designs to be better than others. How do I assess the level of "good"-ness? Well, as I gained more experience with software development, there were a number of common issues that made delivery of requested changes more difficult. As I developed more code, sometimes creating these common issues along the way or running into a code base that already had them, I began to create a mental catalog to refer to. I was also able to work with many other developers who shared their own mental catalogs of common issues. It has been my experience that there is nothing better than dealing with common design issues to help someone assess the "good"-ness of software design.

With the introduction of each common issue into a component, the application's integrity decays. Applications and components with fewer of these common issues tend to be easier to work with and allow for changes even as the code base grows. Thinking back, I realize there were a few characteristics that these better-designed applications exhibited:

- A full build and deploy could be executed from source control with little to no configuration.
- Test cases existed, either manual or preferably automated, with good coverage of the application.

- It was easy to find the place where a change should be made.
- A change in one area of the application did not adversely affect other areas unexpectedly.

If teams are able to work on their applications without grappling with design decay each day, they will deliver better-designed software faster. By delivering working software faster, they can increase the amount of feedback from customers. With frequent feedback, applications evolve into software that fits the needs of the users, and fewer defects are found outside of the team's development process.

Assessing the "good"-ness of software design does not follow one simple set of rules. The most fundamental design qualities are high cohesiveness and low coupling. Although these are wonderful principles to guide software design, their application to code can be blurry depending upon team member experience and background with the platforms and domain of the application. Depending upon the context of the application being developed and the makeup of the team, important design decisions could be perceived differently. Procedural programmers may not appreciate the separation of concerns or abstractions created in an object-oriented software application. Experienced programmers may not see the value in writing automated unit tests for a significant portion of the code because they can figure out where to make changes easily enough already. Manual testers may not see the value of automation because their organization has compliance concerns and the independent verification and validation group will execute all the automated tests manually anyway.

The characteristics of applications with good design listed previously might not work for every project. Rather than following a list of suggestions for how to make good design decisions, it is important to identify how the application design is decaying as early as possible. With this information you can work on fixing the design issues before they become too costly to fix. Instead of assessing whether the design is satisfactory, look for ways to continuously improve the design each day.

Incremental Design

When they are first introduced to Agile methods such as Scrum and XP, people wonder how much "up-front" design is necessary to be successful. This question tends to stem from more detailed questions, such as

- How will we know whether the overall design is consistent and robust?

- If we focus only on what we are implementing this iteration, won't the overall design become chaotic and hard to work with?
- How will we ensure that the software is implemented with the "best" design?
- Won't the software become too complex if we don't create an overall design before coding?
- Won't integrating across dependent teams become problematic if all interfaces between them are not defined?
- Isn't this suggesting that teams just do "cowboy coding" with no accountability?

These are valid concerns, and teams should consider their current context and capabilities to provide the right level of initial design. Unfortunately, too many teams take an extreme perspective of Scrum and XP and remove all documentation from their delivery. It is a myth that Agile teams do not write documentation. As teams get started with Scrum or XP, they should look at each document and figure out if it is still valuable to deliver. For instance, if a high-level design artifact is helpful to other teams that integrate with the application, keeping the artifact up-to-date could be a valuable use of time.

The amount of up-front design needed in an iterative and incremental approach should always be less than in a plan-driven approach such as waterfall. Depending upon the type of application being developed, user-specific design needs, and current infrastructure, the up-front design could consist of anything from a pair of developers quickly sketching on a whiteboard for a few minutes all the way to providing usability studies for particular desired features.

There is a difference in the rigor necessary to design a data-driven internally used information technology (IT) application versus software that monitors a nuclear power plant. The data-driven application does not have the same compliance needs and potential for negative ramifications as the nuclear power plant monitoring software. Therefore, teams should put more emphasis on up-front design on the nuclear power plant monitoring software. When using Scrum or XP on safety-critical applications, there is a need to spend a bit more time in design, but teams should do design closer to the time the software is implemented. The heuristic for how much design should be done up front is:

Focus on aspects of design whenever there is a need to understand internal and external interfaces at a higher level, but focus the design decisions on the functionality needed now.

Many people might find this focus on what is needed now to be short-sighted, but implementing what might be needed adds unnecessary artifacts that must be maintained over time. The statement does not mean that team members involved in the design discussion shouldn't talk about potential needs and leave the implementation open for their inclusion in the future. When an application has a mature validation structure, such as high test coverage and automated deployment and promotion, team members are more comfortable with deferring design decisions. Therefore, define what "needed now" means as a team for design decisions.

Simplify Design

In XP, "simple design" is expressed when the following characteristics are apparent in the software:

1. It runs all the tests.
2. It expresses every idea that we need to express.
3. It says everything once and only once.
4. It has no superfluous parts.

These characteristics, when put into practice, force the code to become simpler to work with. If we are always able to run all of the practical and relevant tests, we can verify the code's behavior continually. If the code expresses every idea it needs to express, the right behaviors will be verified with the tests. If the code expresses a single idea *once and only once*, when a change is needed there will be only one place to change it. If the code does not express ideas that are superfluous, it will be the smallest it can be and therefore lighter-weight from a maintenance point of view.

Incorporating these characteristics of simple design is definitely not easy, but neither is software development. It takes discipline to apply simple design. With that discipline will come highly factored, less coupled, and more cohesive software that retains its ability to change with new functional needs over time.

One of the most common questions in teaching and coaching Agile methods to groups is "How do we design our software while delivering iterations of potentially shippable product increments?"

Scrum asks that each sprint deliver a potentially shippable product increment. There is emphasis on "potentially shippable" because it is quite common that releases involve running multiple sprints to accrue enough value for the users. "Potentially shippable product increment" means the software has the internal quality that a releasable version of the software should include. Each feature implemented during the sprint should be tested, coded, integrated, documented, and whatever else is needed to verify that it is of high internal quality. Scrum teams gain a better understanding of what deliverables are necessary to make this happen by creating a Definition of Done, which was described in Chapter 3, "Sustaining Internal Quality."

If teams using Scrum are focused on delivering the current sprint's features, how does architecture, which is less defined early in delivery, get tended to? I use a diagram that Mike Cohn originally drew to help teams visualize how architecture fits into software development using Scrum. Figure 8.1 shows my interpretation of the diagram.

This diagram shows that in new software product development efforts, more emphasis is put on architecture elements in early sprints of the release cycle. As the architecture is more fully defined and implemented in later sprints of the release cycle, emphasis turns increasingly toward pure feature development. In the last sprint of a release there is little to no architecture implementation left to do. This diagram demonstrates the expectations of early technical architecture implementation to support feature delivery. It also shows that every sprint in the release should deliver features that the customer can review and provide feedback on.

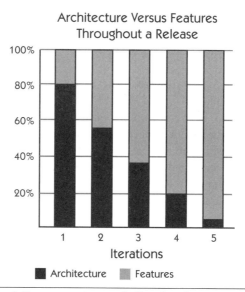

Figure 8.1 The relative percentages of effort for developing software architecture versus developing features during an initial or heavily redesigned software release

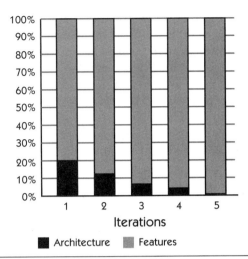

Figure 8.2 The relative percentages of effort for developing software architecture versus developing features during follow-up releases of a software product. The amount of effort devoted to architecture has declined because an initial release of the software has stabilized the architecture so subsequent releases can easily build on top of it.

After the first release of the software, there is usually less architecture emphasis in early sprints of following releases. Subsequent releases build upon an existing architecture in most cases, as is shown in Figure 8.2.

The "Wright Model" of Incremental Design

After I described these incremental architecture diagrams to a developer named David Wright, he approached me to validate his understanding. Within ten minutes of hearing my description of incremental architecture, he had developed a new diagram perspective that I thought was brilliant. His diagram involved two axes, the x-axis representing the surface visible to users and the y-axis representing depth of the architecture. In sprint 1 of a multi-sprint release, a portion of both the surface and architectural depth is realized, as shown in Figure 8.3.

As a release progresses, the amounts of surface visible features and architectural depth implemented are incrementally built upon toward a fully releasable product version. The architectural depth implemented to support the amount of surface functionality grows as shown in Figure 8.4.

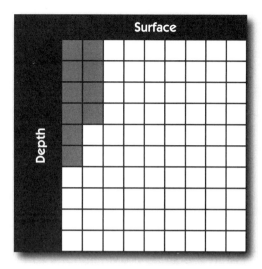

Figure 8.3   Surface, what is being made visible to users, and architectural depth to support the surface functionality in early iterations of a release

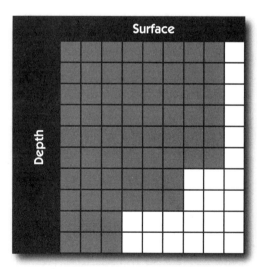

Figure 8.4   Surface, what is being made visible to users, and architectural depth to support the surface functionality in later iterations of a release

The application of an incremental architecture approach comes with a potential issue. Because less is known about the design of the overall release architecture at the beginning, new knowledge could impact existing implementation of architecture elements. In order to manage this issue, we must implement disciplined practices to enable the software to accept change as we gain more knowledge. This is why the XP technical practices such as Test-Driven Development (TDD), continuous integration (CI), pair programming (aka continuous code review), and refactoring have become so common on Scrum teams. With TDD, there is an executable way to prove the existing functionality at the component and application levels has not been broken. This does not negate the need for exploratory testing by a person, but it keeps manual testing to a manageable level. CI automatically runs builds, automated tests, and deployment scripts for the application, then provides feedback to the team about the current state of the integrated system. Pair programming increases knowledge transfer across the team and provides coherent communication of the product's domain into the tests, code, and supporting artifacts. And finally, refactoring is used to continually improve the design of the application. As a team gains new knowledge about the application's architecture, they will find opportunities to improve the design of internal components. If the team has been applying simple design as they go, changes to each component will be focused in a single location for each new design idea to be expressed. Figure 8.5 shows that refactoring of existing components may be needed as the team gains more knowledge about the implementation.

Each refactoring may consist of small changes but lead to a larger positive impact on the application design over the span of a release. Effective use of refactoring keeps the architecture flexible and therefore able to meet evolving business needs. Extensive automated test code coverage that is executed frequently against the application and its integrations along with modularity that can come with isolating components for testing enable a team to have confidence when larger refactorings are needed.

I have used David Wright's model to describe incremental architecture to clients in conjunction with the original diagram from Mike Cohn. It has helped provide a clearer picture of incremental design and how to incorporate it into real-world projects. With David's permission I named it the "Wright Model" and will continue to use it in the future. Thank you, David.

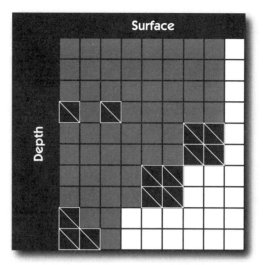

Figure 8.5   Surface, what is being made visible to users, and architectural depth to support the surface functionality in later iterations of a release. The feature under development has uncovered new understandings about the application's design. The team decided to improve the application's design through refactoring (represented by black cells with diagonal white slashes) of existing components to support the functionality.

TEAM TOOLS FOR EFFECTIVE DESIGN

In the past, I misunderstood the value of software tools to help in the design process. I believed that the tools would cause teams to implement effective designs. We used some expensive UML modeling software to enable design and development, yet the software had many of the same issues we had before using the tool. How could this be? As Gerald Weinberg expresses in "The Second Law of Consulting":

> *No matter what the problem is, it's always a people problem.*[1]

Although we were using good software tools, success was based on our own effectiveness as a team working on the project. This realization did not come overnight. Through some fortunate circumstances I found myself on teams

---

1. Gerald Weinberg, *Secrets of Consulting: A Guide to Giving and Getting Advice Successfully* (Dorset House Publishing, 1986).

that used team consensus and visible charts to capture common understandings about how team members worked on the project together.

Over the years, I have found that these team tools fall into the following categories:

- Design tools
- Common environment
- Working agreement

Teams use design tools to enhance communication within and outside the team. Creating commonality in essential parts of a team's environment permits tighter collaboration and sharing across the team. A working agreement sets expectations about how each team member should approach the software delivery and thus provides a stable platform for individual accountability within the team. Each of these team tools will be detailed in the following sections.

Design Tools

Agile teams that I have worked on don't just design software at the start of the project. The team instead takes the viewpoint that we should . . .

Design continuously throughout the project.

To support continuous design, teams need tools readily available to use for communicating about design. In most situations, I have found that a whiteboard is the most useful design tool there is. A whiteboard allows team members to gather around it and share control of design discussions, and it assists participants in aligning their design ideas quickly. An example of the output from a whiteboard session is shown in Figure 8.6.

There are many opinions out there about how much time should be spent on design without writing code. Ron Jeffries in the book *Extreme Programming Installed* suggested the following:

> *Get a few people together and spend a few minutes sketching out the design. Ten minutes is ideal—half an hour should be the most time you spend to do this. After that, the best thing to do is to let the code participate in the design session—move to the machine and start typing in code.*[2]

---

2. Ron Jeffries, Ann Anderson, and Chet Hendrickson, *Extreme Programming Installed* (Addison-Wesley, 2000)

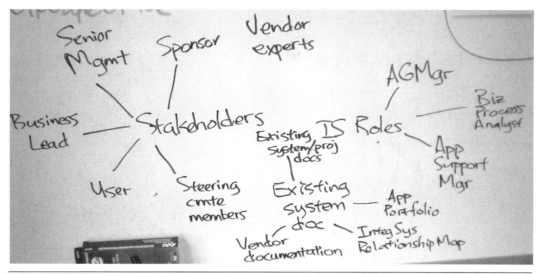

Figure 8.6 A role interaction diagram drawn on a whiteboard that provides a stable point for discussion between the customer and the team

Here are my rules of thumb for how long to design outside the code:

- If your team is doing Test-Driven Design (TDD) and continuous integration (CI) effectively, you should spend less than 30 minutes in any whiteboard design session. When using TDD with automated builds, teams are able to write experimental tests that can evaluate one or more design solutions quickly. This is preferable to thinking harder and longer about what the "best" design is. If team members are taking longer than 30 minutes, there is enough ambiguity that experimental tests will provide needed clarity.
- If your team is not doing TDD and delivering using Scrum or a similar iterative and incremental approach, I suggest that whiteboard design sessions last no more than an hour. If this is not enough time, the ambiguity is sufficient to cause need for clarification. I suggest that teams create one or more "spike" solutions, writing throwaway code that verifies a potential solution. This will give the team essential understanding of the benefits and problems of a potential solution so the team can again conduct a whiteboard design session to choose a collective direction.

Traditionally, teams were expected to launch modeling software and document their design decisions. Unless there are business reasons, such as regulatory and enterprise guidelines, teams should not go directly to beautifying

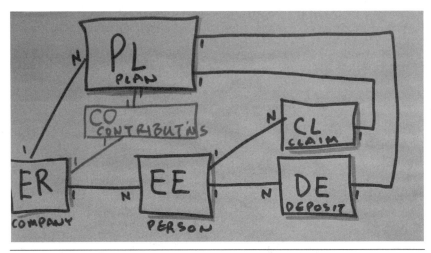

Figure 8.7   The results of a whiteboard session describing the major components of a workflow processing system

their design decisions in a software tool. If the whiteboard drawing is not readable, it can be redrawn quickly or put into a tool for clarity's sake. It is much cheaper to spend money on a digital camera with sufficient resolution to take a picture of your whiteboard design session output if it must be documented. Remember, it may be sufficient to just have the design session and not document the design at all because the people who are involved in its execution were in the room. Sometimes, a team member is not there or capturing the information is considered important, in which case you can take a picture and email it to the entire team or place it onto a wiki. Figure 8.7 shows an example whiteboard session captured for later consumption.

There are plenty of tools out there that can generate visual models for multiple viewpoints of software. Some teams might leave whiteboard session output up on the wall in their common team area. Other teams find it useful to put a printed chart of these visual models on the wall. It is common for me to see database schemas and API visual charts hanging in an Agile team area. Please remember to remove old versions and charts that are no longer necessary.

Common Environment

As teams initially form, there are usually conflicts about tool usage, accepted practices, and essential artifacts for successful software delivery. To resolve these conflicts there is a need to create the foundation for a common environment that the team agrees upon and is comfortable enough with. Creating a common environment supplies the team with explicit expectations and boundaries for internal interactions and delivery.

A common environment includes one or more of the following:

- Work area configuration
- Team room
- IDE
- Coding standards
- Location of common team tools
- Build and deployment profiles

Making these environmental attributes explicit allows team members to contribute their perspectives, enabling the team to address conflicts early. Conflicts around these attributes of a project tend to stifle productivity as team members cobble together ways to collaborate through problematic environmental conditions.

Work Area Configuration

A team's work area can have a profound effect on the software that is delivered. Even a potential walk to ask someone a question can cause communication to be delayed for a substantial period of time. Documentation can help somewhat but is prone to misinterpretation and lacks the appropriate detail. Software tools can offset some of the communication delay but is lower-bandwidth communication compared to face-to-face conversations. Based upon context, whether collocated or remote, it is important to set up the highest-bandwidth communication channels possible to increase the frequency of needed interactions. This reduces indirection, misinterpretation, and rework later in the software delivery cycle.

There are a few common work area configuration topics that affect software design directly:

- Access to whiteboards
- Collaboration tools
- Proximity of team members
- Ability to work together
- Height of walls

Access to Whiteboards. Teams that have accessible whiteboards tend to use them. They use whiteboards to establish a common understanding of software design, user interactions, and other attributes of the deliverables. When teams do not have easily accessible whiteboards, they improvise by relying on more written communication and tools to communicate with each other. Although documentation and tools are useful in specific contexts, it is important that team members not rely too heavily on them to communicate with each other. Whiteboards support frequent and quick collaboration among team members that can be applied immediately to their deliverables.

Collaboration Tools. If your team is not collocated, what do you do? Teams must compensate for their lack of physical presence with software collaboration tools. Teams use tools such as the following to enhance remote communication:

- Instant messaging (IM)
- Online whiteboard tools
- Voice over Internet Protocol (VoIP)
- Virtual network computer (VNC)
- Internet Relay Chat (IRC)
- Telephone conferencing
- Remote video
- Documentation
- Email

Software collaboration tools with voice and video work well except that they are sometimes unreliable because of issues outside the team's control. When video and voice do not work, teams can fall back onto telephone conferencing solutions.

Tools such as IRC and IM enable team members to have a continuous presence with each other, but communication is shallow and difficult at times. IRC and IM are good for quick, specific questions or comments that are not as prone to misinterpretation.

Online whiteboard tools are great for sessions where visualization helps the communication. Online whiteboards and VNC sessions are usually supplemented with VoIP or telephone conferencing to allow conversation about the pictures being drawn. It can help to find online whiteboard tools that allow multiple people to lead the session. VNC is best used for two people to pair on deliverables.

Documenting the results of conversations after using the software collaboration tools mentioned earlier can be helpful to assess whether all participants have the same understanding. Email could be the tool used to disseminate or capture the documentation, but it has been my experience that email is the least reliable communication tool. People are inundated with email these days and tend to pay less attention to lengthy messages.

Proximity of Team Members. In some working environments team members are located in offices on the other side of the building, on different floors of the building, or in an entirely different building or location. Feedback between team members is delayed just because of team member location. Even walking down the hallway or taking the stairs or elevator is an obstacle to necessary communication. It is exacerbated if team members are in different time zones or on opposite sides of the world.

If these obstacles exist in your team, software artifacts will be integrated less frequently and design decisions will be delayed or made with less consistency across the team. It is common for teams in this situation to attack a similar problem, such as logging or data access, with entirely different solutions. This causes internal team discussions to commence after each team member has already made assumptions and value judgments and integrated the design. This makes the conversation about the design more difficult than it would be if the team members had been collocated.

Collocating team members in the same area, within a couple of meters or yards from each other, on the same building floor is optimal. A couple of different configurations of team members are highly effective for close collaboration in a collocated team. The first configuration involves team members sitting in a circle or rectangle with their backs to each other. This arrangement allows them to focus on their work, either in a pair or individually, facing away from the rest of the team. It also enables ad hoc collaborative sessions among team members through a single motion of turning around. The second configuration involves desks with team members facing each other with only their monitors in between. The monitor location supports focus, but again ad hoc collaboration is supported with team members leaning to the left or right and talking.

If you cannot be collocated with your team, setting up communication tools such as IM and continuously running online communication channels such as IRC are helpful. If all team members have an IRC client running continually, they get used to watching for questions or important information from others on the team. This increases communication and feedback, thus enhancing team decision making and consistency.

Ability to Work Together. Problems in software development are complex and many times necessitate more than one person working on them. If individual work areas do not easily allow people to work together, solving complex problems becomes more difficult. Having more than one person work in a single development environment is beneficial to designing an appropriate solution quickly when the problem is complex.

If you are using XP technical practices, your team probably has pairing stations. Pairing stations are configured in a manner that allows two team members to conduct software development activities together. Many teams that use the practice of pair programming only implement production code at a pairing station. These teams become more effective at working together because they practice it through pair programming.

Even if you are not doing pair programming, setting up your work area to allow others to collaborate with you comfortably is helpful. Instead of sitting in a corner, find a way to configure your work area so that you are able to sit side by side with another member of your team. This way you give the other person equal access to make changes and provide feedback. When a person sits behind or at an odd angle to the person in control of the workspace, he or she is less able to provide adequate feedback.

Height of Walls. Many organizations have cubicles. Some organizations do not allow the cubicles to be modified into unsanctioned configurations. To optimize team member interactions and feedback, it is important to empower teams to configure their own environment. Reducing the height of cubicle walls between team members is helpful if allowed by your organization.

If the cubicle walls are not easily modified, your team could find ways to work in common areas. Some teams take over conference rooms so that they can communicate and provide feedback more quickly. Find ways to keep the walls between team members from becoming an impediment to collaboration. Walls negatively affect the frequency of interaction and feedback, which delays design, integration, and consistency.

Working Agreement

Creation of a working agreement is an essential step for establishing healthy interactions within a team. Although there is no single reason or way to facilitate a team in the creation of its working agreement, here is an exercise that can get your team started.

As a facilitator, you can help the team understand the reason for creating a working agreement by discussing the increased collaboration needs when using an Agile approach. Becoming a team involves commitment to working together and supporting each other in the team's common goals. This commitment is supported by writing what all team members believe are important protocols for the team to comply with to maximize their capabilities to deliver faster and with higher quality.

For Scrum teams the following topics are a good starter list for creation of a working agreement:

- Time and location of the Daily Scrum
- Testing strategy (unit, functional, integration, performance, stress, etc.)
- Build and infrastructure plans (shared responsibilities)
- Team norms (be on time, respect estimates, help when needed, etc.)
- How to address bugs/fires during a sprint
- Product Owner availability (phone, office hours, attendance at the Daily Scrum)
- Capacity plan for initial sprint(s)

A common way to facilitate the creation of a working agreement is to put these topics on a whiteboard or piece of easel pad paper and then ask the team(s) to create their working agreement with these topics as guidance. If they find other topics that are important, please add them to the list.

SUMMARY

Designing software that meets the needs of users is a learning experience. Being able to identify all of the requirements before constructing the software is usually a false hope. Software organizations have put significant effort into generalizing processes for all projects. The thought is that if they control the processes for all projects, the projects will become predictable. Yet, this practice has not led to predictable success and only results in an illusion of control. Once users touch and feel the software, they will have feedback that affects the design.

Instead of attempting to control requirements, project teams should incrementally deliver portions of the application and gather feedback. Application design is evolving continuously throughout the construction, and teams must be able to identify design issues so they can be managed effectively. This chapter described many team tools for applying effective design in an iterative approach. These tools help teams take responsibility for the application design. This is essential because "good" design happens each day and must be a result of decisions made close to functional implementation.

Chapter 9

COMMUNICATING ARCHITECTURES

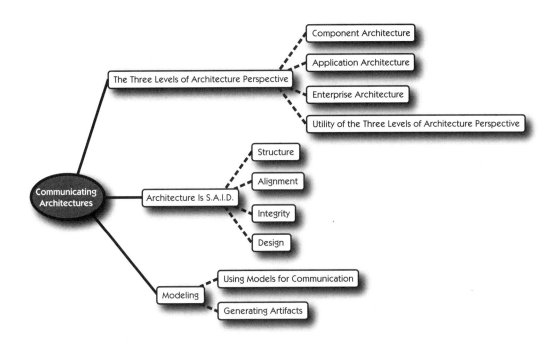

Software architecture is not about longevity. Long-lasting software is a result of an architecture and design that are able to evolve.

—author

THE THREE LEVELS OF ARCHITECTURE PERSPECTIVE

Software implementation and integration decisions have implications at multiple levels of architecture within an organization: enterprise, application, and component. Understanding what level of the architecture is being impacted informs teams how to approach the implementation and who

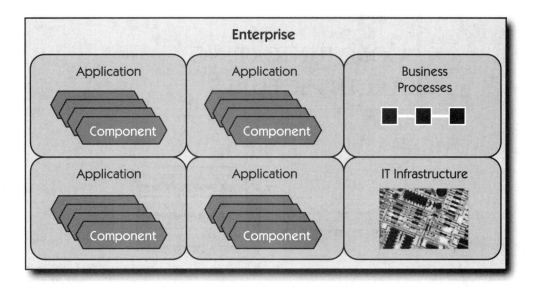

Figure 9.1   The three levels of architecture perspective within a software organization: enterprise, application, and component

should be involved or consulted. Decisions at an enterprise level can affect levels of service, operational integrity of deployed systems, and the costs associated with their maintenance. Application-level decisions impact end users and project delivery dates and cost. At lower levels of the architecture, component design and integration have ramifications for maintainability, reliability, deployment, and other software quality attributes, which percolate issues up to higher levels of the architecture. This is the reason that teams that focus on building highly cohesive components with interfaces that reduce coupling to other components more easily evolve their applications and enterprise integrations. Figure 9.1 shows an abstract view of an enterprise including all three levels of architecture perspective.

Component Architecture

Components within an application are self-contained units of functionality that provide specific interfaces to work with. The internal design of a component is focused on optimizing its capabilities in terms of software quality attributes such as performance and reliability. External views of a component are usually made available through an API or service interface that describes how to interact with the component.

It is not unusual for users of the component to interact with it in unexpected ways. This means that the internals of the component should permit changes to how users interact with its interface. The main concerns for components are how friction with future changes can be minimized and how the component adapts to new needs.

A basic example of a component could be a data access library. The component provides capabilities to support C.R.U.D. (create, retrieve, update, and delete) operations to a relational database. As anyone who has worked with multiple relational database implementations knows, each implementation has its own quirks to optimize performance and results. Therefore, deciding which relational database implementations to support in the data access library is essential. The development team can then evolve the library to support these implementations while still exposing a single API to users. Reducing changes to the API enables users of the library to upgrade to newer versions without significant rework.

Application Architecture

Applications are composed of components to provide assistance with or enhancement of an end user's work or lifestyle. The focus of an application is meeting the user's needs through the use of specific domain logic, a supportive user interface, and integrated components. When building applications, teams attempt to satisfy user needs while establishing a maintainable internal structure. Maintainable applications tend to have highly cohesive components and low coupling to specific component implementations. If the need arises, a component should be replaceable with another implementation or able to be rewritten with little effect on the rest of the application's user functionality.

An interesting twist to the three levels of architecture perspective is that applications can become components of other applications. A simple example of this is UNIX command-line tools. As a power command-line user, I commonly use tools such as grep to search through files for a particular pattern of text, which I can do simply from the command-line shell like so:

```
$ grep foo my_file.txt
There is a foo in my file on this line
...
```

Using grep can also include interaction with other command-line tools. For instance, I could count the number of times that a text pattern is found in the file using wc. To create an application user interface for this new utility I could create a script that encapsulates the use of `grep` and `wc` from the user but gives the user the ability to find the information needed: a count of how many lines in the file contain the specified pattern of text. Here is the shell script code I might devise:

```
#!/bin/bash
grep ${1} ${2} | wc -l
```

As you can see, applications can be turned into components of another application to supply a new capability. In fact, this is a common technique for interacting with legacy software. Knowing that the existing application is being used as a component is important to the design of a new application. The more interactions with the component application take place through an interface, the more maintainable the application will be in the future.

Enterprise Architecture

An enterprise is composed of applications along with business processes and IT infrastructure. Architecture at the enterprise level is concerned with application integrations, optimizing organizational business processes, vendor management, extranet interactions, and the internal infrastructure to support all of this.

People involved in enterprise architecture take a macro view of the organization and its technology. These are some of the questions they might attempt to answer for an organization:

- How can application assets be leveraged to provide new business capabilities?
- Which business processes can be automated to improve quality and throughput of our operations?
- How do vendors enable and support enterprise capabilities best?
- What business partners interact with our company and how do those interactions affect new development efforts?
- Is our internal infrastructure sufficient to support upcoming desires of our business?

As with software architecture, there are many different definitions of what enterprise architecture is. Traditional viewpoints on enterprise architecture describe it as one or more of the following:

- The structure and interactions of internal and externally facing business processes

- Diagrams describing the structural design of internal and externally facing business processes
- Specific methods resulting in artifacts describing the structural and logical design of internally and externally facing business processes

A somewhat different focus is documented in the Massachusetts Institute of Technology (MIT) Center for Information Systems Research definition of Enterprise Architecture:

> *The organizing logic for business processes and IT capabilities reflecting the integration and standardization requirements of the firm's operating model.*[1]

As opposed to the traditional viewpoints on enterprise architecture, the MIT definition does not focus on the artifacts. I believe this to be an important distinction because I have found many enterprise architecture groups that are more focused on the artifacts than on communicating the *organizing logic for business processes and IT infrastructure*. Enterprise architecture should be about communicating the current operating model for the intended purpose of supporting strategic planning.

Utility of the Three Levels of Architecture Perspective

Throughout this book, the three levels of architecture perspective (component, application, and enterprise) are referenced. The idea is to describe how particular practices, processes, and tools affect each level. Knowledge of these effects gives teams ideas about how to identify needs for communication and coordination on architecture concerns. Teams that discuss these concerns can put their own agreements together on how to handle them. Some questions they can answer in those agreements are:

- Whom should we work with to address this concern?
- Where can we find information on how these concerns have been handled in the past?
- What impacts will our decision have on the application design?

---

1. "Enterprise Architecture," MIT Sloan School of Management, Center for Information. Systems Research, http://cisr.mit.edu/research/research-overview/classic-topics/enterprise-architecture/.

Asking effective questions about each level of architecture to the appropriate people within your organization will increase the success of current and future architecture decisions.

ARCHITECTURE IS S.A.I.D.

Communicating architecture decisions to project stakeholders who may be impacted is not always straightforward. Teams produce communications about these decisions using methods all the way from filling out a design template to drawing sophisticated design models. The resulting artifacts may or may not be useful to impacted stakeholders or supportive of essential strategic decisions.

Agile teams look for ways to spread knowledge across the project team and its technology stakeholders as much as possible. Stakeholders, in this case, include software developers, testers, end users, business sponsors, subject matter experts, managers, and others. Knowledge about software architecture decisions and how they affect stakeholders cannot be communicated using a single method. Figuring out the perspective of the stakeholder is essential to effective communication. The acronym S.A.I.D., based on a form of communicating, helps teams focus on the perspectives of different stakeholders:

> **Structure:** how the pieces (components) create a solution (application)
>
> **Alignment:** the degree to which the application or enterprise structures align to current business objectives and strategy
>
> **Integrity:** the components that provide stability to the structure (application or enterprise) (i.e., automated tests and builds, service-level agreements, network infrastructure, etc.)
>
> **Design:** a way to conceptually communicate the planned or implemented structure of a component, application, or enterprise (i.e., system of names, XP practice of Metaphor, information radiators, etc.)

Each part of S.A.I.D. gives a different perspective on architecture decisions. Technical stakeholders interested in using or testing a component or application want to know its structure. Business folks want to know how the decision meets objectives in their overall strategy. Project teams want to know what processes, techniques, and tools they will use to sustain integrity of the software. Management and analysts want to understand how it meets the needs of users in terms of the domain. When teams are figuring out how to work with stakeholders, S.A.I.D. helps them gain a broader perspective and generate more effective communication techniques. The following sections will go into more detail about each part of the S.A.I.D. acronym.

Structure

Structure is the reality of the application's construction. The way components of an application depend on and interact with other components indicates its structure. When people ask about an application's architecture, they are usually interested in a description of its structure and the platforms supporting it. Diagrams are usually a good way to communicate an application or enterprise structure.

A common way of representing an application's structure is a block diagram, identifying key components and how they relate to each other. Rectangles with text inside them and lines that connect the rectangles are used in block diagrams to represent dependencies and interactions. Block diagrams are simple to draw by hand. Along with a conversation and a whiteboard, block diagrams can be used to show cohesive components and how they are coupled to other components. At an enterprise-level perspective, Unified Modeling Language (UML) deployment and component diagrams are useful in that they show how applications and infrastructure are structured in a particular environment.

Another way to diagram an application's structure is through a UML package diagram as seen in Figure 9.2. Packages encapsulate components of an application and interact through specific interfaces. Understanding how packages relate within an application supports communication of its internal structure. UML class diagrams depict the internals of components and, in many cases, how they interrelate with other components.

The structure of an architecture should be communicated using a minimalist approach. Only what is necessary to describe what a stakeholder will use should be put into diagrams. Team members and dependent teams use diagramming sessions to get in alignment about how components will be structured and interfaces will be maintained. The outputs of these diagramming sessions are usually useful for only a short period of time. There may be no need to document the diagrams that are created. Instead, just erase the whiteboard once everyone understands the diagrams well enough. If there is a need to capture the diagrams and other related information beyond the session, email and digital cameras are usually sufficient to disseminate them.

An application whose structure consistently resists changes to meet new business demands is brittle. Brittleness is usually a result of high coupling,

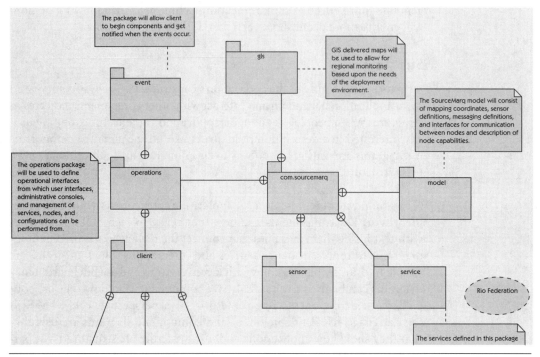

Figure 9.2   A UML package diagram where packages represent components of an application and how they relate to and depend on each other

low cohesion, or an overly complex application structure. If you have been in the software development industry for even a short period of time, you have probably seen applications that are extremely brittle. Even the most basic functional change involves excessive analysis and extreme hesitancy.

Applications with a satisfactory structure are modular and ready to accept new business demands. Changes are isolated to particular components and have few surprising side effects. When working with an application that has a "good" structure, logic is found where you expect it to be and the artifacts associated with the software are easy to read and understand. On top of that, there is little duplication in the software artifacts, so changes are easily isolated to a single location.

Alignment

Business needs change rapidly. Traditional software processes resist change at the expense of business needs. This resistance leads to deteriorating value of software assets because they become less able to change in response to new business needs. Software is a business asset and should be treated as such. If the enterprise or application structures do not align with current business needs, their value to the business depreciates.

Deteriorating alignment of software assets and business needs can occur in many different ways:

- Project teams resist making changes to the current architecture and instead force-fit new business needs into it. This is done because in the past it was the right architecture to implement business needs.
- The organization paid a bunch of money for the components of the existing platform and consequently is unwilling to sink those costs to move onto another platform.
- The application has become too brittle to work with and therefore the project team tries not to make any changes unless they are absolutely necessary.

Continual restructuring of architecture to meet today's business needs is essential to maintaining the value of software assets. Software applications and their current business alignment should be discussed periodically beyond the last release date. Creating a small project to make the necessary changes while they are still comparatively small can rectify misalignment. This misalignment could be identified by an IT governance body or product management group and prioritized just like other features and initiatives in the organization. Documentation of user scenarios through applications can help with future decision making about necessary changes. Use cases and other methods for documenting user scenarios should be considered in some cases.

Integrity

Understanding and maintaining the level of integrity of software applications involves infrastructure, monitoring, early detection, and discipline across all project and operational roles:

> *integrity*—noun: an unimpaired condition: soundness [free from flaw, defect, or decay]

Organizations maintain the integrity of their software assets by managing software debt. It is not possible to avoid generating some software debt, but organizing staff and creating the infrastructure that enables identification of trends toward a buildup of software debt early can keep it manageable. The main concepts in the definition of integrity align well to sustaining it:

Free from flaw: A flaw is any fault that affects the end user of an application. Development teams will not remove all flaws that end up in an application during implementation. On the other hand, allowing the project's issue tracker to get denser with flaws while pushing for adding significantly more functionality on top of the flaws will affect the integrity of the application. The chapters on "Quality Debt" and "Executable Design" describe some ways that project teams can reduce the frequency of flaws not being found and reduce the number that do not get fixed.

Free from defect: A defect is any fault that produces incorrect results when users interact with the application. These issues tend to be created in the development process because certain paths through a component of an application have not been tested or issues found are not resolved. The source of defects could be within a component's dependency or within the logic of the application code itself. The chapters on "Technical Debt," "Executable Design," and "Design Debt" give advice on process, practices, and tools that can increase earlier feedback on changes in the small that result in defects in the large.

Free from decay: Decay is accelerated in applications that get delayed feedback on flaws and defects in their components and their integrations. The more delay there is, the greater the chance that a component will decay. This happens often on projects where code is developed for weeks, months, and sometimes over a year before being given to the testers to find the flaws and defects. Another factor in software development that causes a decline in integrity is waiting to integrate components. Delayed integration can be a result of mistrust of the current integration process or how the teams are configured and divide up modules of an application. The chapters on "Quality Debt," "Configuration Management Debt," and "Platform Experience Debt" discuss ways to reduce the impact of integrations and team configurations that will force issues across team dependencies to be found earlier.

There are those who believe architecture should not be concerned with the details of quality assurance, programming, and team configuration. It is my belief that understanding how delaying feedback on flaws, defects, and decay affects the integrity of an application and its potential for meeting the business needs of the future is essential to good architecture strategy. Agile teams will find more long-term success for themselves and their customers if they can improve their ability to handle integrity issues closer to real time with the implementation.

Design

Design is a technique for planning and communicating the conceptual structure of components, applications, and enterprise assets. Communicating the conceptual structure is a way to provide essential information about how the components will function in particular scenarios. Communicating design helps project team members (existing and new) and project stakeholders gain perspective on how the components and applications interact and behave without drowning in the details of code.

Providing people with sufficient information on these structures can involve verbal, tactile, written, and visual examples. For each audience, the appropriate choice of example and perspective may be different and should be considered by project teams. For business stakeholders, user interface design, business process workflows, and automation of manual tasks might be an interesting perspective. On the other hand, a software development team is more interested in integration interfaces, technical infrastructure, and domain-specific entities they will deal with during construction of software functionality. Understanding the needs of your audience is essential to creating the correct form of design artifact.

A common misconception about Agile teams is that they do not perform design activities. This perception is a result of associating design with traditional design document templates and "big design up front." Filling out design documentation, such as detailed designs, has become synonymous with "good" design. Yet most software is riddled with flaws, defects, and decay even though this documentation has been created. Also, writing design documentation, and the practice of evaluating the soundness of the designs, slows the development process and delays essential feedback from stakeholders and users on software they can interact with directly.

Instead of taking a fully up-front design approach, Agile teams design all the time. This does not mean they don't do some up-front design. Rather they focus on essential design for the upcoming functionality desired by the customer. A tool that is useful for establishing a quality focus is a software quality attributes rating tool, as shown in Figures 9.3 and 9.4. People outside the software development team, such as architects and management, do not use such a tool to force the project team to comply. Rather, business and technical stakeholders of a project use it to get alignment about the highest-priority software quality attributes to focus on. Understanding how different software quality attributes are more important when trade-offs need to be made will allow for better decision making and identification of risky technical issues earlier. This information can also be useful when discussing, designing, and estimating work items as software is developed incrementally using Agile methods.

Software Quality Factors	Emphasis Ranking (score 1-5)	3 Must Haves— Business	3 Must Haves— Technical	Notes
Suitability				
Interoperability				
Compliance				
Security				
Maturity				
Fault Tolerance				
Recoverability				
Usability				
Learnability				
Operability				
Performance				
Scalability				
Analyzability				
Changeability				
Testability				
Adaptability				
Installability				
Conformance				
Replaceability				
How to Use:				
Intent of software quality factors rating tool	This tool is not to decide what software attributes will be present in the software product getting developed. It is used to identify which software quality factors the team should put more emphasis on when making trade-off decisions between them and budgeting work tasks. NOTE: If the software quality attributes identified above are not easily understood by customers, ask them for their own terms for similar quality attributes.			
Emphasis ranking	Have the customer score each software quality factor from 1 to 5 (1 being less applicable and 5 being more applicable) in terms of the software product. This activity should involve business and technical stakeholders.			
3 must-haves— business	Ask the business stakeholders what are the three software quality factors they want most and stack rank them from 1 to 3.			
3 must-haves— technical	Ask the technical stakeholders what are the three software quality factors they want most and stack rank them from 1 to 3.			
Notes	Use this column to capture any specific decisions about the software quality that would help during implementation of the software product.			

Figure 9.3   A tool for business and technical stakeholders to identify the most important software quality attributes to focus on in a project. The idea is not only to focus on the identified software quality attributes but also to support trade-off decision making and high-level expectations from business and technical viewpoints.

Characteristics of Software Quality	Terms	Description
Functionality	Suitability Interoperability Compliance Security	Functionality is suitable to all end users Functionality interoperates with other systems easily Functionality is compliant with applicable regulatory guidelines System is secure: confidentiality, integrity, availability, accountability, and assurance
Reliability	Maturity Fault Tolerance Recoverability	System components are proven stable by others System continues operating properly in the event of failure by one or more of its components System recovers from failures in surrounding environment
Usability	Understandability Learnability Operability	Able to use system with little training Supports learning of system functionality with little external interfacing Ability to keep a system in a functioning and operating condition
Efficiency	Performance Scalability	Perceived response is immediate Able to handle increased usage on the appropriate amount of resources
Maintainability	Analyzability Changeability Testability	Ability to figure out how the system functions Ability to change the system components to meet new business needs Ability to create repeatable and specific tests of the system and potential for some to be automated
Portability	Adaptability Installability Conformance Replaceability	Ability to change out system component functionality quickly Ease of installation and reinstallation Conformance to industry and operational standards Ability to replace system in the future

Figure 9.4   Short descriptions of different software quality attributes and categories of focus they align to

Some elements of software architecture are candidates for up-front design. The deciding factor for whether or not to do some design up front on a software architecture element is the following:

> If a team is not able to implement upcoming functionality as working software, meaning usable by the intended users, even without a design decision right now, the team should figure out how to move forward with minimal design decisions made. Delaying design decisions in most cases will allow more valid information to be available at the time a decision gets made.

Some frequent candidates for early project decisions are programming languages, deployment environments, persistence platforms, test automation tools, source code repository, and development tools. In larger organizations, centralized bodies such as enterprise architecture guide some of these early project decisions. It is important when making these early decisions to consider the larger enterprise from operations and maintenance points of view. You might notice that code structures and interface definition are not part of this list. As the development team begins developing desired functionality, based on business value priority, they will decide when these types of design decisions are best made. Not all design decisions can be made right before implementation, so teams should be careful to consider instances when some lead time is needed.

When teams need to make a design decision, it is common for them to use some type of modeling technique to create a common understanding among team members. The rest of this chapter will discuss how modeling, at a high level, works in an Agile approach.

MODELING

I spent quite a bit of time during my technical career learning modeling languages, UML notation, model-driven methods for delivery, and ad hoc design techniques. I spent enough time working with UML that I started teaching classes on its notation. I used model-driven techniques while working on three separate projects along with one other project that I consulted on. I would describe myself as a once heavy-duty user of UML and other standards from the OMG (Object Management Group). The time I spent learning UML and other associated standards was not wasted. My experiences with UML have prompted me to better understand how it is used most effectively and also to probe for more techniques with which to create models.

Modeling can be done using textual formats, but there is an overwhelming tendency to create visual models for communication. Depending upon the audience, textual or visual models are the appropriate formats. On most teams that I work with, using textual representations, either through pseudo code or actual code examples, for integrating libraries or external services into the project is preferable to, but does not exclude, using visual models. It is common for teams to conduct modeling sessions to gain a high-level understanding of how they will work together on a particular area of the project. These modeling sessions usually involve some visual representations to validate understanding with the group. Although visual models are useful within a team, they are also useful for communicating aspects of a project to people outside the team. Examples of visual models for communication outside the team are business process workflows, high-level architecture diagrams, and deployment diagrams.

Using Models for Communication

Deciding on the appropriate format to produce diagrams of models for communication purposes does not start with the diagram format itself. First consider the needs of those who will consume the models before choosing from a plethora of diagram formats available. To choose an appropriate format for your models, consider the following in order of priority:

1. Whether the diagram will be saved for later consumption
2. How formal a format the audience expects the diagram to be delivered in
3. Style of diagrams the intended audience is used to receiving

Diagrams are not always generated so that they can be useful today and into the future. In fact, most diagrams are short-lived and offer just enough information to get a small group of people aligned about how to move forward. If the diagram will not be used in the future, it can be thrown away as soon as it no longer adds value. For short-lived diagrams, transitory media such as whiteboards, pieces of paper, and the back of a napkin are sufficient to make the concepts visible to the group. If you are working with people in remote locations, a virtual whiteboard application or sharing an appropriate application across the network can support effective collaboration around a diagram. Allow diagrams that are transient in nature to be erased, thrown away, or deleted when their stakeholders no longer have a need for them.

When diagrams will be useful for future reading and maintenance, think about how they will be used to decide on the appropriate format. Teams can use photos of diagrams drawn on whiteboards in documentation, even when they are presented to executives. Teams I have worked with have been complimented on not wasting time with beautifying design artifacts and instead focusing on communicating the message.

To understand what form the intended audience for a model finds valuable, I find it best to ask. Answers could range from flow charts to user interface wireframes to state machine diagrams. The format and tool to produce them are important because the members of the intended audience are not always able to extend their capabilities for reviewing new modeling formats. This can be frustrating if the team uses different operating systems or tools from the intended audience, but having a user-focused mentality goes beyond the software delivered to include the maintenance and product strategy. If the intended audience uses Visio to review diagrams, find ways to provide a format that is viewable in Visio if you work in a non-Windows environment. If the intended audience will not be editing the diagram, make it available in a digital image format that can be viewed easily on multiple operating systems.

Finding an appropriate diagram format to convey a model succinctly is important. When describing a business process workflow, showing representations of people involved in a flow diagram rather than a box with text inside communicates a step more effectively. If the business process workflow is automated, using the *Business Process Modeling Notation* (BPMN) to be executed on platforms that understand this standard should be considered in addition to generic flow diagrams.

Generating Artifacts

Creating models is not always necessary before implementing features of an application. This does not mean teams should not gather around a whiteboard to have a discussion about the feature, but a model may not be the appropriate focus of the conversation. At the same time, there are times when models are useful after the fact. Models for design review, maintenance, or getting new people up to speed can be generated from the software instead of created up front. By generating artifacts after the application has been implemented, a team is able to reduce wasted efforts creating artifacts that may never be important. Also, generated artifacts do not necessitate rework because they are a representation of the actual, rather than the expected, implementation. Teams should find tools that will help them generate models from the actual implementation and try them out so that they are able to exploit the tools' capabilities.

SUMMARY

Thinking about software architecture in terms of what level of architecture perspective (component, application, or enterprise) is being discussed helps focus the information that must be communicated. When describing each level of the software architecture, teams can use the S.A.I.D. framework to help them provide appropriate coverage of architecture concerns. When people in the software industry think of architecture, they usually relate it to the *structure* of components, applications, and enterprise infrastructure. It is important not to forget about how the architecture at each of these levels provides *alignment* to business goals and objectives. When describing the architecture, it is not only important to describe the structure but also to illustrate how the internal *integrity* will be validated and maintained over time. To communicate structure, alignment, and integrity of the software architecture at all levels, teams use *design* artifacts to communicate the essential elements for their respective audiences.

At each level of the architecture, keeping stakeholders, either inside or outside the project team, apprised of architecture decisions is useful to coordinate incremental delivery of software components and applications. Be attentive to project stakeholders' perspectives and communicate architecture decisions in a form they can consume. Modeling can be a tool for creating understanding within a group and also for communicating that understanding to others outside the group. Putting models into documentation for communicating proposed designs, architecture decisions, or aspects of software for future maintenance should be done at an appropriate level, considering the value of each model on its own. If documenting models makes sense in the current context, finding the simplest way to incorporate them will reduce wasted effort. An example of this is taking digital pictures of whiteboard diagrams and incorporating those into the document rather than re-creating the diagrams in a formal diagramming tool.

This chapter focused on how software architecture can be communicated within and outside a project team. Rather than filling out software design artifacts as part of a larger process, the focus should be on communication with appropriate stakeholders so that architecture decisions can be validated. Project teams doing incremental delivery of software make software design decisions continuously and should find ways to communicate with stakeholders about the decisions that have the most potential to impact them. Use the three levels of architecture perspective, the S.A.I.D. (structure, alignment, integrity, and design) acronym, and effective modeling techniques to help focus these communications.

Chapter 10

TECHNOLOGY EVALUATION STYLES

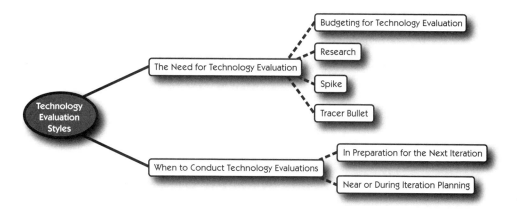

True genius resides in the capacity for evaluation of uncertain, hazardous, and conflicting information.

—*Winston Churchill*

THE NEED FOR TECHNOLOGY EVALUATION

Product requirements evolve throughout the life of a project. As they evolve, technical aspects of the product implementation also evolve. Some features involve technology, skills, and knowledge that the development team does not currently have. In order to help the customer understand the cost of these features, the team needs to gain enough of the skills and knowledge necessary to estimate the implementation. The team may ask a customer to budget for this skill- and knowledge-gaining time so that it will be properly accounted for and used in prioritization of features. Agile teams use the following technology evaluation styles to meet the evolving needs of the product:[1]

---

1. Although these terms were defined individually elsewhere, a team that I worked with defined them succinctly during a project in 2004. This team included Mickey Phoenix, Paul J. Dupuy, Charles Liu, and Jonathon Golden. Thank you, all.

- **Research:** broad, foundational gaining of knowledge to decide what to spike or to obtain the ability to estimate features desired in the future
- **Spike:** a quick and dirty implementation, designed to be thrown away, to gain knowledge about a larger feature or integrating technology
- **Tracer bullet:** a narrow implementation in production quality of a large feature to be implemented into the product later that will enable the team to better estimate the remaining feature work

Research and spikes are used when the team does not have enough skill or knowledge to estimate a feature. The team must find a potential solution (research) or experiment with a potential solution (spike) in order to give an estimate for the feature. A tracer bullet is used to break down a large feature into a part of the feature that will enable the team to understand its entirety. This usually involves implementing the "happy path," the path through a feature when everything works as planned with few to no exceptions, through the technology stack involved in the full feature implementation. As a team implements functionality using an iterative and incremental approach, they use these technology evaluation styles to create knowledge and understanding and apply them to the rest of the product's development and beyond.

Budgeting for Technology Evaluation

Research and spikes are budgeted activities that are estimated by the team and proposed to the customer for deciding on their priority. These technology evaluation styles can affect product plans negatively, such as when unexpected costs and risks are found too late in the release cycle. The release could be in jeopardy if the customer and team are not able to respond effectively to the new risks. Therefore, the customer is involved in deciding whether the budget should be used to further explore solutions or to move on to other priority features of the product that do not require these evaluation costs.

The customer should not take the need for a technology evaluation by the team lightly. If the team has a question related to implementation of an upcoming feature, the evaluation process allows for risk to be reduced significantly and could save downstream costs to the customer as new features are implemented into the product. Some projects delay technical risk areas until later in the release cycle. If the customer is fairly certain that the feature will be needed for the release, the idea of delaying technical evaluation should not be entertained. Delayed risk on release implementation unknowns results in late surprises, leading to additional costs and missing the scheduled release date.

Tracer bullets, on the other hand, are used to take a small slice of a complicated feature to figure out how difficult it will be to implement the remaining portions of the feature. Therefore, it is treated as a normal elaboration of the feature request and not as a budgeted activity. From this narrow implementation the customer can get a better estimate of the work remaining to implement the feature. The team can help the customer describe a tracer bullet of functionality that will inform them about technical unknowns and still establish progress toward the completion of the larger feature.

Research

When a team does not already have a potential solution to an issue or for an upcoming feature, they have to conduct some research. Research has become considerably easier with the quality of search engines, information provided by vendors, open-source forums, and passionate developers who enjoy sharing their experience with the online community. Teams, and indirectly their customers, are able to take advantage of increased and higher-quality information that is provided online to build better products faster. In addition to the web, there are many magazines, books, and local special interest groups that represent potential sources of information.

Research usually begins with a list of desired solution attributes for an issue or feature. While working on a Multimedia Messaging Service (MMS) performance-monitoring tool, our team recognized the need for a Wireless Application Protocol (WAP) stack. The WAP stack would allow our tool to connect with the WAP gateway to send an MMS message through the cellular company's network. Some of the desired solution attributes for the WAP stack were:

- To initiate an MMS transmission through the WAP gateway
- Could be developed in Java and interfaced with the WAP stack API
- Configurable at runtime

Based on this short list of desired solution attributes, we were able to search for some potential solutions. Our team took one week to search the web, ask experienced WAP stack developers, and score the tools based on our initial criteria. Upon completion of this research we found a WAP stack that met our needs well enough. We were unable to find a mature WAP stack written in Java, so we went with one that was written in C++. I had done a fair bit of Java Native Interface (JNI) development in the past, so we decided we could easily integrate the WAP stack into our tool.

Research should be discussed with the customer to help the customer understand what the team will achieve through the research. The discussion should include providing the customer with an approximate cost for the research. In the preceding story, we explained to the customer that we needed one week of two people's time to complete the research. At that point the customer is able to make a decision about whether the issue or feature is worth spending this portion of the budget on. In our case, connecting with the WAP gateway was an essential feature of the tool and it was a no-brainer to move forward with the research.

Spike

An issue arose when a team I was working with was developing an application that captured metadata around mobile content. We needed to find a technical solution that delivered mobile content and played it in the web browser without giving access to the actual file. The current client application was using Macromedia Flash as the client presentation technology. Our team researched which media formats and bit qualities could play in the Flash Player, and the results seemed mixed about actual content specifications that worked for our needs. The mobile content we delivered came in seven formats, each with multiple bit qualities. We decided to conduct a spike in order to figure out which of the formats and bit qualities actually worked.

Since the mobile content server platform already allowed us to find all of the media file variations for a particular piece of content, we created a small integration test that played these files in the Flash Player client. The tests reloaded the client with each format and bit quality of the media content, then reported success or failure results back to the server. Upon completion of this test we were able to verify the various content formats and bit qualities that worked. This information showed our customer that this solution worked well enough to put out version 1.0 within the Flash Player.

The spike that was conducted in this scenario was a quick and dirty implementation of a potential solution to learn if it met the customer's desired feature criteria. Our team knew that the code written for this spike would be thrown away but that its intent was to verify the potential solution. There is an essential element to conducting spikes that should not be taken lightly:

Code written for spikes should always be thrown away.

This may seem arbitrary, but when testing a potential solution, teams do not focus on the design of the code. Instead, they put much of their effort into just getting it to work. In my experience, if emphasis is not placed on the act of throwing away the code from a spike, this code may slip into your production deployments.

Tracer Bullet

Dave Thomas described the use of tracer bullets in gunnery artillery this way:

> *If your target is moving, or if you don't know all the factors, you use tracer bullets—little phosphorous rounds intermixed with real rounds in your gun. As you fire, you can actually see the tracer bullets. And where they are landing is where the actual bullets are landing. If you're not quite on target—because you can see if you're not on target—you can adjust your position.*[2]

The idea behind a tracer bullet is to get feedback quickly about how close we are to the target. In software this means that we take a thin slice of a feature and implement it through the entire architecture. If we are too far off the requested target, we can redirect our efforts and have only lost the time to construct a thin slice. Through that low-cost effort we have gained valuable knowledge about the entire feature. If we are close to what is requested, we can give the customer a fairly good cost estimate for the rest of the feature.

From a planning perspective, a tracer bullet is estimated just as a team would estimate any other feature request. A tracer bullet is to be implemented in production quality and is kept in the product. Many times the initial tracer bullet is enhanced during implementation of subsequent portions of the larger feature. This means that it is important to make the initial tracer bullet implementation easily changeable using good design constructs. I am not advocating designing up front but rather leaving the implementation in a healthy state upon completion.

During one of my consulting engagements, a large feature was identified that had some technical obstacles that had to be overcome before the teams felt comfortable breaking it down or estimating its cost. The teams were implementing a system using an enterprise service bus (ESB) to integrate multiple platform data sources. Most of the team members had not worked with the ESB platform before, so they needed to learn more about it. One team took

---

2. Bill Venners, Artima Developer, "Tracer Bullets and Prototypes: A Conversation with Andy Hunt and Dave Thomas, Part VIII," April 21, 2003, www.artima.com/intv/tracer.html, p. 1.

on this knowledge-gaining activity by breaking out a small slice of functionality from the original feature and pulling it into their iteration plan. This was the original user story:

> **As a customer service rep, I want to find a customer's information from all of our systems so that I can quickly respond to the customer's needs.**

The team members discussed how they should break up this large user story into a slice that would minimize data manipulation and still integrate data from all applicable platforms they were working with. They wanted to put emphasis on the technical challenges rather than the user experience because this is what they knew least about at that time. They decided that presenting the customer's name along with associated unique identifiers from all platforms would prove that they understood the technical integration issues and were able to present data to the users. Here is the user story that represented a tracer bullet sliced from the original feature:

> **As a customer service rep, I want to see a customer's uniquely identified information from all systems so that I am assured more information can be retrieved later.**

After implementing this user story in the product, the team understood the configuration of the multiple platform integration interfaces on the ESB along with potential data management issues to be worked out in later iterations. The team then helped the customer break down the larger user story into a list of smaller user stories that could be estimated.

A tracer bullet allows the team to take a thin slice of functionality from a larger feature and learn about its technical implications. Once the team understands more about the technical solution, they can focus their efforts on delivering the rest of the feature to the users.

WHEN TO CONDUCT TECHNOLOGY EVALUATIONS

There are a couple of options regarding when to conduct the actual evaluation activities. Many teams identify the need during or fairly close to actual iteration planning activities. In these cases the amount of time available for conducting the evaluation is limited and usually not enough to allow the team to make a commitment on the desired feature that produced the need. Therefore, there is another option that teams have used successfully: Conduct technology evaluations for high-priority features during the last half of the previous iteration. How much time is needed and whether that amount of time will impact the current iteration should be considered. If the technology evaluation can be supported in the last half of the current iteration, sufficient information could be available at the next iteration's planning meeting so the team can commit to delivering the high-priority feature.

In Preparation for the Next Iteration

Many teams using an Agile delivery model meet with the customer and other product definition people to discuss what is coming up around mid-iteration or just thereafter. The purpose of this meeting is for the customer to provide the team with clarity about upcoming features and for the team to provide an estimate of cost for each feature. At times the development team identifies the need for a technology evaluation for one of the upcoming features. The team creates a new work item prefixed or somehow identified as an evaluation item and then provides the customer with an estimate for the amount of time needed to find out what they need to estimate the original work item. This might take the form of "Bill and I need two days each to figure out how to integrate with our billing system." Now the customer has an estimated cost and can decide whether this would be a good use of budget for the feature and the overall priorities. If the customer is willing to allocate budget to clarify technical implementation unknowns for the feature, the team can decide to work on it before the end of the current iteration.

It is recommended that 5% to 10% of a team's potential iteration capacity be used planning for the next iteration.[3] This allotment is usually sufficient to conduct short evaluations while in the current iteration. Teams can use this time for evaluations and other improvement activities that will enhance the future product delivery. They should make sure that putting effort into this evaluation does not impede their ability to meet their current iteration commitments.

If the team is able to conduct the evaluation before the upcoming iteration planning meeting, the customer does not have to wait an entire iteration to get the desired work item into an iteration. The team could learn enough about the technical implementation for the work item that they commit to deliver all or part of it during the upcoming iteration. If the results of an evaluation show the work item is going beyond the budget allocated to work on it, the team should work with the customer to see if more time should be allocated to the evaluation.

---

3. Ken Schwaber, *The Enterprise and Scrum* (Microsoft Press, 2007).

Near or During Iteration Planning

Sometimes the evaluation estimate is too large to conduct in the current iteration or it is identified too close to iteration planning. In this case a team brings the evaluation into the next iteration and asks the customer to wait for the actual feature implementation until the following iteration. The reason a team does not commit to both the evaluation work and the desired feature is that they cannot commit to highly ambiguous work. If the team believes the technical implementation has enough unknowns that an evaluation is necessary, the cost for delivery could vary greatly for the desired functionality. This ambiguity in estimated time to deliver the functionality could affect delivery of other functionality the team commits to during the iteration.

If the customer asks for both the evaluation and the functionality to be worked on during the same iteration, a team should set aside enough buffer for potential budget overrun. The lack of technical understanding surrounding the functional implementation of the desired feature can easily get out of control. Anybody who has written software that introduces a new capability, found a surprise issue, and then begun to debug the issue knows that this process could take an unpredictable amount of time to finish. This approach should be used rarely and with caution.

SUMMARY

A team uses technology evaluations when there are unknowns associated with upcoming features. Teams use technology evaluations to gain a better understanding of how the actual implementation can be done effectively given the feature's needs and constraints. After the team has enough knowledge about the technical implementation, the customer can get a fairly good estimate of cost for the desired functionality.

Spikes and research activities are budgeted so that the customer can decide if the evaluation process is worth pursuing in relation to other feature priorities. The customer should not take the need for an evolutionary evaluation lightly or wait until it is too late in the release cycle to prioritize its execution. This could put undue risk on the release, which can result in missed dates and increased cost to the customer.

Tracer bullets are used to break down larger features so that the team can understand their technical implications better. Usually this involves breaking a feature down into a work item that involves implementing a "happy path" through the technical components that will be impacted by the feature. From this exercise the team can better understand the entire feature and how to break down the larger feature with the associated estimates.

Chapter 11

PLATFORM EXPERIENCE DEBT

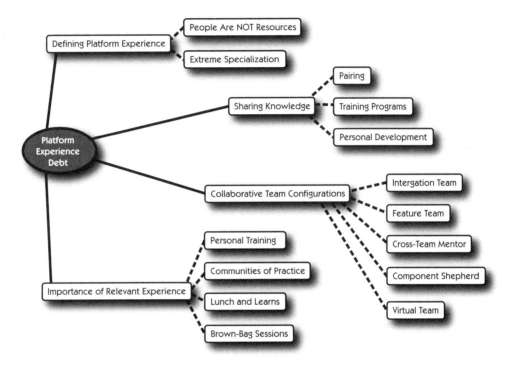

As in Nature, if an organization is too inflexible or stands still too long it will get eaten.

—*James Burke (author and historian)*

DEFINING PLATFORM EXPERIENCE

Software is a knowledge-based industry. Each year brings the emergence of new technology options, new ways of applying technology, and new business models that involve software. The methods that project teams use to deliver software continue to be enhanced through tools, process, and education. Platform experience is *the skills and knowledge inherent in developing software.*

Software development takes knowledge and skill. People do not acquire this knowledge and skill without spending years delivering software. There is a need to specialize in specific functions within the software development realm in order to play a part in projects early in our careers. We might be programmers, testers, analysts, or project managers. With each day we get a little more proficient in a specific functional area. It feels good to be competent in our jobs.

People Are NOT Resources

Software development has become more complex with each passing year. How to parcel out work to efficiently deliver software is a difficult problem to solve. Companies have "resource" managers who are given the responsibility to put people into positions that will fit the constraints of multiple projects. These people, sometimes referred to as "resources," are allocated to different project teams based on their particular skills and knowledge. It is a shell game. Our industry manages projects based on wrong estimates and incomplete requirements, then people are moved around as "resources" to keep them busy and persuade stakeholders that everything is being done to get their project finished.

People are NOT resources!

That is, at least not in the sense that resources are equivalent to widgets in a factory. A person who has only been a Visual Basic programmer cannot be expected to thrive as a C++ programmer. But the person is a programmer, right? Manual testers cannot easily jump into a software development engineer in test (SDET) role if they have not coded before. But they are testers, right?

The focus on role and project causes true progress to be opaque to stakeholders. The analysis is "done," but we still have to build the software. The code is "done," but we still have to integrate it. The code is "done" and ready to test, but we still have to write some code to fix the bugs that are found. The testing is "done," but we still have a number of bugs that have not been resolved in the bug tracking system. Each person, in his or her role, is "done." And yet the project is not "done." Stakeholders are left to deal with learning about the software not being done too late in the project and are not able to make appropriate plans to mitigate the project issues.

There are principles in the Agile Manifesto that give guidance on working with stakeholders:

Our highest priority is to satisfy the customer through early and continuous delivery of valuable software.

Welcome changing requirements, even late in development. Agile processes harness change for the customer's competitive advantage.

Deliver working software frequently, from a couple of weeks to a couple of months, with a preference to the shorter timescale.

Business people and developers must work together daily throughout the project.

Working software is the primary measure of progress.[1]

Each of these principles focuses on transparency and visibility as important aspects of developing software and showing progress to stakeholders. Agile software development methods flip the problem on its head. The ability to deliver on a bunch of projects is not significantly enhanced by moving people around. The capability of a software development organization to deliver a bunch of projects faster is based on how the people in that organization learn to work together more effectively.

> **Rather than creating teams to work on projects, let's find ways to give projects to cross-functional teams.**

It is how those teams create knowledge, learn surrounding skills, share information, and evolve their capabilities that will enable better delivery of valuable software. Extreme specialization, knowledge silos, and not enhancing skills are what will stifle the capabilities of an organization to meet the needs of the business.

Extreme Specialization

The good feelings associated with doing our job function competently are also accompanied by ideas about how our job should be done. We might isolate ourselves so we can do our job function without dealing with others who don't understand it as we do. As we continue to isolate ourselves, we become masters of our domain and other people ask for our help because they need the knowledge and skill we have. Others in the organization depend on us too much to get their work "done." In larger organizations this situation is common and usually involves specific functional departments, such as database administration and configuration management.

---

1. "Principles behind the Agile Manifesto," www.agilemanifesto.org/principles.htm, 2001.

Effective software development involves many disciplines: analysis, design, database administration, programming, testing, configuration management, and system administration. Extreme specialization tends to show up where there are crosscutting concerns for projects, when server environment usage needs to be optimized across many project teams, when database modifications can negatively affect other project teams and existing software installations. Companies tend to isolate these crosscutting concerns into silos, and this begins the process of isolating knowledge. These are sometimes referred to as "knowledge silos" and cause delivery of software to be throttled based on the capability of the silos to meet demands on their services.

Organizations with legacy software that is 20 or more years old often suffer extreme specialization problems. One organization with 20-plus applications that are over 20 years old found itself in a bind. One year prior to my consulting with them on Agile methods, a COBOL programmer had retired after about 20 years with the company. Unfortunately, this programmer had been the only person who had worked with five systems in the past 10 to 15 years. The company learned that this was a problem quickly when other programmers were not able to make requested changes to these applications in a timely manner. This was not going to suffice because there were critical updates that had to be implemented quickly because of regulatory concerns. The retired programmer was not interested in working temporarily for even a hugely increased wage. This was not the full extent of the company's problem. There were five more programmers who had been in a similar situation over the past 10 years and they were likely to retire within 2 to 4 years as well. Silos of knowledge create the potential for stoppages in delivery and can lead to heavy losses for the organization. The fact that I have been to two more companies in similar situations to consult on Agile makes this problem even scarier.

At some point, someone other than us will have to maintain our systems. In the push for "productivity," management continues to look for functional specialists who can perform a particular task faster. The thought is that if all job functions necessary to deliver a release are performing optimally, handoffs will be quicker, individuals will become more productive in their functional roles, and there will be fewer mistakes. Running software development in this manner is an attempt to create an assembly line. The problem is that software is not put together with existing parts using highly repetitive tasks as is necessary with assembly lines. The assumed individual productivity gains give way to centralization of knowledge and difficulty keeping a holistic view of the system as it is being developed. These issues are the foundation of platform experience debt.

Sharing Knowledge

In the paper "The New New Product Development Game,"[2] a strong influence on the creation of the Scrum framework, one of the characteristics recognized in the researched companies was their ability to transfer learning across the organization. Sharing individual and team learning with other teams supports continuous improvement in an organization. There are a few ways that I have seen organizations share knowledge effectively across Agile teams:

- Pairing
- Training programs
- Personal development
- Collaborative team configurations

Taking an approach that includes pairing, training, personal development, and collaborative team configurations moves knowledge around inside a software development organization and puts more people in positions to contribute to successful and sustainable technology outcomes.

Pairing

It is obvious that pair programming provides an opportunity to move knowledge between two people. The act of working together on the same software artifacts, designs, and scripts allows continuous information exchange. Pairing can be taken a step further to support additional knowledge sharing within and across teams.

In the practice of pair programming, one person from the pair acts as the *driver* and the other person acts as the *navigator*. This focus on roles within the pair gives each person a responsibility. The driver is focused on writing the automated unit tests and implementation code, and the navigator observes and points out issues as the driver types. This has been shown to reduce defects considerably and increase team morale.[3]

---

2. Hirotaka Takeuchi and Ikujiro Nonaka, "The New New Product Development Game," *Harvard Business Review* (January–February 1986).

3. Alistair Cockburn and Laurie Williams, "The Costs and Benefits of Pair Programming," *Proceedings of the First International Conference on Extreme Programming and Flexible Processes in Software Engineering* (XP2000).

In 2003, a variation on pair programming was written about on c2.com called the *Ping Pong Pattern*.[4] The basic pattern involves two team members whom I will name "Dave" and "Alice":

1. Dave writes a unit test and shows it fails, then passes control to Alice.
2. Alice writes the implementation code that makes the test pass.
3. Alice writes the next unit test and shows it fails, then passes control to Dave.
4. Dave writes the implementation code that makes the test pass, and so on.

Refactoring is done at any point during the pairing session when the tests are passing. This approach allows both pairing participants to switch between navigator and driver every few minutes. It focuses less on a person taking a role in the pairing session and more on sharing ideas through the software under development.

Going beyond a single pair working together, Arlo Belshee suggested the idea of a *pair net*[5] to describe the effects of promiscuity in pair programming partners and the spreading of knowledge across a human network. When a pair of programmers work together for a session or more, they share knowledge between them. When pairs are switched, the knowledge shared between the original pair is radiated to their new pairing partners. Thus, there are now four people with the shared knowledge. The network created through promiscuous pair programming proliferates the shared knowledge, and the most useful information can be acted upon.[6]

Promiscuous pairing was based on the idea of *beginner's mind:*

> *In the beginner's mind there are many possibilities, but in the expert's there are few.*[7]

I am still surprised by how much I learn from others, whether a teammate, someone with whom I am consulting, or someone I meet in passing, on subjects about which I believed myself to have a lot of knowledge. It is my opinion that having an open mind to whatever will be revealed next is an essential element in sharing knowledge. Although one of the pairing partners is suppos-

---

4. http://c2.com/cgi/wiki?PairProgrammingPingPongPattern.
5. Arlo Belshee, "Promiscuous Pairing and Beginner's Mind: Embrace Inexperience," *Proceedings of the Agile Development Conference* (2005), pp. 125–31.
6. Mitch Lacey, "Adventures in Promiscuous Pairing: Seeking Beginner's Mind," *Proceedings*, Agile 2006, pp. 263–69.
7. Shunryu Suzuki, *Zen Mind, Beginner's Mind* (Weatherhill, 1973).

edly more senior or knowledgeable in a particular area he or she is working in, allowing for the other partner's participation in the development activities results in better knowledge sharing and usually learning for both partners.

Promiscuous pairing can be used beyond the edges of the team, as well. At times, one team may have skills and knowledge that are needed on another team for some amount of time. If teams are able to negotiate a plan around the transaction, a team member could provide services for 50% or more of his or her capacity per iteration to the other team. The negotiation could include a pair instead of an individual to provide the services to the other team. This would allow knowledge sharing to be radiated to the other team in incremental doses. Over time, it is possible that the other team will gain competency in the skills and knowledge they desired and then be able to radiate that knowledge to others.

Training Programs

When the gap between those people who have substantial knowledge about the technology and the domain and those who are novices is too large, pairing alone probably does not suffice. There are decisions and instinctual acts that those who are extremely familiar with the software have developed during their daily work. These are the parts of software development efforts that enable some people to move faster than others because of their knowledge and familiarity with a technology or application. Finding a way to capture this knowledge for broader consumption is a way to share the knowledge. Training programs can be created within an organization to help move knowledge beyond the team. Development of training materials involves at least the following:

- Making instinctual knowledge explicit
- Describing important structures as simply as possible
- Finding teaching methods that support the learning process
- Defining exercises that provide realization of content

This list of items is not easy to put into practice. It takes considerable focus to provide effective training. The benefit training can provide is that knowledge can be spread to many more people faster. This is especially valuable when a company is growing rapidly beyond a base group of individuals. The gap in knowledge can be enormous, and therefore finding ways to close the gap is essential to establishing positive growth. This book will not go into methods for developing training materials; that is a book unto itself. Instead, find people, maybe outside of your company, with competencies in developing training materials to help with this process.

Personal Development

Getting stuck in a technology rut can become a debt to the organization, as well. Tools, libraries, and platforms are evolving and improving continually. When a company does not incorporate updated technologies, it is in danger of becoming outdated. This leads to the company not getting the best talent and reduces the chances that the software design will evolve to meet new business requests in the future.

It is not easy to keep up-to-date with technology changes. There is a skill in identifying the technologies that are worth incorporating into an organization's software development efforts. Individuals and teams have to experiment with different technologies regularly to keep up and to choose appropriate ones for the organization's needs. Some organizations institutionalize personal development time, such as requiring all team members to work on an open-source project for four hours every Friday.

Personal Development Day

Our team inherited a mobile application platform that had 1 million lines of code, 16 SQL Server databases, 15 programming languages, and absolutely no test cases, not even manual test scripts. After continually breaking the code while trying to implement new features, a team member named Paul Dupuy brought in a tool he had developed off-hours that he thought might help us work with this platform. After three iterations using the new tool, now called StoryTestIQ, the team was delivering at four times its previous throughput.

Our team and customer found this new tool so helpful to the development effort that we decided to work on this and other tools every Friday. This allowed us to enhance StoryTestIQ and ultimately helped the team to deliver six times throughput in three months of its use for our customer. StoryTestIQ was not the only technology that the team worked with during this time. We also found better ways to perform continuous integration and relational database optimizations.

Your organization may find other ways to allow teams to experiment and improve their software development efforts. In return, they will optimize the value they deliver with the same amount of effort expended.

COLLABORATIVE TEAM CONFIGURATIONS

When software development on a single platform or product scales beyond one team, the way those teams are configured can heavily influence whether knowledge is shared or not. Project teams that scale and want to use an Agile software development approach should think about how to create small, cross-functional teams. Cross-functional teams represent a collection of individuals with different but complementary software development skills who are able to deliver increments of software from feature definition to release.

Putting in place an organizational design with cross-functional teams at its core is not easy for organizations. Creating truly cross-functional teams in an organization can be counter to the existing culture and management hierarchy. The current software architecture could be too complicated for any one team of five to nine people to take a feature all the way to potentially shippable. The existing legacy software could be in a state that makes it difficult to get all cross-functional roles of a team efficiently working on it. Change is difficult. Project teams must decide whether they are willing to make the transition to cross-functional teams and work through the issues inherent in such a change.

Once a team decides to ascribe to being cross-functional, there are some team configurations that could help them get started and support scaling to multiple teams:

- Integration team
- Feature team
- Cross-team mentor
- Component shepherd
- Virtual team

The *feature team* configuration for scaling of teams provides the most flexibility and focus on value delivered out of all these patterns. Flexibility is supported because there is more than one team that has knowledge about how to implement the next most valuable backlog item. Value is delivered by each team staffed to fully deliver independent features. The feature team configuration is the most difficult to implement for organizations and project teams.

When the feature team configuration creates significant issues for the current organizational structure and architecture, using the *integration team* configuration can be a good transitional approach. These challenges tend to stem from extreme specialization and an overcomplicated or less maintainable product architecture. The integration team configuration pattern uses component-focused teams with continuous integration teams to ensure frequent integration.

The *virtual team* and *component shepherd* configurations can be used with either feature team or integration team configurations. The *virtual team* configuration supports the coordination of decisions across teams. The *component shep-herd* configuration is used to help distribute knowledge about a particular component in the software's architecture to more people while maintaining a consistent design. Each of these team configurations will be discussed in the following sections with their respective pros and cons.

Integration Team

The integration team configuration is used to break up larger product features across multiple teams working on different aspects of the solution. Each team focuses on an area of the product or component of the architecture involved in the solution. A single product roadmap and vision drive the development across all teams and are managed by the *Chief Product Owner*. Since the pieces involved in the solution are too numerous for the Chief Product Owner to know all the details, a *product definition team* supports that role in breaking down larger initiatives on the product roadmap into a Product Backlog associated with each component. The product definition team includes people from areas beyond product ownership such as quality assurance, enterprise architecture, and business analysis. Each Product Backlog has a person in the role of Product Owner managing it and maintaining alignment with the Chief Product Owner.

All of the Product Backlogs are prioritized by the Product Owners and esti-mated by the team(s) that will be pulling and implementing items for their component. The teams are still cross-functional, so they are able to deliver finished features on their component of the solution. These teams are usually referred to as *component teams* because they focus on a single component of the application's architecture.

It is recommended that all teams conduct planning on the first day and reviews of their deliverables on the last day of the iteration together. The iter-ation planning meeting involves the entire project team. The Chief Product Owner describes the higher-level focus for all teams during the iteration at the beginning of planning. Then each team breaks out into their own groups focused on their Product Backlog items aligned with the focus described. The teams break down Product Backlog items into tasks describing how they will implement the functionality. When necessary, each team coordinates its planning with other teams they are dependent on. Figure 11.1 portrays the integration team configuration in relation to product definition and compo-nent teams.

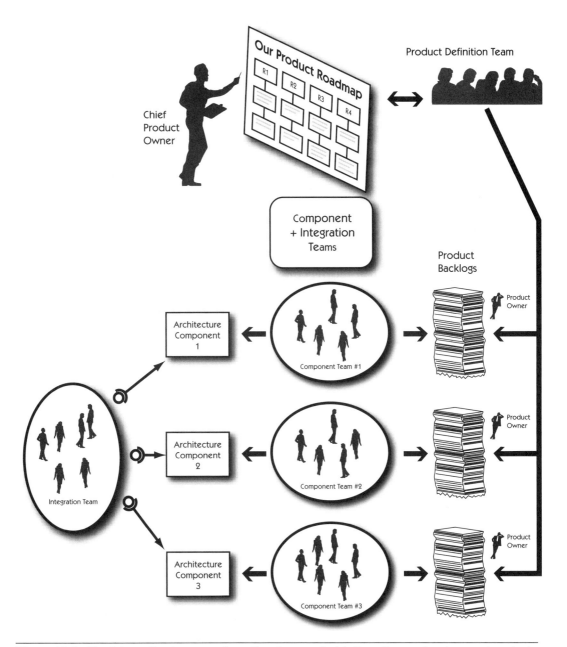

Figure 11.1 The integration team configuration for a scaled Agile software development project. Component teams work off their own Product Backlogs, and the integration team integrates component functionality to provide the solution desired.

During the iteration, each component team constructs features. There is still a need to integrate their parts of the solution with other component implementations happening in parallel. This is where the integration team comes in. The integration team is responsible for implementing the integration plumbing across components for features being implemented and showing that they work together by the end of the iteration. This is quite different from traditional software development where a similar team might hand design documentation to a team to implement the needed integrations. This would include interface specifications and protocols. The integration team in this case is expected to implement these and therefore must have access to software artifacts for each component to integrate them together.

On the last day of the iteration, the entire project team conducts a review of the deliverables with stakeholders. Project teams I consulted with in the past set this up like a science fair. Each component team has its own table in a large room or multiple rooms in an adjacent area. The teams put up posters describing what they implemented that iteration along with any supporting iteration data. The integration team also has a table where they show all of the component implementation functioning together. Stakeholders are able to come in during a 90- to 120-minute time box and provide feedback on the deliverables. This allows each stakeholder to focus on aspects of the delivery he or she is most interested in and keeps the review session to an appropriate duration.

The feature team configuration, to be discussed in the next section, is the preferred method compared to the integration team configuration because

- The integration team configuration continues silos of knowledge for components of the solution architecture.
- The breakdown of larger product features based on components in the solution architecture causes project teams to not always work on the highest feature priorities.
- The focus on components of solution architecture perpetuates the isolation of specialized roles and reduces cross-fertilization of skills and knowledge.
- It is difficult to track the progress of a single feature across team deliverables.

Although the feature team configuration is the preferred method for implementing Agile software development across multiple teams, there are reasons that an organization might choose the integration team configuration:

- The project team has extreme specialization. One organization at which I consulted was developing a VoIP platform for commercial installations. The number of protocols, hardware aspects, and technologies involved combined with previous methods of breaking up work had left the project team with only a 2-to-1 ratio of people to specialization across six Scrum teams of around eight people each.
- Components in existing architecture are too numerous, disparate, and complex on their own. A client I consulted with had four different COTS packages and four more custom applications that were all going to be integrated to provide a solution. There were five teams to work across all eight components with a need to scale knowledge out to almost half of all the teams about each component.

The integration team configuration pattern could be used as a transition toward the feature team configuration. Project teams that wish to move toward becoming feature teams need to find ways to share knowledge across component teams and simplify the solution architecture or how they work with it. This could include big changes to the solution architecture's structure and components. When possible, the integration team configuration should be avoided. Instead, focus on implementing the feature team configuration to the best of the project team's ability.

Feature Team

Feature teams are described in great detail in Craig Larman and Bas Vodde's book *Scaling Lean and Agile Development*[8] in Chapter 7. They have done a wonderful job of going into great detail about feature teams, and it is highly recommended that you read their book when implementing the feature team configuration across an organizational unit. This book will not re-create the content from their book but there will be some overlap. In this section, we will focus on how to implement the feature team configuration and attributes that enhance its effectiveness.

Just as in the integration team configuration, the Chief Product Owner manages the product vision and roadmap with the support of a product definition team to gather inputs across the domain and technology stack. Rather than breaking up items on the product roadmap across multiple Product Backlogs, the product definition team, in conjunction with the Chief Product Owner, creates a single Product Backlog. The product definition team priori-

---

8. Craig Larman and Bas Vodde, *Scaling Lean and Agile Development* (Addison-Wesley, 2008).

tizes the Product Backlog, and when there are conflicts the Chief Product Owner is the tiebreaker.

All teams are now feature teams and pull from the top of the Product Backlog alongside the other feature teams. The feature teams work together to estimate the Product Backlog items and distribute them based on priorities across teams. This reduces the risk of any single team not delivering all of the highest-priority features in the iteration. The feature teams conduct planning and review together just as in the integration team configuration. During the iteration, representatives from each feature team should get together daily and solve any integration issues that cross team boundaries. Figure 11.2 shows the feature team configuration in relation to product definition and architectural components.

The following is a list of reasons why the feature team configuration is effective for Agile software development:

- Skills and knowledge are transferred based on need to more people in the organization.
- More people are put into a position of making decisions local to implementation concerns when more information is available.
- Teams are always working on the highest priorities.
- Each team delivers functionality that meets the needs of application users directly.
- Software architecture is naturally simplified to enable a single team to deliver features.

Here are some common issues that occur when instantiating the feature team configuration within an organization:

- Not every team has the skills and knowledge needed to implement the next-in-priority Product Backlog item.
- The design of feature implementations across components of the solution architecture could become haphazard.
- Feature teams could get stuck on design decisions.

Each of these issues has additional configuration nuances that help mitigate their impact. It is natural for there to be times in a feature-team-based project when people must learn new skills. For some individuals this can be scary and uncomfortable. Using the cross-team mentor configuration allows members from another team with the skill set the individual needs to learn to mentor the person directly during the iteration. To keep the design of a com-

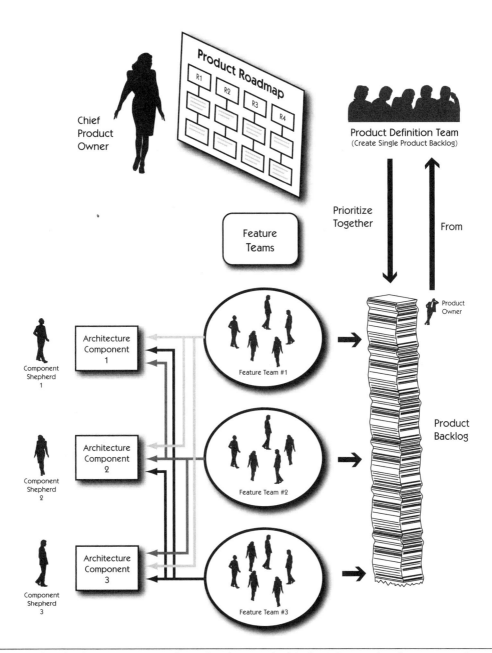

Figure 11.2 The feature team configuration for a scaled Agile software development project. Feature teams pull from a single Product Backlog defined by the product definition team and Chief Product Owner.

ponent that is being updated by multiple teams maintainable, one or more component shepherds could be asked to watch updates to the component and a cross-team mentor could work with individuals on specific design issues. When design decisions become large enough to impact the structure of the architecture being implemented upon by multiple teams, it could be difficult to gain consensus. A virtual team that crosses the boundaries of each feature team can bring new design issues, work with peers to develop the planned solution, and communicate it back to their own team. The next sections will go into more detail about each of these cross-team configurations.

Cross-Team Mentor

Sharing knowledge across teams is sometimes necessary when multiple teams are implementing features throughout an application's structure. The need for support is usually identified during iteration planning. If teams are planning at the same time, one team may make a deal with another team that has someone who can help them as a *cross-team mentor*. The cross-team mentor plans to use 50% or 100% of the iteration capacity to provide hands-on support to the team in need.

The cross-team mentor configuration can also be done in pairs. If both teams are doing pair programming in a disciplined manner, moving in pairs may be more natural. The pairs should use promiscuous pairing techniques to mingle with members of the other team.

When using the cross-team mentor configuration, it is important to validate the planned team capacity impacts with the appropriate Product Owners for the team's Product Backlogs. When the teams are part of a feature team configuration this is less problematic because they will be working from a single Product Backlog. The teams are then thought to be doing what is best to implement the highest-priority Product Backlog items.

Component Shepherd

Teams implementing Agile software development methods at scale quickly find there are people who have specialized skills and knowledge needed by all teams to implement vertical slices of functionality through all components of the application. In the past, these people might have been described as "shared resources" and were the go-to people for making changes to that application component. Having a single person or not enough people with the ability to change an application component that has even small, but continuous, changes to support new functionality causes the entire project to move more slowly. Making changes to this application component becomes a wait state in the delivery process as the specialist serially works through the requests.

The *component shepherd* configuration changes this by allowing teams to make changes freely. Of course, each team makes an assessment of its abilities to actually make the changes necessary before doing so. When team members are not confident about their ability to make the changes satisfactorily, they ask for a cross-team mentor. If they do feel comfortable enough to make the necessary changes, the component shepherd will find issues with any changes, usually by watching check-ins to source control, using 50% of planned capacity. When the component shepherd identifies a design issue with a change, he or she works with the team that made the change to help them understand the issue and how to enhance the implementation. By doing this, the component shepherd moves skills and knowledge to more teams based on the actual needs of the software under development.

Being a component shepherd is a significant responsibility. It is difficult to consult with a team without being perceived as an interruption or, even worse, a dictator. A component shepherd should be trained to work with teams in an effective manner.

Virtual Team

Scaling up small, cross-functional teams to work on a single application release involves heavy coordination across teams. This coordination involves alignment of plans, direction, and technology. Building software at scale necessitates coordination of architecture decisions across teams. The *virtual team* configuration is a way that representatives from each team in a scaled application development situation can coordinate architecture decisions. Figure 11.3 portrays how team members from each team can participate in a virtual team configuration.

Creating a virtual team is not as simple as it sounds. Jim Highsmith describes the difficulties of creating virtual teams in this quote:

> Interaction across feature team boundaries is harder than internal interactions . . . the common mission provides a mechanism for cooperation.[9]

---

9. Jim Highsmith III, *Adaptive Software Development: A Collaborative Approach to Managing Complex Systems* (Dorset House Publishing, 2000).

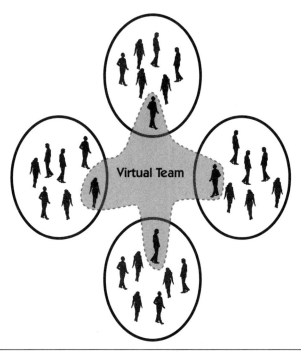

Figure 11.3   A team with representation from multiple teams working on a single application release with the charter to coordinate architecture decisions is called a virtual team.

The need for a common mission is essential. This goes beyond the vision for the product all of the teams are delivering. The virtual team must have a charter that describes how they will manage issues within the team and make decisions on solutions. The difficulties in creating an effective virtual team are not technical, as Jessica Lipnack and Jeffrey Stamps describe in *Virtual Teams*:

> *It's 90 percent people and 10 percent technology. Social factors above all derail the development of many virtual teams.*[10]

Creating a team charter that considers the following questions can help a virtual team start off well:

- How often will the team meet?
- Which components of the application have the most architectural risk associated with them?

---

10. Jessica Lipnack and Jeffrey Stamps, *Virtual Teams* (John Wiley & Sons, 1997).

- What is our plan to support feature team empowerment when this team makes decisions that affect them?
- How will the team capture the architecture roadmap?

There could be other questions specific to the domain of your application, but these are a good start. Do not take the answers to these questions lightly. It is essential to obtain agreement on how to coordinate the activities of the virtual team. Without agreement, the direction provided by the virtual team becomes confusing and creates unnecessary conflict without a means for resolution.

There are some issues inherent in using the virtual team configuration:

- It singles out specific roles on feature teams with special responsibilities beyond those of the team.
- It could easily lead to top-down architecture decisions that create conflict with feature team members.
- The virtual team could gain significant influence on the Product Backlog priorities and inflate what is "necessary" for release.

The virtual team should support the product vision and application release. It should not have direct control of defining what is necessary for release. Balancing the need for coordinating architecture decisions in support of the release with empowerment of feature teams and those responsible for feature priorities is the main goal of the virtual team.

IMPORTANCE OF RELEVANT EXPERIENCE

Decisions are made daily that affect software design in positive and negative ways. How does a team make more positive decisions than negative? Although it may seem obvious, I find the following statement to encompass one of the most important ways to enhance software design:

Nothing is a substitute for relevant experience.

Each year I am in the software industry I learn something new that improves my skills. As I gain broader experience and dive more deeply into particular areas of software development, I am further enabled to provide effective delivery and consulting to customers. You'll know you are considered to be experienced in an aspect of software development when others look for your help.

Relevant experience is not sufficient on its own for getting a better design, but it goes a long way. The problem is that finding an experienced team in any particular software development effort is difficult. As an industry, we must find ways to guide and support teams with diverse skills and experience. This is approached in many organizations by setting up programs such as personal training, communities of practice, lunch and learns, brown-bag sessions, and regular open-space meetings.

Personal Training

Training is thought of as a wasteful and costly activity in many organizations. Training does not have to be costly. People within the same organization can train each other. This type of training takes minimal investment and results in a more effective workforce. Investment in the people within your organization will have positive effects on their ability to deliver.

Software development is a knowledge creation industry. Knowledge of the domain and technology is essential to delivering valuable software. Creating knowledge is not free and takes investment over time. Organizations will enhance their investment in people by allowing room for sharing knowledge continually rather than relying on external training opportunities.

Communities of Practice

Agile teams should not lose sight of the need for deep knowledge in discrete topics associated with software development. There is lots of focus in the Agile community on building great teams that are able to organize around the work and blur roles to enhance their team capabilities. It is important for specialized knowledge to still be nurtured in conjunction with learning about surrounding practices.

Communities of practice (CoPs) are created by groups of people who have common interests and decide to learn more about them together. CoPs emerge from within teams and organizations and are usually started by individuals with a passion for a specialized area. Organizations can support and nurture CoPs by furnishing them with access to books, facilities, and other learning tools.

Lunch and Learns

People are known to collaborate more effectively when they are fed, and they are more likely to communicate over a meal. Also, when people are hungry, they have difficulty concentrating and tend to be less affable. Putting together an event where people come to learn while getting fed will enhance the knowledge transference and collaboration among participants. Many organizations hold lunch and learns once a week and choose topics suggested by their employees to present. Some organizations bring in outside thought leaders to speak on particular topics.

Brown-Bag Sessions

Just like lunch and learns, brown-bag sessions are events where people get together to gain knowledge while congregating around food. Instead of the company providing the food, the people who attend bring their own lunch and eat it while they participate in the session. It is common for brown-bag sessions to be started by a team or community of practice.

SUMMARY

To combat platform experience debt, organizations must find ways to continually share knowledge about all aspects of their software, and team members must interact more often to maintain a shared understanding of the design. Using the practice of pairing on development efforts provides an opportunity for sharing knowledge to at least one more member of the team. When pairing is used in a promiscuous manner, by mixing up pairing partners frequently, the knowledge is shared beyond those two people and is proliferated to a larger audience. When there is a considerable gap in knowledge about the depth of the software under construction, developing training materials to disseminate this knowledge further into the teams can start filling the gap. Providing mechanisms for immediate feedback during the construction process gives teams indicators of the essential function of the software. Automated tests can provide these mechanisms for giving feedback when they are able to be executed by teams.

Team configurations can influence how teams isolate and share knowledge among them in a scaled software development project. The integration team configuration supports frequent integration of disparate components of the application architecture but can isolate knowledge of the integration and muddle feature priorities across component-focused teams. When possible, using the feature team configuration for scaling to multiple teams on a single application release supports sharing knowledge further and focusing on feature priorities. There are difficulties associated with implementing the feature team configuration in organizations. Therefore, there are team configurations that help manage these difficulties: cross-team mentor, component shepherd, and virtual team.

Investing in people is probably the most effective way to create sustainable software. Going beyond the basic interview process of asking questions and evaluating answers to short working sessions with the candidate and hiring team can provide better understanding of their capabilities. Sharing knowledge across the organization creates the possibility of distributing ways to optimize software delivery to more teams. Finding ways to support individuals and teams with training, communities of practice, lunch and learns, and brown-bag sessions increases the knowledge sharing across team boundaries.

WHAT IS AGILE?

Agile software development techniques were born before they were codified into values and principles at Snowbird, Utah, in 2001. The software industry has continued to mature in process, practice, and knowledge throughout the years. Its lineage goes back through systems thinking, complex adaptive systems, Lean thinking, object-oriented design, and pattern languages up to specific methods such as Extreme Programming (XP), Scrum, Feature-Driven Development (FDD), Crystal, Lean software development, and Dynamic Systems Development Method (DSDM). The codifying of a "Manifesto for Agile Software Development"[1] provided an opportunity to promote a common understanding of how development organizations could work with their business partners to optimize the value of their software assets.

Agile is not a methodology. Instead, it is a collection of four values and 12 principles that describe how process, practices, and people work together in Agile software development. These values and principles provide guidance for a team or organization when deciding how a situation they face should be handled. Figure A.1 is a snapshot of www.agilemanifesto.org where the four values and 12 principles are made publicly available.

The topics discussed in this book should be broadly relevant to all Agile software development methods. Most of the topics are also relevant whether or not your team or organization is using an Agile software development method. There are places in the book where the focus is on particular Agile software development methods, Scrum and XP in particular, so that examples can be shared effectively.

Scrum

Scrum is a project management framework invented by Jeff Sutherland. He first used Scrum at Easel Corporation in 1993. The framework constructs practiced at Easel Corporation are almost the same as those that Scrum teams practice today.

---

1. "Principles behind the Agile Manifesto," www.agilemanifesto.org/principles.html, 2001.

Manifesto for Agile Software Development

We are uncovering better ways of developing
software by doing it and helping others do it.
Through this work we have come to value:

Individuals and interactions over processes and tools
Working software over comprehensive documentation
Customer collaboration over contract negotiation
Responding to change over following a plan

That is, while there is value in the items on
the right, we value the items on the left more.

Kent Beck	James Grenning	Robert C. Martin
Mike Beedle	Jim Highsmith	Steve Mellor
Arie van Bennekum	Andrew Hunt	Ken Schwaber
Alistair Cockburn	Ron Jeffries	Jeff Sutherland
Ward Cunningham	Jon Kern	Dave Thomas
Martin Fowler	Brian Marick	

Figure A.1   Snapshot of the "Manifesto for Agile Software Development"
taken from www.agilemanifesto.org/

The term *Scrum* was identified in an article titled "The New New Product
Development Game" by Hirotaka Takeuchi and Ikujiro Nonaka for the *Harvard Business Review* in 1986.[2] This paper discussed six characteristics of
product development teams at highly innovative and successful companies.
These characteristics are described briefly as

- **Built-in instability:** Management provides a challenging goal to a
  team and gives them extreme freedom to implement a product that
  meets the goal.
- **Self-organizing project teams:** Teams are introduced to the product
  goal and must organize around this work across functional disciplines.
- **Overlapping development phases:** As opposed to the relay race or
  handoff approach to optimize functional phases of product development,
  teams synchronize their delivery and force interactivity
  between functional roles to meet delivery goals.

---

2. Hirotaka Takeuchi and Ikujiro Nonaka, "The New New Product Development Game,"
   Harvard Business Review (January–February 1986).

- **"Multilearning":** Multilearning involves learning at multiple levels (individual, team, and corporate) and on multiple functions. Team members, through close interaction with external entities and within their team, acquire new knowledge and skill sets to assess and use this new knowledge quickly.
- **Subtle control:** Emphasis is put on a team's internal self-control. Management provides sufficient checkpoints to minimize instability, ambiguity, and tension in pursuit of a challenging goal.
- **Organizational transfer of learning:** Teams work to transfer their learning to others outside the group.

If the small taste of the six characteristics described in "The New New Product Development Game" interests you, you can pay for and read the original article to gain more understanding of how these characteristics were applied to real product development. The Scrum framework exhibits these characteristics in relation to software product delivery. A focus on these characteristics of Scrum can generate breakthrough innovation, performance, and quality when used effectively.

Another significant influence on Scrum was empirical process control. Ken Schwaber visited Babatunde "Tunde" Ogunnaike at DuPont Experimental Station in 1995 to discuss methodologies that were not working well in software development. What was learned from this meeting was the difference between defined (plan-driven) and empirical process control models.[3] A defined process assumes that the work can be fully understood. Software projects are more complicated with surprises throughout all aspects of the development process. Empirical process controls use an "inspect and adapt" monitoring of progress to manage the complexity inherent in particular processes such as software development.

The influence of "The New New Product Development Game" and empirical process control led to the ostensibly simple Scrum framework. Here is a short overview of the Scrum framework.

> In Scrum, there are three roles: Project Team, Product Owner, and ScrumMaster. Scrum starts when a Product Owner comes up with a product vision. The Product Owner generates the Product Backlog that describes this product vision in more detail. The list of items contained

---

3. Babatunde A. Ogunnaike and W. Harmon Ray, *Process Dynamics, Modeling and Control* (Oxford University Press, 1994).

in the Product Backlog is prioritized in stack-rank order and estimated by the Project Team.

When the Product Backlog contains enough work for the Project Team to implement in a single time-boxed iteration, called a Sprint, the team conducts a Sprint Planning Meeting to decide what to work on. The Sprint was 30 days in the original Scrum literature but it is common to conduct Sprints in three-, two-, and even one-week increments. In the Sprint Planning Meeting, the Product Owner starts by describing the highest-priority Product Backlog items to the Project Team. The Project Team members ask questions about the Product Backlog items to gain clarity about the feature requirements. Once they have covered what seems to be a sufficient number of Product Backlog items to fill the Sprint duration, the Project Team focuses on coming up with a plan for how they will deliver those Product Backlog items in their own Sprint Backlog. As a full Project Team, they break down the Product Backlog items into smaller tasks incorporating all aspects of software development represented on the cross-functional Project Team, such as testing, coding, integration, and documentation. The Project Team commits to a Sprint Backlog after they have sufficiently tasked out a set of Product Backlog items to work on.

After the Project Team commits to a Sprint Backlog, they start work. During the Sprint, the Project Team gets together each day for a 15-minute time-boxed meeting called the Daily Scrum. They discuss what they have done since the last meeting, what they plan to do, and bring up any impediments blocking their work. The focus of the Daily Scrum is not reporting status but rather for the Project Team to figure out if they are still on track to deliver on their commitments for this Sprint. If they are not on track, action can be taken immediately.

At the end of the Sprint, the Project Team demos the software created with the Product Owner and any other interested stakeholders who attend the Sprint Review Meeting. The team is expected to have created a Potentially Shippable Product Increment. This means that it contains all of the quality a shippable product would include, thus giving the opportunity, if the Product Owner decides, to deploy the software to the users. After the Potentially Shippable Product Increment is reviewed, the Project Team conducts a Sprint Retrospective where they look at the process used this Sprint and try to find ways to improve it. The Sprint Retrospective results in a list of improvements the Project Team will make on the next Sprint, which starts the next day with a Sprint Planning Meeting.

The Scrum framework has three built-in "inspect and adapt" opportunities. At the Daily Scrum, the Project Team inspects their current Sprint progress and adapts based on their ability to meet Sprint Backlog commitments. The Sprint Review Meeting allows the Product Owner and other stakeholders to inspect the Potentially Shippable Product Increment and the Project Team adapts the Product Backlog contents and priorities based on their feedback. In the Sprint Retrospective, the Project Team inspects their software development process looking for ways to improve and adapt it in their next Sprint. Figure A.2 is a visual representation of the Scrum framework described above.

Applying this simple framework has been shown to be incredibly difficult for many organizations. Some organizations try to apply Scrum "by the book" but don't comprehend the focus on "inspect and adapt." Others incorporate a subset of the Scrum framework and call it "Scrum." This is referred to as a

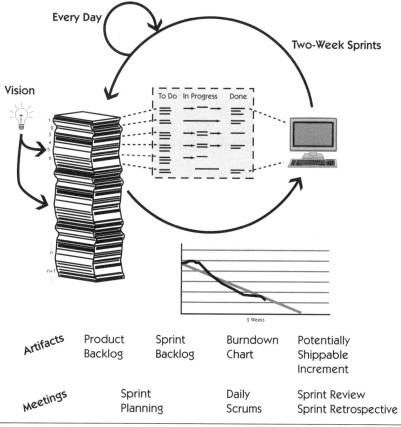

Figure A.2 Overview of the Scrum framework

Scrum but implementation of Scrum. For instance, "We do *Scrum but* we don't meet for a Sprint Retrospective." Or "We do *Scrum but* we do coding in one Sprint and then do testing in the next Sprint so the Sprint does not result in Potentially Shippable Product Increments."

Effective use of Scrum enables project teams to deliver increments of software that are potentially shippable in 30 days or less. The Product Owner then decides whether or not there is sufficient value in what has been delivered for deployment to the software's users. It is common for Product Owners to find early release opportunities not easily identified in requirements development. These early releases minimize the amount of investment needed to give additional value to the users.

Extreme Programming

Kent Beck, Ron Jeffries, and Ward Cunningham invented Extreme Programming (XP) during the Chrysler Comprehensive Compensation (C3) System project around 1997. About two years after the first Scrum team successfully delivered product releases, Kent Beck asked for extensive information on Scrum from Jeff Sutherland to incorporate into a new process they were developing. This ultimately made XP a natural component of a well-executing Scrum, and the best Scrum teams today use XP in their development process. Beyond the process, XP is based on the values of communication, simplicity, feedback, and courage.

Communication is important since most problems occur because the right people did not speak at the right moment during a project. Teams should be collocated, sitting together in close proximity, so they are able to communicate quickly about issues that inevitably arise. It is also important that the customer remain close to the team in order to answer questions early in the delivery. This reduces the amount of churn a team goes through when deciding how the customer wants the functionality to behave.

Simplicity is doing the "simplest thing that could possibly work." This is difficult in practice because traditional development methods tell us to analyze and design a solution before implementing it. In XP, disciplined use of practices helps reduce complexity in software development.

Feedback is an essential element of XP. Within seconds during a pair programming session a programmer gets feedback about the code being written. Within minutes test cases are executing successfully for new functionality. Within days users give feedback about new features put into the software. Within weeks the software is deployed to production and there is feedback on how it works for the end users in their daily lives.

Courage to do what is right during a software release cycle can be difficult for teams. When time is running out, the team continues to write unit tests and customer tests because that will enable effective delivery. When an architectural element is not working well, have the courage to throw it out and rewrite it. Try out a new design with just enough discussion to start coding and prove its ability to solve an issue through code.

The XP values are enabled through the use of practices in a disciplined manner. XP focuses on reducing the cost of change during feature development through the use of 12 practices. These practices, as described in *Extreme Programming Explained* by Kent Beck, are

- *The Planning Game—Figure out the features that go into the next release.*
- *Small releases—Release the minimum amount of valuable features to production and then follow up with subsequent releases.*
- *Metaphor—Provide a shared story about the software under development.*
- *Simple design—Design the system for simplicity and remove complexity when identified.*
- *Testing—Team members and customers execute tests to validate the software is in good health and features are working.*
- *Refactoring—Modify the software's structure through small and frequent changes that result in better design without affecting the way it functions.*
- *Pair programming—Two programmers work together on each production artifact.*
- *Collective ownership—Any team member can change any part of the software anytime.*
- *Continuous integration—Build, integrate, and execute automated tests after each task is finished. This happens many times a day.*
- *40-hour week—Work at a sustainable pace and don't put in overtime hours two weeks in a row.*
- *On-site customer—An actual user of the system is available full-time to the team to answer questions and validate features.*
- *Coding standards—Programmers establish guidelines for writing all code to help communication through the software artifacts.*[4]

---

4. Kent Beck, *Extreme Programming Explained* (Addison-Wesley, 2000). Text excerpt from p. 54, © 2000 by Kent Beck. Reproduced by permission of Pearson Education, Inc.

There are plenty of stories about significant performance and quality gains made by teams using XP. It is also well known in XP and other Agile-related communities that most teams who say they do XP are practicing only a portion of the 12 practices. Most of the practices take a significant change in mind-set to be done effectively.

When XP is implemented effectively, it has been shown to significantly reduce entropy as software ages. When scaling to teams larger than ten members, many of the XP technical practices are used within the Scrum project management framework. Jeff Sutherland has written in presentations:

> *It is hard to get a Scrum with extreme velocity without XP engineering practices. You cannot scale XP without Scrum.*[5]

This statement suggests why many teams implementing an Agile approach tend to begin with Scrum and some XP technical practices. The close alignment of Scrum and XP values and principles along with a difference in their main focus in software development elements permits them to be used together effectively.

---

5. "Pretty Good Scrum: Secret Sauce for Distributed Teams," presentation by Jeff Sutherland, downloadable at http://jeffsutherland.com/scrum/prettygoodscrumv5.pdf.

INDEX

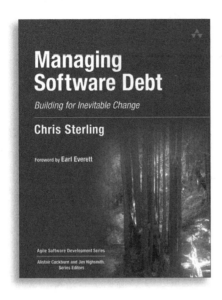

FREE Online Edition

Your purchase of **Managing Software Debt** includes access to a free online edition for 45 days through the Safari Books Online subscription service. Nearly every Addison-Wesley Professional book is available online through Safari Books Online, along with more than 5,000 other technical books and videos from publishers such as Cisco Press, Exam Cram, IBM Press, O'Reilly, Prentice Hall, Que, and Sams.

SAFARI BOOKS ONLINE allows you to search for a specific answer, cut and paste code, download chapters, and stay current with emerging technologies.

Activate your FREE Online Edition at
www.informit.com/safarifree

> **STEP 1:** Enter the coupon code: WHGSIWH.

> **STEP 2:** New Safari users, complete the brief registration form.
> Safari subscribers, just log in.

If you have difficulty registering on Safari or accessing the online edition, please e-mail customer-service@safaribooksonline.com